FLIGHTS
INTO
HISTORY

FLIGHTS
INTO
HISTORY

FINAL MISSIONS RETOLD BY
RESEARCH AND ARCHAEOLOGY

IAN MCLACHLAN

SPELLMOUNT

First published 2007
This edition published 2010

Spellmount Publishers, an imprint of
The History Press
The Mill, Brimscombe Port
Stroud, Gloucestershire, GL5 2QG
www.thehistorypress.co.uk

British Library Cataloguing in Publication Data.
A catalogue record for this book is available from the British Library.

ISBN 978 0 7524 5639-3

Typesetting and origination by The History Press
Printed in Great Britain

To Sue.
Thanks for the continuing endurance.

Contents

Acknowledgements

As with my previous books, I am indebted to those researchers and historians who have generously shared the results of their labours. Their boundless dedication honours the crews involved in these flights into history, and these brave men represent countless others whose stories remain untold.

The list that follows is long and the support from all is much appreciated, but I am particularly grateful to Chris Gotts for making available the results of his research. I am sure he would have performed the author's role admirably had he not become incapacitated by ill health. Bob Collis, a friend of many years' standing, unstintingly provided a selection of stories from his extensive archives, and Peter Stanley generously supplied the story of his friend 'Hadi' Vogt.

These and other researchers remain modestly in the background, anxious only that the airmen whose lives they have touched are remembered. Direct input from some veterans is included, from Dickie Rook, John Bitzer and Harold Church among others. Harold Church had written a lightly camouflaged fictional account in which he replaced his real crew with characters. I felt he would more fully honour his fallen comrades if his account was written in the first person, and the unassuming Harold finally concurred. Lack of space here prevents me from supplying the details of each contributor to this book, but their kindness and generosity are hereby acknowledged with gratitude. Any errors that remain are my responsibility.

A.V. Cannings, Air Forces Escape & Evasion Society, Alan Hague, Alastair Goodrum, Albert Chilvers, Barbara Lockwood, Belgian Aviation Historical Association, Bernard Roper, British Aviation Archaeological Council, Chris Betts, Chris Goss, Chris Gotts, Chris Hearn, Craig A. Fuller, Cynrik De Decker, Dr Georg Konrad, Dan Engle, Danny Morris, David J. Stubley, David Wade, Dennis F. Tye, Derek James, Don W. Pashley, Donald Stowers, Dr Kurt Möser, East Anglian Aviation Research Group, *East Anglian Daily Times*, *Eastern Daily Press*, *Eastern Evening News*, Ed Beaty, Edward Daines, Ernest A. Osborne, *Flypast* Magazine, Geoff C. Jeffries, Gill Powell, Gordon McLachlan, Harold D. Church, Horst A. Munter, Hugh McGill, Iris H. Shuttleworth, Jack Edmonds, Jeff Carless, John A. Hey, John C. Bitzer, Joyce Carter, Julian Metcalfe, June R. Edwards, Kathleen Ellis, Ken Ellis, Kenneth McLachlan,

Louise Metcalfe, Lowestoft Aviation Museum, Maggie Secker, Mark Brotherton, Martin W. Bowman, Merle C. Olmsted, Michel Doutreleau, Mike Bailey, Mike Butler, Mike Harris, Nigel Beckett, Norfolk & Suffolk Aviation Museum, Pat Everson, Pat Marks, Pat Ramm, Paul Thrower, Pauline Fisher, Pete Snowling, Peter J. Pfeiffer, Radio Norfolk, Radio Suffolk, Ray Corke, Ray Jones, Richard Rook, Robert Degrez, Robert Kemp, Roger A. Freeman, Russell George Nichols, S.E. Harvey, Shannyn Scarff, Simon Digweed, Simon Dunham, Stan Bishop, Steve Snelling, Stewart P. Evans, Theo Boiten, Tony North, T/Sergeant Mona Ferrell, Uwe Heintzer, Val Grimble.

I also thank the team at Sutton Publishing for their considerable perseverance. My 'day job', contracting as an Overseas Sourcing Consultant for e2v technologies, entailed much travelling and delayed the submission of the manuscript. The Sutton team deserve recognition not only for their professional skills but also for their forbearance: Jonathan Falconer, Julia Fenn, Nick Reynolds, Clare Jackson and Sarah Cook.

Finally, there would be no book without the support of my family. My daughter Bethan and son Rowan helped with practical research, and I am also grateful to their partners Tom and Eleanor for releasing them to do so! Jake and Maddie turned down the volume while we shared study space, and Jonny and Hannah supported the noise reduction. Above all, I owe my thanks to my wife Sue, whose unwavering support demonstrates her own recognition of the sacrifices made by young airmen before she was born. Their legacy is our freedom. Writing is not a dual pastime and she has had much to tolerate. She puts up with it because, while the obsession is mine, she knows as I do that these endeavours may bring some comfort to those families whose knowledge of what happened remains incomplete, and may perhaps fill some of the gaps in their understanding. It also proves to surviving veterans that subsequent generations have not forgotten, and never will, their flights into history.

Ian McLachlan, 2006
Suffolk, England

Preface

Countless flights took place during the Second World War. As well as combat missions, there were test flights, ferry flights, training sorties and passenger movements. Most passed virtually unnoticed, and the airmen concerned simply wrote more hours in their flight log-books. Some inevitably ended badly, and all too often that meant the end for the airmen aboard.

This book relates fourteen accounts of 'Flights into History' undertaken by British, American and German airmen. Most began as routine flights – if any form of aerial combat through flak-filled skies can ever be considered as such. Many ended dramatically. Some were never recorded by the participants; the closing entries in their log-books were made on their behalf, before their documents and personal belongings were returned to the next-of-kin. In the overall scheme of things these flights may not have been historically momentous, but when they went wrong the impact on the survivors was often emotionally and sometimes physically scarring. Also affected were the families of the fallen. Their lives were devastated, and the subsequent lack of information only exacerbated their misery. Our research into these flights answers some of their questions. We sympathise with those who grieved and pay tribute to the sons, fathers, uncles and brothers whose absence left a perpetual void.

Airmen said that any landing you could walk away from was a good one! Some of the stories in this book record machines that have disappeared for ever, with only tiny fragments or broken assemblies surviving. Archaeological evidence might be all that now remains of aircraft that once soared into the skies, lifting high the hopes and spirits of the young men who rode the heavens. I hope you will celebrate their memory with me.

CHAPTER ONE

Early Nights

Adominant image of RAF Bomber Command is of squadrons of aircraft disgorging a deluge of destruction into the burning heartland of Nazi Germany, of punishment brutally meted out and endured as technologically driven opponents battled for supremacy in the night skies. Radar was used to remove the nocturnal cloak hiding the bombers' targets, but it also stripped away the shielding sanctuary of darkness from the aircraft. By 1944/5 heaven and earth had blended into hell as thousands perished in a battle of monstrous proportions. Britain's iconic Avro Lancaster and its Handley Page stable-mate the Halifax, along with other types, wrought devastation on an evil regime whose populace paid in blood for the abrogation of their democracy. A struggle lasting almost six strenuous years had shortened developmental lead times, so that aircraft and equipment were introduced at a furious pace.

Following numerous disastrous attacks during daylight, the RAF's heavy bombers had been driven into the darkness, but their equipment and methods were exposed as inadequate by the Butt Report of August 1941. A notable civil servant, D.M. Butt from the War Cabinet Secretariat, was tasked with studying and interpreting hundreds of photographs made available following advances in technology. The cameras fitted to the bombers were now synchronised to take pictures of the moment of impact, thus allowing independent target verification. Butt's analysis was devastating for the senior officers of Bomber Command. Over 30 per cent of aircraft failed to bomb their primary objective. Of the remainder, only a third released their bombs within 5 miles of the prescribed aiming point and this figure tumbled to only 10 per cent when the targets were in the strongly fortified industrial regions of the Ruhr. In cloudy conditions reliance on navigation by dead reckoning was subject to error because the calculations were primarily based on predicted wind speed and direction over significant distances. Even on moonlit nights only 40 per cent of aircraft bombed within 5 miles of the objective, and moonless nights saw this figure fall to just 7 per cent.

The equipment may have been lacking, but the valour and determination of the airmen was not and this chapter recalls courage beyond measure when the vanguard of Britain's bomber crews took their machines into combat. Knights errant, they championed the desire of the increasingly beleaguered British populace to strike back. At a crucial period Bomber

Later in his career, Ralph Edwards poses with some of his 115 Squadron crew. (Left to right): Sergeant Bob Shaw, navigator; Sergeant Ken Merriott, wireless operator; Ralph Edwards, pilot; and the rear gunner. The engines are running and the front gunner is rotating his turret in preparation for flight prior to the crew taking off for their night flying test. (*Ralph Edwards via Chris Gotts*)

Command's achievements boosted the morale of people who had 'taken it' for long enough, and gave strength at a time when the war news reeked of potential defeat. Even if their exploits were later exposed as distorted by unintentional self-deception, the lessons learned in those early nights established an inventory of experience – but the cost was high.

During August 1940 the Battle of Britain was approaching a crescendo as the RAF's fighter pilots struggled to hold the enemy at bay. Even so, the RAF commanders knew that, no matter how heroic, defensive defiance would not win the war. While exhausted Hurricane and Spitfire pilots slept, or tried to, their nocturnal bomber brethren retaliated on Britain's behalf. Attacks on the accumulation of barges sheltering in the channel ports for the intended invasion of England were interspersed with deeper penetrations into the Reich's industrial heartland.

Serving with 3 Group's 115 Squadron at RAF Marham in Norfolk, Sergeant Pilot Ralph Edwards was fast becoming familiar with German geography. His log-book now listed Hamm, Hamburg, Cologne, Bremen and Gotha. For his sixth sortie, on 22 August 1940, a new name appeared when they were summoned to briefing: Mannheim. At this stage briefings lacked the strictures subsequently imposed on air-crew, as Ralph later recalled:

> The target was displayed, with the suggested route, defended areas, other hazards, pinpoints, weather to be expected and the time advised to be on target and away from the area. Crews then went away to the crew rooms to plan their own routes and heights to and from the target, and their direction of attack. Some time needed to be spent in the target area to attempt to identify a target often obscured for a variety of reasons, including cloud, smog, fog, defences etc. . . .

For this operation Ralph would be flying as second pilot under the command of another sergeant, the seasoned Neil 'Cookie' Cook, who would be using the occasion to complete a veritable 'Cook's Tour' of thirty sorties. In addition to Ralph, Cookie's crew comprised three more sergeants: A. Overall as navigator, Nathan as wireless operator, and H.V. Watts as front gunner. Manning the rear turret was Pilot Officer G.D. Waterer, the flight gunnery leader, but in accordance with RAF custom he was subordinate to Cookie as skipper. Gathering in the crew room, the six air-crew discussed the opportunities offered by Mannheim. The obvious route lay over Belgium and Luxembourg to south-eastern Germany, where the confluence of the rivers Rhine and Neckar had undoubtedly influenced the foundation of this attractive city. Rivers aided navigation and Alan Overall's task was made easier by Mannheim's quadrate grid pattern. Unique in Germany, this square-patterned city plan dated from the seventeenth century but its grace and symmetry were appreciated by the crew only for the benefit it offered in target identification. Using the street plan and the town's famous Art Nouveau water-tower in Friedrichsplatz as reference points, they hoped to locate railway bridges and industrial targets such as the marine diesel engine factory. Sixty-five years earlier Karl Benz had driven the world's first automobile in Mannheim and he had left there an engineering legacy that continues to this day. There were numerous factories, including one producing U-boat engines, as well as other potential targets, including a paper works, a rubber factory and a plant producing celluloid – but first the air-crew had to get there.

Kitted out with parachutes, Mae Wests, helmets, gloves, goggles and so on, they eventually clambered into the transport taking them to their aircraft. Piled in with the assorted flying apparel were thermos flasks and sandwiches. It would be a long night. Bumping over the airfield's turf, the truck soon approached the squat shape of their aircraft silhouetted against the stars. The premier heavy bomber of its period, the Vickers Armstrong Wellington would earn a reputation for toughness, and the type endured in combat throughout the war. Designed by Dr Barnes Wallis using his renowned geodetic fuselage structure, the Wellington was soon nicknamed 'Wimpy' after a famous cartoon-strip character, the portly J. Wellington Wimpy from the Popeye series. The Wimpy's fabric-covered tubbiness concealed a toughness of character that enabled it to absorb punishment and still get home. Ralph's machine, a Mark 1c, serial R3276, was a comparative youngster, having been with the squadron for only five weeks, during which time it was allocated

A Wellington taking off. This aircraft was the most successful of the RAF's pre-war bombers and its lineage continued through the postwar Vickers Viking airliner, the Valetta transport and the Varsity trainer. Sadly there are no airworthy Wellingtons extant. (*Via Mike Bailey*)

aircraft letter B and wore the squadron code KO-. Ralph realised the Wimpy's record owed much to the dedication of its ground-crew:

> One recalls, as dusk fell after the activities of the day – the air-test; bombing up; refuelling; briefing etc. etc. – we, the air-crew, would be driven out to our dispersal point at the far corner of the grass airfield and the ground-crew would greet us cheerfully, assuring us that everything was OK, that such important points for morale had been

attended to . . . The wing tanks contained those few extra gallons of precious 90-octane petrol for the de-rated Peggy 18s [Bristol Pegasus XVIII radial engines] which might be over the official fuel load . . . The leading edges of the wings had a good coating of grease to help prevent ice accretion . . . and there was an extra coat of anti-glow paint on the engine exhaust manifold rings on the leading edge of the cowling, which we fondly imagined dulled the brilliance of the fluorescent glow from the heat of the exhaust gases, [preventing us] from being spotted by night-fighters or tracked by infra-red equipment. . . . Another important factor was oxygen. The number of bottles carried was limited and, with six crew members all breathing in steadily, the oxygen could be used up much too quickly, especially as the type of face-mask worn was of a dense cloth material, which at the top allowed oxygen escape and wastage. The later, tighter-fitting rubber mask, with oxygen on demand, was very efficient.

The ground-crews had been busy as over fifty Wellingtons and Hampdens were readied for the night's activities against six targets in the Ruhr and Rhineland. In addition, Blenheims raided enemy airfields in France and even the outmoded Fairey Battles were busy nipping at E-Boat bases. Some of the aircraft carried mines, which were to be sown in key shipping routes and on the approaches and entrances to ports and harbours. This activity was nicknamed 'gardening' and it made a significant contribution to enemy shipping losses, but that night the majority of aircraft carried high explosives, with Wellingtons shouldering the heaviest burden. Nestling sinisterly on board KO-B was the payload: 3,500lb of high explosive. Drawing in a final draught of summer-scented night air, Ralph climbed into the fuselage and was immediately assailed by the less comfortable aromas associated with his trade. The taut fabric stretched over the airframe had its own fragrance, which mingled with the scents of oil, fuel and rubber from their workshop in the air. Aboard KO-B, the crew prepared for flight. Settling into his seat, Cookie commenced the familiar routine but with no hint of complacency. Experience had taught him the importance of being methodical; their lives depended on it. Outside, the ground-crew had manually rotated each propeller to avoid an accumulation of oil causing the pistons to lock. As they stood clear, Cookie flicked the starter and booster coil switches as a mechanic primed the induction system. Needles flickered and danced, and dials began to glow as power flowed into the aircraft's electrical system and the bomber stirred into life. Shuddering out of its slumbers with the first crack of combustion, the Wellington awoke and its engines were soon grumbling like lazy workers beginning their nightshift. Testing each engine for any hint of reluctance, Cookie took them up to the raucous tones of take-off boost; once satisfied, he throttled back and continued his checks. Brake pressure, fuel pressure, oil pressure, switches and tabs, trim and controls, gauges galore. Only when he had finished to his complete satisfaction did he release the brake lever on his control yoke and gun the aircraft into motion.

There were no concrete runways at Marham so KO-B trundled over the turf to her take-off position and awaited clearance. Green given, Cookie powered forward and Ralph felt the vibrations lessen as the mysteries of aerodynamics shifted the stress from the undercarriage to the wings and they eased off the grass, climbing purposefully into the clear night sky. In the crew room they had agreed on an attacking altitude between 10,000 and 13,000 feet. Now a gradual, fuel-conserving ascent was made, untroubled by cloud or course alterations, other than those to avoid areas of known flak concentrations. Alan Overall plotted their course and was undoubtedly pleased that the three-quarter moon and starlit skies gave excellent conditions for astro-navigation, while even the darkened landscape yielded signs. As Ralph explained: 'A sweep of moonlight across a stretch of water could often provide a swift clue to one's position deep over enemy territory, from lakes and rivers in relation to targets. The moon helped crews to keep a look-out for night-fighters . . . although one felt vulnerable alone on a bright night, the light tended to diffuse somewhat the stark intensity of searchlights.'

Nearing Mannheim, the crew became aware of searchlights seeking out the intruders, and bursting flak added brief stars of violence to the spectacle. Finding your aircraft 'coned' by searchlights was frightening and stomach-churning, as Ralph recalled:

> I would like to mention that carrying out evasive action with a [Wellington] 1c, whilst carrying a full bomb-load, and fuel, generally in a fully laden condition, at a height of 10,000 feet plus, was a somewhat 'fragile' operation. To maintain height and airspeed whilst carrying out manoeuvres to avoid attack, especially when caught in searchlights, needed much concentration. When fully loaded, climbing at standard boost and revs was, above 7,500 feet, a case often of plus 200 feet, minus 100 feet on the climb and dive indicator.

Reducing the risk from such dangerous gyrations, Cookie now employed a trick of his own to deceive the defences. He deliberately de-synchronised the engines to confuse the listening devices he suspected were employed by the enemy. It was thought such apparatus could tune in more readily to harmonised engines and direct the guns accordingly. Both sides believed the other had extensively deployed sound locaters, but in reality neither side found the devices effective and few were in use by the end of 1940. At this time German flak was principally directed by searchlights with only limited guidance from sound locaters. The latter had a range of only 6,000 yards and it took some 20 seconds for the locater to pick up the engine noise, so it could only indicate where the aircraft had been, not where it was – and the bomber would have travelled about a mile in the meantime!

While the crew were de-synchronising the engines and dropping flares to illuminate their target, they remained within range of the enemy guns and the Wimpy sustained slight damage from shrapnel. Whether this affected their fuel situation is unclear but Ralph became anxious and felt they could ill afford any delay if they were to get home. In the past their fuel status had proved at times 'somewhat critical', especially in the face of the prevailing westerly head-winds.

Soon they located a suitable target and Ralph was relieved when their bombs tumbled into the darkness. Neil Cook had flown most of the time, with Ralph undertaking a series of mundane but essential activities, including pumping oil to the engines, releasing flares down the chute and making general observations from the astrodome. At times he had difficulty keeping his balance when Cookie's evasive weaving became too energetic. Straight and level flight over the target area was far too dangerous, so the pilot would weave his aircraft vigorously from side to side. Ralph, grasping for the nearest hand-hold, noted how 'the brilliance of the searchlights, seen at various angles when we were weaving, lanced through the interior like a floodlit, lattice-work, ice cold greenhouse'.

On leaving the target area it was customary for the second pilot to take over and Ralph duly made his way to the cockpit. Grasping the handgrip overhead, Cookie eased out of his seat and squeezed aft into the main cabin, where a rudimentary bunk offered a degree of comfort. Meanwhile Ralph followed the course given by Overall and KO-B cruised homewards, her journey untroubled. Crossing the North Sea, the aircraft gently descended on track towards Marham as dawn slipped silver fingers over the earth's rim. Ahead a tracery of breaking waves sketched the dark outline of Norfolk's landmass but such serenity still harboured dangers and the crew remained alert for enemy intruders. Making landfall at about 3,000 feet, they continued their descent and could be forgiven for thinking of bacon and eggs for breakfast. But it was not to be. Daylight filtering through the long Perspex window weakened the shadows on board as Alan Overall posted himself into the astrodome atop the central fuselage, partly for navigational purposes but primarily to provide an additional observer to look out for enemy aircraft. With its undercarriage and flaps down and the pilot concentrating on his approach, an aircraft was very vulnerable as it landed. Alan's sudden yell over the intercom startled Ralph, but it was not an intruder. The navigator's anxious alarm call announced that there was 'black smoke coming from both engines!' Simultaneously Ralph felt both motors begin 'to surge and lose power and the instruments fluctuated wildly'.

Leaping from the bunk, Neil Cook came swiftly forward to the cockpit, gesticulating for Ralph to vacate the captain's seat. As Ralph slid clear, Neil yelled at him to get Henry Watts out of his position – the front turret was no place to be. They were virtually out of fuel and, with no airfield immediately available, a crash-landing was inevitable. Tucking his intercom plug and oxygen tube into his harness and flying suit to prevent them snagging, Ralph dropped down the step from the second pilot's position to the bomb-aimer's compartment below the cockpit floor. The bomb-aimer's feet extended aft beneath the flight deck when the bombsight was in use. Forward of this, perched on the Wimpy's nose, was a Frazer Nash gun-turret with twin .303in Browning machine-guns. There was little space in the turret, and 20-year-old Henry Watts, being small in stature, was well suited to the tight confines and bore well the rigours of his post. Unlocking the bulkhead door sealing off the front turret, then tugging open the small double doors for the turret itself, Ralph shouted for Henry to get out. Startled, Henry swung round, clearly wondering what was happening, and began to struggle free. But cramped and frozen, he needed assistance.

Suddenly the engines stopped. The two men were close to the forward exit and parachute storage, but there was no time to attach their parachutes and bale out. Hastening aft to their crash positions, Ralph encouraged the semi-frozen Watts with a good shove then turned and

A scene akin to, and possibly even of, the crash at Corpusty. Personnel from 54 Maintenance Unit dismantle a crashed Wellington. (*Frank Harber family*)

shut the bulkhead door; they would need all the impact resistance available. As they headed towards the flight deck, the eerie silence of their descent was nerve-wracking for Ralph: 'The only sounds were the rush of air past the rapidly descending plane, the drumming of the fabric stretched tautly over the geodetics, and the swish of the wind-milling, three-bladed, non-feathering airscrews.'

Ralph managed to get on to the aluminium step leading up into the second pilot's position. Grasping the cockpit coaming, he pulled himself up to look through the windscreen – and was just in time to see a row of trees directly ahead. In the last moments before impact, trees filled the windscreen, a green wall concealing brutally sharp branches and rugged trunks. The aircraft slammed into the foliage at about 100mph, and the absence of fuel now became a blessing as the Wellington was torn apart but did not catch fire. The tail section was ripped off with poor Waterer still inside. He was found upside-down in his severed turret some distance from the rest of the aircraft. Bursting through the branches, the rest of KO-B slammed to earth and skidded onwards amid a savagery of structural disintegration. When the wreck finally came to a halt, Neil Cook was trapped in his seat. He was suffering from severe head injuries, plus a fractured right femur. Henry Watts lay unconscious in the debris, bleeding badly, while Ralph had been catapulted out of the cabin and smacked heavily to earth, also bleeding. He too had broken his right femur and sustained head wounds, rendering him unaware of events even though he was struggling to get up. Alan Overall had a broken arm but was otherwise unharmed and mobile, as was Sergeant Nathan, whose injuries were fortunately only minor.

The crash had occurred at 05:15 on the B1149 Saxthorpe–Heydon road near the Norfolk village of Corpusty, but the isolated location and the early hour meant that no assistance appeared. Without the sound of engines overhead, and in the absence of an explosion, their brutal arrival had actually gone unnoticed in the community. Alan Overall finally decided to seek help and eventually found a farmhouse whose occupants alerted the authorities. In response, Norfolk Civil Defence officers ordered three ambulances to the scene but some time elapsed before they located the crash. Tragically they arrived too late for Henry Watts – the young gunner had bled to death. Waterer was still alive in his rear turret but grievously wounded with major head and facial injuries plus a fractured tibia and fibula. Rendering emergency assistance, the medical personnel then dispatched the wounded in the Cromer Civil Defence ambulance to the Norfolk and Norwich Hospital in Norwich. Some official records state that there were only two injured airmen and that Ralph Edwards was unharmed. In fact Ralph was badly hurt but remembered nothing until he regained his senses in the caring hands of medical staff at the hospital.

All five survivors were in one ward and 'were looked after wonderfully well by the nursing staff'. Overhead the air war continued and from his hospital bed Ralph listened as 'the air-raid sirens were constantly sounding. One at the Caley [chocolate] factory was particularly noisy.' On one occasion he heard bombs exploding, and later learned that two German air-crew, perhaps responsible for this commotion, were also in the hospital but segregated in another ward. Elsewhere the air raids had been intense and after two weeks the RAF beds were earmarked for casualties from London, so Cookie and his crew were moved by RAF ambulance to the new RAF hospital at Ely. There Ralph spent some months, first in Thomas splints and then in plaster of Paris. During this time he celebrated his 20th birthday and was honoured to meet the king and queen when they paid an official visit. Shortly afterwards, he and Cookie were transferred to a rehabilitation centre in Blackpool for recuperation and physiotherapy. Cookie had healed faster than Ralph and, unwilling to rest from operations, he returned to Marham at the end of May 1941. Some six weeks later, during an attack on Duisberg on the night of 15/16 July, the newly promoted Flight Sergeant Cook and his crew fell to the guns of Hauptmann Werner Streib of 1/NJG.1 – there were no survivors.

Ralph never again saw any of the others from the crash at Corpusty but later inherited a crew of his own and completed his tour, despite having a close encounter with a night-fighter and another less severe crash-landing:

Returning from a Nuremberg 'op' on the night of 12/13 October 1941, whilst in a searchlight cone at 4000 feet in the Frankfurt area . . . we had a short combat with a night-fighter. Some mild weaving of the aircraft was in progress when suddenly streams of sparkling tracer came streaking by, on and through the starboard side of the aircraft from

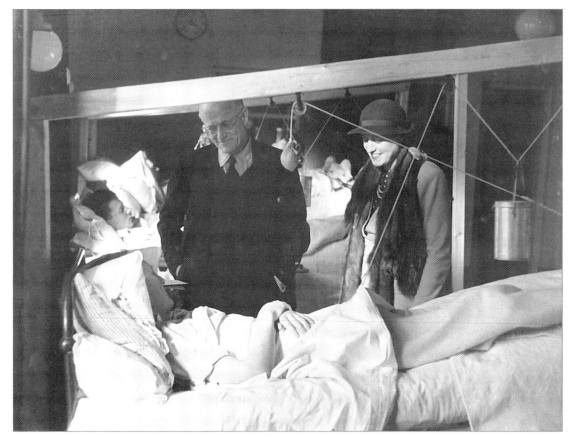

Neil Cook looks like the reluctant pilot of some weird aerial device as he (nearest camera) and Ralph Edwards are visited by two American VIPs touring the RAF hospital in Ely, October 1940. Both airmen are in traction, which will help heal their fractured femurs – note the weight suspended on the right (*Mrs J.R. Edwards*)

the rear . . . The rear gunner Sergeant Lester was alert and shouted, 'Fighter! Fighter!' and blazed away immediately with his twin Browning machine-guns. There was a pungent smell of burnt cordite throughout the aircraft. Then came a yell from the second pilot, on his first op, P/O Little, who was at the astrodome. He had been hit . . . after swift evasive action, we lost both the searchlights and the fighter. As the starboard engine was vibrating, I throttled it back a little and we stooged slowly homeward.

So, we had the second pilot wounded and out of action, one engine damaged and the hydraulic system out of action. I had to gain the attention of Bob, the navigator, for a course to steer because he was with Ken, the wireless operator, back in the cabin making the second pilot as comfortable as possible. We flew back to base. It was a dark night and, after circling around waiting for other squadron aircraft to land, [we] carried out the procedure to prepare for a belly landing. We had tried to manually pump the wheels down, for a long time, but without success. I prepared to carry out an approach for a belly landing on the dark side away from the flare path so as not to obstruct any other aircraft landing. With the crew in crash-landing positions, . . . the rear turret was rotated manually . . . to the side, to allow easy egress. The astrodome was unclipped and pulled down inside and the handle for the pilot's escape hatch was ready for pulling down to open. We came in for landing. It was very dark. With a harsh, grating roar and bumping friction, we skidded along in the darkness, finally coming to rest in a cloud of smoke and steam. The port airscrew was hurled, bent and twisted, some distance away but otherwise there were no injuries. The fire engines and ambulances were promptly on the scene, but there was no fire. The crew were rapidly out of the exits, and the wounded second pilot lifted out to the ambulance.

Later commissioned, Ralph became an instructor on Wellingtons and participated in the first 1000-bomber raid on Cologne on 30/31 May 1942. His instructional duties continued until December 1943, when he secured a posting to 7 Pathfinder Squadron flying Lancasters from Oakington near Cambridge. Here he completed another operational tour (including the disastrous raid on Nuremburg on 30/31 March 1944 when ninety-five Lancasters and Halifaxes were lost). In June 1944, now a flight lieutenant, Ralph was awarded the DSO for being 'a highly skilled and fearless captain and pilot whose fine fighting qualities have been reflected in the efficiency and determination of his crews'. During September 1944 he was posted to Transport Command, and retired from the RAF as a squadron leader in 1958. Ralph Edwards had experienced and survived the transformation of Bomber Command from puny pinpricking nuisance raids to the massive attacks that contributed so much to the defeat of Hitler's Reich. Sadly Ralph has passed away since relating this account.

* * *

Another early nights adventurer was Pilot Officer David Penman from 44 Squadron, part of 5 Group and based at Waddington in Lincolnshire. David had enlisted in 1937 and fledged on that ubiquitous biplane trainer, the de Havilland Tiger Moth. In those days many of the front-line aircraft were also biplanes and David's career took him on to the graceful Hawker series of Audax and Hart light bombers. Completing his tuition, he reached 44 Squadron in October 1938 during the political turmoil of the Munich Crisis, when war seemed imminent. Conflict was narrowly averted when Britain and France failed to support Czechoslovakia and allowed Hitler to occupy part of that unhappy nation. Had war broken out, the RAF would have been woefully ill-prepared but 44 Squadron, having recently re-equipped with the Bristol Blenheim Mk 1, had at least gone beyond the use of open cockpit biplanes. The origins of the Blenheim, a twin-engined, medium day bomber, stemmed from the private-venture Bristol 142 'Britain First' executive aircraft sponsored by Lord Rothermere, owner of the *Daily Mail*. Embarrassingly for the RAF, in 1935 the newspaper baron's personal transport proved faster than contemporary front-line fighters and the Type 142 spurred the development of a bomber derivative. Advanced and innovative on its introduction, the

Pictured before the war, David Penman is seen here with a silver-doped Hawker Hart or Audax. This Hawker series saw some operational service during the early part of the Second World War. (*David Penman via Chris Gotts*)

The narrow fuselage of the Handley Page Hampden is evident from this head-on view. Inadequately armed, and with flawed flying characteristics, it soldiered on as a front-line bomber until September 1942. Modified with a deepened bomb-bay, the aircraft had some success as a torpedo-bomber. (*Via Mike Bailey*)

Blenheim design was soon outmoded by the advent of war but the heroism of its air-crews and the feats they performed are remembered with pride. David Penman was not enamoured of the type – 'serviceability was not good and the Blenheim had a bad accident record' – but relief of a sort was at hand when 44 Squadron re-equipped with the Handley Page Hampden. David related: 'We were glad to receive the first of our Hampdens in February 1939. The Hampden, though not quite as fast as the Blenheim, was a much better aircraft all round.'

Designed, like the Wellington, to Air Ministry specification B9/32, the Hampden entered service later than its companion but was likewise intended to perform primarily during daylight. A very narrow forward crew compartment, from which extended a slender fuselage tapering back to a twin-tailed configuration, soon saw it nicknamed the 'Flying Panhandle'. If anything, the Hampden was even less suited for its role than the Wellington. Lacking any power-operated turrets, it was poorly defended and soon transferred to nocturnal activities. David Penman was more supportive of this type:

It was a single pilot aircraft and no dual could be given. To me it was a delightful aircraft to fly, though others might not agree; it had a large roomy cockpit, which offered an excellent view. The controls were light and responsive, and with large flaps and also leading edge slots, it handled well at low speeds. However, it could swing badly on take-off, had a very poor single-engine performance and could get into a stabilized yaw which caused many accidents . . .

The 'stabilized yaw' was a notorious feature of the Hampden that derived from a design flaw. If the controls were not smoothly coordinated in a turn, the aircraft would side-slip. In some situations the forward fuselage then blocked airflow over the rudders, rendering them ineffective. Given adequate height (and sometimes the use of throttles), a pilot could recover but at low altitude there was never enough time to retrieve the situation. Pilots were also warned to avoid flat turns, for the same reason. Despite the aircraft's reputation, David Penman was comfortable in his cockpit:

The Pegasus engines were very reliable and each consumed around 70 gallons per hour – total fuel load, 656 gallons. I cannot recall any shortage of aircraft once we were fully equipped and they were replaced quickly. We were short of crews, having two flights each with six crews, and replacements were slow to arrive. The very high accident rate at the Hampden Operational Training Unit did not help. For pilots just out of training school with little over 150 hours on Tigers and Oxfords, it would not have been easy. I was lucky to have 450 flying hours, 75 of them on the Hampden, when the war started. When we set out for Berlin on 25 September 1940, I had over 600 hours, including 190 hours on the Hampden, 52 of them at night.

Berlin became the last resting-place for many a bomber during the years of increasingly savage struggle, while the destruction they wrought reduced great swathes of the city to rubble and thousands perished. Residents of the city had an unpleasant foretaste of this during the night of 23/24 September 1940 when Bomber Command, untypically for the times, focused its attention on the German capital. A mixed force of 129 aircraft, Wellingtons, Hampdens and Whitleys, optimistically sought eighteen precision industrial and logistical targets. Three aircraft failed to return from this skirmish but 112 claimed positive bombing results, despite the difficult conditions caused by ground mist and burgeoning enemy defences.

Returning to more disparate operations, the RAF continued to pinprick Berlin and David Penman found his crew tasked for a small raid on the city on 25 September. On 11 September he had been allocated Hampden X2916, coded KM-D. It was a brand new machine, although as David reflected wryly, 'very few survived long enough to become old'. Would his be an exception? His crew that night were all sergeants. His navigator was Frank Stott, who had qualified as a pilot but was assigned as a navigator pending a crew of his own. Sergeant Duffy, a regular on the Penman crew, took care of the radio communications while defending the Hampden was the primary task of air-gunner Sergeant Hird, who was flying only his fifth operation with Penman as pilot.

Berlin was at the limit of their operational capabilities, and KM-D, fully laden with fuel and four 500lb high explosive bombs, weighed heavily on its undercarriage as it taxied out. Waddington would not be blessed with concrete runways for some months yet, and there was always the risk that a fully laden aircraft would become bogged down. Fortunately KM-D reached the take-off point unhindered and commenced final take-off preparations. To everyone's relief the take-off was similarly uneventful and the ensuing climb became a laborious process. They were aligned on a regular aerial corridor taking them eastwards until they could identify Skegness on the Lincolnshire coast. The town provided a useful navigational fix before their aircraft slipped across the featureless North Sea, toiling slowly upwards at some 120mph towards 10,000 feet. Frank Stott now relied on dead reckoning and his sextant skills for star shots. Their track was simply a straight line for Berlin and Frank did his best to avoid any deviation but the vagaries of wind speed and direction always made the navigator's job more difficult. Supporting Frank, Sergeant Duffy struggled to get wireless fixes and loop bearings from British radio stations but David later remarked that these proved 'very difficult to get'. The Hampden droned uncertainly onwards. The crew were at least blessed with a peaceful sea crossing and an undisturbed track in over the enemy coast. Some time later David saw heavy flak filling the sky ahead and called Frank to discuss their position. He was worried. A few rough calculations using airspeed and elapsed time told him it could not be Berlin. Supporting this assessment was the area of flak which, although dense, was not as widespread as that experienced over Berlin. Gauging the area of gun flashes and supporting searchlights, plus what little they could determine of the city's outlines, the crew concluded they were over Magdeburg, south-west of their objective. Turning north-east, they set course for Berlin, which, if this *was* Magdeburg, would be some 70 miles away. The twin Pegasus engines pounded away the miles but no target appeared and it became unhappily apparent that they were lost. Checking his fuel levels, David knew they were approaching the limit of their endurance and began searching for a target of opportunity. Below, in the moonlight, the straight lines of an autobahn appeared, 'so four 500lb bombs went down on it'. Still lost, they established a course that would, they hoped, bring them in to some recognisable part of the English coast, from where they could get a bearing for Waddington. To the east, the first hint of dawn lightened the horizon and the blackness beneath slowly faded to a greyish hue. The strengthening light eventually revealed nothing to help identify their exact location as a solid blanket of cloud covered the countryside. Disconcertingly, Frank Stott now guessed they were somewhere near Heligoland, a notorious place for the RAF. During 1939 Luftwaffe fighters inflicted heavy casualties in this area when the RAF persisted with daylight operations. Severe losses had finally demonstrated the vulnerability of unescorted daylight raids, and as dawn broke David sensibly concluded that it was 'not a good place to be' and sacrificed fuel for speed and distance. Further calculations tried to establish how far it was home, and whether they could make it, judging by their rate of consumption and their fuel reserves. There was no doubt about it: they were in serious trouble. With luck, they might just make the eastern extremity of England around Cromer on the Norfolk coast. With luck.

As the danger of interception receded, so their most pressing enemies became weight and distance. David instructed his crew to discard any surplus equipment. Everything not nailed down, including all their machine-guns and ammunition, splashed into the North Sea. Eking out their fuel, David throttled back as far as possible and with both Pegasus engines puttering on low revs he trimmed the bomber for maximum endurance and a gradual descent. Soon their shadow danced from cloud tops ahead of them, racing like a puppy in the park. Then, kissing the cloud tops, the Hampden finally married its ethereal image and disappeared. Flying on instruments alone, David kept the artificial horizon level but allowed the aircraft symbol on the indicator to stay just beneath the line on the instrument's face. Gently coasting the air-currents within the cloud, the aircraft rose and fell. The crew's anxiety increased – would land be visible when they broke clear? At last the clouds grew thinner and the aircraft shed the final, vaporous tendrils to emerge over a sullen seascape unendorsed by even a hint of land. Peering down, David took little solace from the relatively calm sea conditions that might assist if they ditched, but he ordered the crew to prepare. The fuel gauges now flickered to zero and the empty vista ahead offered no hope. Then – was it just imagination? The horizon surely had a density suggesting land. But none appeared and their hopes now felt as empty as the fuel tanks. Again the horizon thickened. Land? Yes – no – maybe – please God. YES. Looming out of the mist was a coastline, all sandy curves with beautiful greenery beyond. They all searched unsuccessfully for a recognisable feature but could only assume it was Norfolk – somewhere. Suddenly the aircraft shuddered as first one engine backfired, then the other. The final drops of fuel swirling in the tanks caused their loyal Pegasus engines to splutter and cough like old men with the day's first fag. Each motor was fed from its own tanks with no capability for transferring – not that it mattered, since all the gauges indicated a firm and final zero.

Any hopes of a crash-landing on one of Norfolk's firm flat beaches were soon dispelled. The tide was in and the little strips of soft sand were unsuitable even without the dunes, cliffs and plethora of protruding anti-invasion poles, now clearly visible. Worse still, this deterrent extended inland for field upon field, robbing them of another option. They were now below 1,000 feet as both engines, sucking vapour, lost power. Any opportunity for parachuting after reaching the shoreline had disappeared as they lost height and David ordered the crew to adopt their crash positions. He also felt the aircraft offered its pilot only a poor chance of survival if he baled out – the likelihood was that he would strike the tail unit. Searching a landscape spiked with countless poles, David knew he had to choose a smaller, unguarded field where there might be a slim chance of squeezing in. Picking the best available, he opted for a wheels-down landing because he wanted to save his aircraft if humanly possible. Selecting undercarriage down, he was gratified to see the green lamps come on, and with the engines still spluttering he chose a flap setting that would stretch his glide when they quit, as they inevitably would. Holding his shallow approach, he nursed the Hampden towards the nearest boundary hedge of the chosen field. His mind now juggled the options available and he decided to risk overshooting the first hedge on the simple basis that it would be more expedient 'to overshoot and hit the far hedge slowly than undershoot and hit the first hedge hard'. Either way, the field looked uncomfortably tiny and, closer now, distinctly uneven. A lack of waves on the shoreline had indicated very little wind so he made allowances as the bomber settled. However, having been aloft so long, his machine now seemed reluctant to touch down. Empty tanks and the lightened airframe caused it to float high over the first hedge, which, he now realised, had concealed a dip on the far side. Precious distance disappeared before X2916 touched down. David braked hard. The wheels locked but his speed barely dissipated. Perhaps the early morning dew on the meadow was causing the bomber to aquaplane? Still travelling fast, they reached a mound that divided one field from the next and bounced over, momentarily airborne, before crunching down hard on the undercarriage. David did his best to level the wings in time but the impact was so severe that one wheel sheered away and the bomber slewed crazily round on the other, dragging its wing and skidding sideways in a flurry of scattered soil and grass. Sliding askew for a little distance, the Hampden finally came to rest looking very much the worse for wear.

In the seconds of silence that followed, the crew realised that their perilous homecoming was complete, after a flight that had lasted a gruelling 9 hours and 20 minutes. Relief washed over David as he unclipped his harness and clambered from the cockpit down on to the sweet-scented meadow. Every blade of grass looked beautiful. Several soldiers were hurrying towards the stricken bomber as the grateful but exhausted airmen emerged to find out precisely where they were. They had landed close to the church of St Mary in the Norfolk village of Northrepps – perhaps there was a touch of divine intervention in their survival.

Those that wanted lit cigarettes – there was no likelihood of spilt gasoline – and then gazed around as more and more people arrived until a welcoming throng surrounded David's decidedly bent bomber. He was taken to a local homestead where a kindly lady provided breakfast and then the luxury of a bed for the weary airman. Others of the crew received similar hospitality but their RAF masters were less understanding and David was woken 'long before I wanted to be' and fetched back to Waddington by an RAF vehicle. There was no tea and sympathy there. Instead he found himself being berated by the station commander, who was aggrieved about the misshapen aircraft and felt that David 'should have found an aerodrome to land on'. David's protestations regarding their fuel status were ignored, although he was certain there was no fuel in the tanks when he touched down and 'even a minute more would have meant no engines and no choice'. He felt equally sure that a belly-landing would have meant the aircraft slithering into the mound they had bounced over and the crew would have been injured – or worse – in the resultant crushing of the fuselage. However, after this admonishment David heard no more about the incident, and the Hampden was recovered and repaired. It continued in service until lost with all its crew during a night training exercise on 11 August 1941.

Three nights after his Northrepps mishap, David returned to duty on a sortie to Stuttgart. Airborne for 6 hours 55 minutes, he successfully diverted to North Coates aerodrome to land when adverse weather closed Waddington. The aircraft's limited endurance continued to handicap Hampden operations. One of David's friends, Pilot Officer David Romans, ditched twice in the space of a week owing to lack of fuel, first off Salthouse, then off Lowestoft. Meanwhile, on another operation Frank Stott made amends for his earlier navigational mishap by getting the Penman crew to Berlin and safely back to Waddington 7 hours 45 minutes later. This time they deposited four 500lb bombs on the city. To extend the Hampden's range, Handley Page devised additional fuel tanks that were attached to the under-wing bomb racks and provided an extra 140 gallons. As one of the squadron's most experienced pilots, David undertook several raids using the long-range tanks, which would provide 'a story in themselves', including one sortie to Bordeaux carrying a 1,500lb magnetic mine. 'The take-off was not easy and we just cleared the hedge. Climb was 120mph which appeared to be just above the stall. We flew level at 2,000 feet for 2 hours at 120mph to lighten the load before climbing higher.' On another sortie to Berlin, again using the long-range tanks, he had all the fuel tanks switched on for take-off but, 'having reached 2,000 feet, there was the nerve-wracking business of having the wireless operator switch off the port main fuel cock, wait a while, then the starboard. There was no way of knowing what fuel was left in the overload tanks and all we could do was fly for around 1 hour 40 minutes, then switch on the mains again, then switch off the overloads and hope there was no air lock. The wireless operator's control of the overload consisted of two rings with a wire from them to the cocks on the tanks on the wing.'

David completed his tour with 44 Squadron in February 1941 and went to RAF Finningley as an instructor on Wellingtons. He then converted to the ill-fated Avro Manchester before returning to the Wellington with 97 Squadron at Coningsby. 'We went to Wilhelmshaven on 10 January [1942] and then, with a sigh of relief, converted to the Lancaster on 15 January: 'the conversion was one circuit of 15 minutes'. Six months later he returned to 44 Squadron to command its conversion flight using both Manchesters and Lancasters. The Manchester's twin Rolls-Royce Vulture engines proved temperamental and the type was soon withdrawn from front-line operations. However, history now records how the magical Merlin engine was married to the basic Manchester airframe to create the majestic Lancaster. David served another full year on Lancasters and continued in the RAF for a further thirty but even then was not ready to relinquish his coveted wings. He flew as a pilot with 10 Air Experience Flight using the de Havilland Chipmunk to introduce Air Training Corps cadets to the delights of flying. As they clambered apprehensively into the rear cockpit, few of them knew that their chauffeur had been one of the RAF's early night adventurers, one of their heroes.

With the onset of winter in 1940, the RAF moved some of its Blenheim bombers to night operations, as recalled by navigator Sergeant Richard 'Dickie' Rook: 'Having spent the first six months of the war in Coastal Command searching for mines and submarines ahead of the Royal Navy and Merchant Navy convoys in the Western Approaches, heading out into the Atlantic, in June 1940 I was posted to 114 Squadron equipped with the Blenheim Mk IV aircraft. [We were] stationed at Horsham St Faith, near Norwich, and then went on to Oulton, a satellite aerodrome where we were billeted in Blickling Hall.' In March 1937

Blenheim boys. Paddy Murray (left) and Dickie Rook epitomise the indomitable spirit that typified Bomber Command. (*R. Rook*)

Dickie's new squadron had been the first to operate Blenheims when the type was regarded as the 'fastest medium bomber in the world' – eminently suitable for the squadron whose cobra-headed badge bore the motto, 'With Speed I Strike'. Times had changed markedly by the time the unit went to France in 1939, and the German Blitzkrieg through Belgium and the Low Countries in 1940 found the outclassed and hard-pressed Blenheims of 114 Squadron bombing columns of the advancing Wehrmacht. Following the defeat of Britain's allies, the squadron was withdrawn to Wattisham before moving to Horsham St Faith, where, as Dickie recalled it, they 'spent most of the summer months engaged upon targets in Europe and shipping around the Dutch coastal areas'. On his arrival at 114 Squadron, Dicky crewed up with fellow sergeants Peter Waigh as pilot and Irishman Paddy Murray as wireless operator/air-gunner (or Wop/Ag). Although this was the first posting for both Peter and

Paddy, following completion of their training, the trio got on well, together frequenting the local pubs, playing darts and chasing damsels. In Peter's case, the latter was a very successful pursuit as he met his future wife, Penny, in Norwich. The new crew soon had several successful operations to their credit when the change of tactics saw 114 Squadron increasing its nocturnal activities. One of their earliest night attacks saw six aircraft, including Blenheim R3594 with Sergeants Murray, Rook and Waigh aboard, on the battle order for the night of 27 November. At briefing that afternoon, they learnt that Bomber Command was targeting five objectives in Cologne with a force of sixty-two aircraft. They were to take off from Oulton but return to Horsham St Faith because the satellite base lacked night-flying facilities. Dickie remembers:

> It was a bitterly cold and damp day with low cloud, brisk winds and hazy drizzle when we made our way to the dispersal point and boarded the aircraft. I was feeling the signs of an approaching cold and remember thinking that bed would have been a much more appealing option but this quickly passed as I prepared my charts and implements on a very damp chart table.

Meanwhile, moisture had permeated the airframe and all the metal fittings had a sheen of dampness as Paddy settled into his position. In the cockpit Peter pushed his parachute into its bucket seat and commenced his pre-flight preliminaries: hydraulic selection lever 'down', likewise the undercarriage lever, and there were three comforting greens when he flicked on the indicator lamp switch. Lightly grasping the spectacle-type control column, he checked it and the rudder pedals for unhindered movement of the flying controls. Next, he set the carburettor air intake beside his left elbow, adjusted the engine cowling gills and confirmed that the propellers were set to fine pitch. Conversant with the Peter's ritual, the ground-crew waited for confirmation then primed the engines and connected the external power supply. Peter cautiously nudged the throttle levers forward a half-inch along the quadrant. Go too far and you risked neat fuel being pumped into the air intake and then gulped back on start-up with the consequent possibility of an engine fire. Burning out one of His Majesty's Blenheim bombers would not enhance a young pilot's flying career. Checking there were no personnel near the propellers, Peter switched on the main magnetos and pushed the first starter, his left hand poised on the throttles in case an engine decided to 'spit back'. Fortunately, both behaved and the twin Mercury engines were soon chortling contentedly, with oil and engine cylinder temperatures looking fine. Peter indicated to the ground-crew to disconnect the external power supply magnetos and they quickly secured the priming pumps as Peter tested his flaps using the engine-driven hydraulic pump. After confirming he had adequate brake pressure, he released the parking brake and boosted the machine into steady progress over the wet turf while he completed his pre-take-off checks of hydraulics, trim tabs, fuel mixture and propeller pitch settings. All was fine and he swung the Blenheim into wind and straightened up before notching up a final burst of power with the brakes applied. The all clear was received – they were ready to go. Both engines chorused their enthusiasm as the power increased and Blenheim R3594 gathered speed. Counteracting the type's characteristic starboard swing, Peter felt the undulations diminish as the undercarriage oleos absorbed less strain and aerodynamics took over. The swathe of grass illuminated by the Blenheim's lights blurred and at about 90mph he eased the bomber into the air, retracting the undercarriage as he continued to gain speed. The airscrew settings were switched from fine to coarse and the boost was adjusted to maintain a steady climb through 150mph. Dickie gave Peter the required heading – there would be no clear navigation this night. With no stars or visual pinpoints, it was dead reckoning all the way.

Dickie described the trip:

We were airborne at 17:45 hours and climbed steadily into the dark murky cloud and mist which enshrouded the aircraft reducing outside visibility to zero. We were now dependent entirely upon the pilot's fluorescent instrument panel and the skill of the navigator to take us across the North Sea and into Germany and our intended target, as wireless transmission silence was enforced. As we approached our intended height we began to get some rapid ice accretion; as the temperature was critical, we decided to take steps to counteract this and began to climb higher to come into lower temperatures where ice would no longer form. (This was because the water droplets would already have formed ice crystals and these would not adhere to the airframe.) We found the right conditions between 18,000 and 20,000 feet where the temperature was in the region of minus 40° C. At this altitude eyebrows and eyelashes, in fact any exposed hair, very soon became white with frost as exhaled breath immediately froze in the extremely low temperatures.

As we approached the enemy coast, searchlights illuminated the clouds from below and we felt one or two unusual lurches of the aircraft, which we associated with some random anti-aircraft fire but this caused us little concern. The dense cumulus cloud showed no signs of a break and we discussed what tactics we should adopt when the target area was reached. It was agreed that, should the target area not be visible, we would bomb on ETA (Estimated Time of Arrival) rather than carry the bombs all the way back home and indeed this is exactly what we did.

As soon as the bombs were released we swung round on an almost reciprocal course heading for home. Now we had only the dense cloud and impending icing problems to contend with, and it was not long before it became obvious that that was quite enough. As we descended into warmer air, with the aircraft temperature still below freezing, ice began to build up at a rather alarming rate. Soon, as the temperature began to slowly rise in the lower and rather less cold regions, some ice began to loosen. As it broke away, it would impact on the fuselage with a heavy thud, similar to the noise made by shrapnel strikes, while bouncing off the props it sounded like rapid rifle fire. At this time a misty rime frost began to cover the inside of the aircraft, tending to obscure the flying instruments. The pilot, who was wearing two pairs of gloves, an inner of silk and the outer of heavy leather, began wiping the frost from the glass fronts of the various instruments, one of which was the altimeter. The significance of this will become clear later.

Our descent continued until we reached our ETA at Horsham – when nothing but the intense dark of the winter's night could be seen. After circling and attempting, without any success, to contact base on the R/T, the pilot, as was not uncommon in such cases, immediately blamed the navigation, assuming that we were out of range. To disprove this I suggested that we headed for the coast again where, providing there were no intruder aircraft in the area, I would locate Happisburgh Lighthouse, which I was sure would be showing. Off we went and on ETA, sure enough, we located a strong light through the lower mist and cloud. This was sufficient confirmation for me that my calculations had been accurate. A new course was given for the return to the aerodrome but, on ETA, not a thing could be seen in the inky blackness. We circled again, hoping to see perhaps the twinkle of a poorly masked car headlight in or around the city of Norwich but there was nothing and no reply to our constant R/T calls to base. All this time every effort was being made to locate something, anything, to give us a clue as to our position. It was then that, while peering through the front nose panel, I happened to glance across my table at my altimeter. It was my practice to set this at aerodrome level before take-off, whereas the pilot set his at mean sea level. To my absolute horror it was reading zero! Immediately I called the pilot and screamed, 'You're on the deck – climb immediately'. To my astonishment, a calm voice replied, 'I've got 600 feet here and that's plenty in this area'. I immediately pointed out there was ample space above and we should use it, and at this moment the lights went out.

We had, according to witnesses, struck the gable end of a house a glancing blow with the starboard wingtip, hit a tree and eventually finished up, in many pieces, in the middle of Catton Deer Park, less than 2 miles from the aerodrome. It is my belief that, while the pilot was clearing frost off the instruments earlier, on our homeward flight, he had inadvertently altered the [altimeter] setting.'

If this were the case, it was understandable in the circumstances. The altimeter had a protruding adjustment knob that pulled out to alter the hands, rather like a watch. If Peter's gloved hand caught this knob, he might well have accidentally altered the setting and been oblivious of the fact. It is also possible that the instrument had failed in some other manner. Although primitive by today's standards, altimeters of the period were, according to a technical manual, 'accurate to within 1 per cent of the recorded height, except possibly at heights below 2,000 feet but, even after a somewhat rapid descent from a considerable height, the error on landing will not normally exceed 20 or 30 ft'. This would be fine in good visibility but not in pitch darkness and travelling at over 165mph. Doubtless Peter would have checked his altimeter on Dickie's call but it was already too late for any debate. Peter described what happened next: 'The last thing I remembered was the canopy being torn asunder and rivets popping out as though some great hand was brutally tearing open a zip fastener. All then went black, blacker than the night around us.'

Geoff Hawes and his wife had been sitting indoors when the bomber smashed into the gable end and chimneystack of their home. A large chunk of the aircraft and pieces of rubble crashed

The broken-backed Blenheim lays crumpled on what has since become a housing development on the outskirts of Norwich. The guard, hands in pockets and collar turned up, tries to stave off the winter's chill. (*R. Rook*)

Both engines and one propeller were ripped off as the aircraft was torn in two. The nose and crushed cockpit are to the right. (*R. Rook*)

Amazed that anyone could have survived, RAF personnel stand close to what had once been a cockpit and the navigator's station. (*R. Rook*)

into their garden, wedging shut their back door. Anxious neighbours ran to assist but fortunately the couple emerged unharmed apart from a covering of soot that had erupted from the fireplace when debris tumbled down the chimney! In his home nearby, 9-year-old Bernard Roper was startled by the roar of a low-flying aircraft, and then came the crash and a sound like 'a lot of tin cans being tipped out of a wheelbarrow'. The next moment he heard someone yelling for his father Cedric, who was a first-aider and, as the youngster reached the stair top from his bedroom, the front door slammed shut. His father dashed into the darkness with others from the neighbourhood, all running towards where the noise told them an aeroplane had crashed. Whether it was British or German was unknown. Chasing over several gardens, Cedric and his companions climbed a bank and through a hedge surrounding the meadow known as Dixon's Fold. Further into the field lay the Blenheim's bedraggled carcass. The aircraft's back was broken. The torn-off tail plane lay askew, both engines had been ripped off and the forward section was just a crumpled mess. Miraculously, from within the remains, what sounded like a Canadian voice yelled 'Get me out of the bloody plane!' Presumably the locals mistook Paddy's Irish brogue for a Canadian accent, but the certainty that the crew were Canadian soon settled into local folklore. Being further aft, Paddy was possibly more vocal than his more seriously injured companions, but soon all three were found.

Peter Waigh never fully recovered from
the injuries he sustained in the crash.
(*Mrs Patricia Marks*)

Peter recalled:

I came to thinking I was in bed looking at the stars through the window but soon realized
I was in a field unable to move. Then men's voices in the distance and soon one close by
saying, 'This one doesn't look too good – he's bleeding badly'. A light flashed in my eyes
and the voice said, 'Are there any bombs on board?' I managed to say, 'We left them on the
other side'. 'Good,' he said. 'Have a cigarette.'

   I next remember waking up in the Norfolk and Norwich Hospital with a leg in plaster
and a torn up face.

Dickie Rook had fared little better:

I became semi-conscious lying on the ground with some dear old soul supporting my head
and very soon someone else produced a hot drink. I have no idea whether I drank it or not.
We were then placed into the ambulance and I remember nothing more until some days

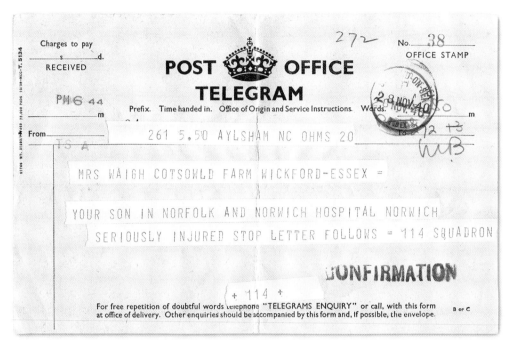

In the days before e-mails and mobile phones existed, telegrams told families the news both good and bad. This one must have caused great anxiety to Peter's mother. (*Mrs Patricia Marks*)

later I was aware of being in a darkened room with a nursing orderly speaking to me and being told that I was allowed no light in the room because of serious concussion. I was not allowed a pillow, my hands were heavily bandaged and I had to be fed by an orderly, a situation which continued for about a week.

Paddy Murray was in a bed opposite with concussion and frost-bitten feet. Being less seriously injured, he was soon independently mobile again and quickly returned to flying duties.

Noting how local people had ignored the dangers of fire and explosions to rescue the men, the commanding officer from RAF Horsham St Faith wrote to them to express his thanks and the letter received by Edgar Betts is still treasured by his family. It reads:

I wish to express my appreciation on behalf of the aeroplane which crashed in the vicinity of OLD CATTON on the 27th November 1940, and to which I add my own thanks for the assistance you kindly rendered them following the accident . . . It was most kind of you. The assistance you gave is the more valuable as the pilot, the observer and the gunner had been flying in extremely difficult weather conditions and without your aid the injuries to them may have been much worse than they have turned out to be . . .

Some weeks later Dickie was able to express a more personal appreciation in the bar of the Woodman pub, but it was to be six months before he passed a full medical in the RAF hospital at Halton and was pronounced fit for flying duties. Following this, he was posted to 105 Squadron at Swanton Morley, where he met Paddy again, and together they crewed up with Squadron Leader Judson. For the next five months they flew many of the hazardous low-level operations for which the squadron and its parent, 2 Group, became renowned. Both men were then taken off combat operations and Dickie later became a station navigational officer. He last met Peter Waigh in 1945 when the latter was instructing on the Link trainer at RAF Bramcote. Peter had been in hospitals and rehabilitation centres for many months and had had a steel plate inserted in his leg, which prevented further operational flying. It would trouble him for the rest of his life. He died in July 1986. Despite the fact that it may have been his error that caused the crash, there were no ill-feelings from his former crew. Together they had contributed much during a period of trial and error for the whole RAF, and Bomber Command in particular.

* * *

With 1940 drawing to a close, it became evident that the RAF had secured a significant victory and saved the British nation (and arguably the free world), at least for the time being. Fighter Command undeniably deserves the credit for securing air superiority and gaining vital time during which the nation could re-arm and strengthen its resources to repel the invasion that many felt would come during 1941. The early achievements of Bomber Command lacked the definition of the daylight fighter victory and it clearly needed aircraft more suited for the role, additional training and better methods of target location and identification. However, the survivors of those early nights of blundering blindly over Europe provided a nucleus of expertise that would later be used to establish a better-equipped strategic striking arm capable of pounding the Third Reich to its knees. Neither they nor those who came later were given any form of campaign medal – although their courage is often recalled, their contribution remains sadly unrewarded. There was no separate recognition of their efforts. With the benefit of hindsight, and with the threat of Nazi tyranny now lifted, one may argue about the morals of the Allied bomber offensive. But there can be no doubt about the courage of the young airmen involved.

CHAPTER TWO

Swastika Stories

While the RAF eventually recognised its inadequacies and planned to rectify them with the development of a strategic bombing capability, the Luftwaffe failed to establish an equivalent and primarily focused its efforts on supporting its ground forces. Had the German authorities chosen to invest earlier in a powerful strategic bomber force with suitable long-range fighter escort, then the outcome of the war might have been very different, but the reality is that the Luftwaffe's endeavours to attain air superiority over England failed. It finally resorted to area bombing. However, horrendous though the British casualty figures were in the towns they blitzed, the Germans lacked the delivery systems to wreak such havoc that the British nation would be forced to capitulate, through the collapse of morale or infrastructure. Four years later Allied air power similarly failed to undermine German morale to bring about the cessation of hostilities. However, strategic air power as used by the British and Americans rendered invaluable assistance by destroying the oil refineries and other elements vital for a modern power to maintain its military capabilities.

Hitler further compounded the difficulties for his air force by opening a second front during Operation Barbarossa – the invasion of Russia on 21 June 1941. The initial successes of his blitzkrieg tactics ultimately over-stretched his resources and supply lines before freezing to a halt in a campaign that cost millions of lives. The absence of a strategic strike force meant that German bombers lacked the range, capacity and capability to reach the Russian manufacturing plants deep inside the country, and with western support the Russian authorities were able to set about re-arming.

For the British in 1940/1 Hitler's intention to invade remained a real threat until Barbarossa made it an unlikely proposition, as Hitler became preoccupied with wrestling Stalin's giant bear. The threat was very real, and there are reminders of it dotted along Britain's coastline and waterways, in the form of concrete pill-boxes, anti-tank blocks and former anti-aircraft gun emplacements. There is also evidence of Britain's response to earlier threats: Martello towers, for example, recall the failed aspirations of an earlier tyrant seeking dominance over both Europe and Russia, while the remnants of former gun batteries echo a time when the Royal Navy protected our shores and air superiority was a concept unknown to military planners. Just occasionally, further reminders appear on the shoreline or amid the sand dunes. So it was in 1998 that a barnacle-encrusted elevator section from an aeroplane was washed up on the beach near Blakeney in Norfolk. This trophy was picked up by a couple with a second home in the vicinity, and they decided it was intriguing enough to prompt a visit to the Norfolk and Suffolk Aviation Museum (N&SAM) at Flixton. They left their find at the museum gates and went to have lunch at Flixton's famous Buck Inn! While they dined, Bob Collis, then one of the museum's historians and a specialist on Luftwaffe equipment, spotted the relic and had a look at it. He reported:

> It was fairly easy to identify as a control surface, and surprisingly it still had a fair amount of fabric attached to it. Marine life and small dead crabs were in or on the piece, so I knew it had been in salt water, and 15 minutes' work with a soft brush gave us more clues, and part numbers beginning 'R8 111' confirmed it was an airframe piece from an He111. You would have loved to see their faces when they rolled out of the pub an hour later, hauled the relic down to the Blister Hangar and came looking for me. 'Go and see Bob Collis,' the Chairman had told them. 'He's the wrecks and relics man.' Unaware that I had already examined the piece, they invited me to look at it with a view to identifying it. I cast an eye over the elevator, smiled, and said in a laid-back expert voice: 'I should say you found this in the area of Cley, Norfolk?'. They were astonished!

In fact, Bob knew the museum already had items from this machine, He111 Werke-nr. 8747, including an FuG10P radio set, plus the winch for the trailing aerial, and a bomb slip, 'all in superb condition and "liberated" from the wreck at the time'. This collection originates from an aerial duel on 18/19 June 1940 and represents the first in a section of swastika stories recalling the courage of German airmen and their British adversaries.

Peering from the greenhouse that was his exposed position in the Heinkel 111, Oberleutnant Ulrich Jordan was on his first operation over England. It would also be his last. Not many hours earlier Jordan, a staff officer with 4 Staffel, Kampfgeschwader 4 'General Wever', had telephoned Oberst Handrick, the officer in charge of Luftwaffe fighter units in Northern France, Belgium and Holland. Jordan was planning his unit's attack that night and wanted to more fully appreciate the capabilities of British night-fighters. Who better to ask than someone with experience and intelligence resources? He was pleased (and perhaps a touch cynical) to find that Handrick was dismissive of Britain's night-fighters, basing his response in part on a comparison with the inadequacies of German night-fighters. Neither side was a force to be reckoned with. In truth, Handrick was right. The RAF, like the Luftwaffe, was ill-prepared for the nocturnal defence of the British Isles. Air Interception (AI) radar was in its infancy and few of the Blenheim 1F night-fighters carried the apparatus. Their meagre numbers were augmented by Boulton Paul Defiants, single-engined fighters in which the forward-firing fixed machine-guns had been relinquished to make way for the additional weight of a specifically designed Boulton Paul dorsal turret wielding four .303in machine-guns plus a gunner. Lacking forward defences, it was not a success in daylight, and it wasn't long before German fighter pilots became familiar with the Defiant's form and its

Reported as downed at 0357 hours on 19 June 1940, the wreck of He111 5J+DM 8747 lay on the foreshore at Cley for many years before Trinity House decided it was a navigation hazard and ordered it blown up in 1969. The starboard propeller had been feathered and the crash-landing conducted so skilfully that the nose Perspex remained intact. (*Via Chris Gotts*)

Stripped of any equipment considered to be of intelligence value, the wreck became a target for souvenir hunters.

The Blenheim's fine marksmanship – the tail section being 'frizzled away', in Duke-Woolley's words – is evidenced by a missing section of rudder and the remainder riddled by machine-gun bullets.

weaknesses. Defiant losses soared and the type was relegated to the night-fighter role where it and the Blenheim did sterling work until more suitable types – the Beaufighter and Mosquito – became available. Augmenting these new night-fighters were Hurricanes and Spitfires, which were effective by day but less so at night. However, combined with anti-aircraft guns and searchlights the aircraft had some successes against the intruders, and Ulrich Jordan unwittingly assisted the defenders when planning his unit's contribution to the largest assault on Britain yet undertaken. Some seventy bombers would be launched against the UK that night. Coincidentally, almost the same numbers of RAF machines were ordered off in the opposite direction to attack targets in the Ruhr, Hamburg and Bremen areas.

In this tit-for-tat campaign, Ulrich Jordan was determined to punish the RAF for an earlier piece of impudence in bombing his base at Merville. The Germans had captured the airfield from the Allies less than a month previously and II/KG4 had barely settled in to their new home, 20 miles south of Flanders, when Blenheims attacked and put numerous He111s out of action. Such audacity deserved a sturdy response, and orders were received to raid RAF bomber airfields at Honington and Mildenhall. Not anticipating serious aerial opposition, Jordan planned a strung-out assault instead of bunching his resources. This resulted in a steady trickle of raiders, a tactic that benefited the defenders because they had more time to search for individual machines. Jordan knew that many of his crews lacked night-flying experience, and combined with lost aircraft in the RAF raid the number of aircraft available for the retaliation reduced from an intended twenty to less than half that number.

Pictured conferring before take-off are (left to right) Oberleutnant Ernst Dieter von Tellman; Oberleutnant Joachim von Arnim; Major Erdman (Gruppenkommandeur) and Oberleutnant Ulrich Jordan. Von Arnim and his crew were shot down that same night and crashed at Six Mile Bottom in Cambridgeshire. (*Ulrich Jordan via Chris Goss*)

Prior to briefing the crews, Ulrich assessed the strategy with his Gruppenkommandeur, Major Dietrich Freiherr von Massenbach, with whom he would share the honour of being first airborne, in Heinkel 5J+DM. This was not Jordan's regular machine. To his chagrin, his own was still being repaired after some unwelcome attention from the impertinent RAF.

At last, Jordan settled into the cockpit, grumbled inwardly over 5J+DM's additional armour-plating. About 20 per cent of the II/KG4 aircraft carried this additional protection but it was unpopular because the extra weight reduced speed and the He111 was arguably slow enough already. Further aft, Oberfeldwebel Max Leimer adjusted and established settings at his radio station as the flight engineer, Feldwebel Karl Amberger, went through his own pre-flight routine, including checks on the hand-held MG15 machine-guns, even though they were unlikely to be needed. After a final time check, the twin Junkers Jumo 211 engines were fired up under the attentive gaze of the ground-crew. With little further ado, the brakes were released and 5J+DM trundled to its take-off position. The aircraft was painted a dark black-green, so that the darker letters on its fuselage were barely discernible as

The snub-nose and belly gun-pack are evident in this example of a Blenheim I fighter. (*Via Mike Bailey*)

the setting sun elongated the evening shadows over the northern French countryside. Only the white D and the white trim surrounding the swastika on its fin were distinguishable as the bomber bellowed past the watching ground-crew and climbed away.

Some 200 miles away the Blenheim crews of 23 Squadron, based at Collyweston in Northamptonshire, 12 miles from Peterborough, were once again alerted to the possibility of 'trade' that night. Their job was to protect the back gate to England's industrial heartland, and they had been put on alert every night that month, so far without result, but the mechanics and armourers still carefully tended their snub-nosed steeds. Unhappily for the RAF, this description implies a speed these underpowered mounts did not possess. Beneath the nose of each machine lurked a batch of four .303in machine-guns that were intended to bolster the inadequate single fixed forward-firing weapon from the original design. The dorsal turret, mounting a single .303, had also been retained, and the extra firepower meant that the Blenheim was capable, with effort, of destroying German bombers – if it could catch them. They were slower than the sleek Junkers 88 and only marginally quicker than the slim-lined Dornier 17 'Flying Pencil'. Against Jordan's slower He111s, the Blenheim had a speed advantage, but the closing pace from below or level flight was still uncomfortably slow. The seven machines of 23 Squadron made ready, as did five other defending squadrons employing a mixture of Blenheims and Spitfires as the size of the enemy force became evident.

From his seat in the familiar Heinkel greenhouse, Ulrich Jordan observed the great mass of London on his port side, while the moon-silvered sheen of the Thames Estuary glistened to starboard. Suddenly the night sky was segmented by searchlight beams, maybe a dozen or more, each searching the skies for the invaders. Jordan noted the absence of anti-aircraft fire, which meant that British night-fighters were also on the prowl, no matter what Handrick had said. Abruptly a searchlight dazzled blindingly into Jordan's cockpit, and soon three more were illuminating every detail of the Heinkel, despite the German's evasive manoeuvres. Exposed and afraid, the crew awaited the blast of machine-gun bullets but strangely nothing happened. There was no savagery of shellfire, no searing burst ripping apart their machine. In an almost courteous manner, the searchlights passed the plane politely from one cluster to the next, as the Heinkel continued to the north-east. It was, they knew, too good to be true. It was. Sliding in behind the brightly lit bomber, Sergeant Alan Close slowly, slowly gained on his opponent. The guns of his 23 Squadron Blenheim were set to fire and his gunner, Leading Aircraftman Laurence Karasek, was equally prepared. Still concealed in the darkness, the RAF crew knew they would be easily visible to the vigilant gunners in the Heinkel once they emerged into the glare. On board 5J+DM, both Leimer and Amberger were alert and straining their glare-stressed eyes beyond the beams, searching for the dangers they knew must be lurking in the shadows. Close and Karasek were equally ready for the next part of the attack. There was no easy option here: it was kill or be killed.

The exact choreography of events is unclear but an exchange of gunfire rattled across the heavens as .303in and 7.9mm rounds ripped through the darkness. Ulrich Jordan felt strikes on his machine. Whether Alan Close felt anything beyond the first searing agony will never be known. Now blindingly illuminated by the searchlights, his aircraft was targeted by the Heinkel's guns and bullets tore into its fuselage and wings. Lacking self-sealing fuel tanks, the Blenheim burst into flames and Karasek found his world heeling sickeningly over into a terrifying plummet earthwards. The British aircraft scorched its blazing trail through the night sky with its gunner fighting for survival and its pilot already dead or dying, while the Heinkel, seemingly triumphant and unperturbed, continued serenely on course.

Airborne a few miles distant, over Boston in Lincolnshire, Flight Lieutenant Raymond Duke-Woolley witnessed the downfall of his comrades. We might like to think of heroes being spurred into action by such sights, but, as Duke-Woolley himself later admitted, seeing the Blenheim's fiery demise 'did not improve my morale . . . watching this ball of flame that had been our aircraft, I found myself thinking furiously'. Earlier, a jingoistic senior officer, without any combat experience, had announced that it was merely a matter of sneaking up on the enemy to 'let him have it', and the man blustered ignorant assurances about enemy aircraft falling apart after being hit by the Blenheim's 'tremendous armament'. This Heinkel seemed impervious but Duke-Woolley and his gunner, Aircraftman Derek Bell, were determined to do their duty and avenge their compatriots through a combination of wisdom and stealth. Believing the destruction of enemy aircraft was not quite the simple task envisaged by the 'gallant and decorated air commodore from the First World War', Duke-Woolley conceived what he described as a 'nifty plan'. He deduced that Close had been totally dazzled by the searchlights, later remarking that 'if this happened, the light inside our Perspex cockpit was hideously bright and one could barely see the instrument panel, let alone anything outside the cockpit'. He pushed the throttles forward until both engines were straining, and with considerable trepidation the second night-fighter crew to challenge the Heinkel closed in with great caution. Duke-Woolley told Bell that he would continue stalking the bomber, but not attack until it lost the searchlight beams. He also ordered Bell to don his parachute, just in case.

To the He111 crew, it would seem as if the assaults on their machine continued without interruption from one night-fighter to the next. Climbing hard, the latest Blenheim was sensed but remained unseen, although it was now almost in range. At last the searchlights went out. Creeping beneath the bomber, Duke-Woolley first went abreast then slid out to its port side and 'very gently took up station' close astern and just below. He held his aircraft at some 130mph and, still unseen, eased even nearer. From only 50 yards' distance the Blenheim opened fire, the close-set armament pack unleashing a concerted stream of bullets into the bomber. Duke-Woolley saw a series of strikes on the rear fuselage. 'I suppose I fired for about 3 seconds with every second feeling like an hour and sweat pouring off my face. Well, I was frightened! After all, I had only a sheet of Perspex between me and whatever it was that destroyed the other Blenheim in nothing flat . . .'. The He111 suddenly seemed to slow, as if chopping throttle to make the Blenheim overshoot, and its gunners returned fire but this time with less accuracy.

Karl Amberger had been hit in the stomach and one leg so his gun fell silent. Ulrich Jordan's earlier irritation about the additional armour-plating turned to relief as British bullets peppered his aircraft. He hoped his crew's return fire had been just as accurate.

After the first 'interminable' 3 seconds the Blenheim broke away to starboard just as 'great gouts of gunfire' emerged from the embattled enemy and rent the night sky precisely where the Blenheim had been only moments earlier. Close. Very close. Duke-Woolley was now below and to starboard, yet amazingly the He111 still seemed 'utterly unconcerned'.

In fact, the reverse was true, as the Blenheim crew gathered their courage for a renewed strike. They gave it another burst, producing 'bags of strikes'. Then Duke-Woolley rapidly broke to port as retaliatory fire lanced the night sky again, straight through the slot just vacated by the Blenheim, which now slipped to the opposite side of its prey. Not to be outdone, Bell was also blasting away when the opportunity occurred, but now his pilot, edging even nearer to the Heinkel, invited his gunner to 'stitch him up'. Bell could hardly miss and whipped out several bursts before the Blenheim skidded away again, before bringing its fixed guns to bear. The effect of Bell's efforts was 'absolutely and precisely nil', and Duke-Woolley had no choice but to get even closer to their stubborn opponent. Inching closer until they were dangerously near the Heinkel's tail, the Blenheim blasted away. By now they were so close that Duke-Woolley could see the back of the Heinkel being 'frizzled away' by his bullets. The effect reminded him of 'those magic papers' popular at Christmas which smouldered red without actually igniting – unlike the Blenheim pilot's temper. He was 'furious at being ignored', and his rage nearly caused his own aircraft's downfall as he waited too long before banking steeply away to starboard. At point-blank range the Heinkel's gunners 'properly clobbered' the Blenheim.

To the German crew, it felt as if the entire RAF fleet of night-fighters had sallied forth to attack them and Jordan, hunching down in the protection of his armour-plate, estimated the duration of the battle as fully 20 minutes. His bomber had absorbed tremendous punishment but that last attack had seriously damaged their port engine. He could only hope they had finished off their assailant.

As they fell away into the darkness, Duke-Woolley heard Bell yell out that he had been wounded and the Heinkel's port engine was ablaze. The Blenheim pilot was too busy with a damaged starboard motor and loss of power to aid his gunner or celebrate the report that their target was at last on fire. After dropping towards the sea, he managed to level off, but could no longer see their adversary. He thought it had dived away, straight into the drink, he hoped. His own machine was 'in a sorry way' and might soon follow suit. Bullets had cut through the electrical connections just behind him, smashed the radio and ripped away the mounting for the oxygen bottles, causing them to roll loose in the fuselage; worse, poor Bell was still shouting that he had been hit in the face. They were some miles out to sea but it was a 'gin-clear' night and the bright full moon gave clear relief to the coastline so he had no trouble with their position. He was less certain of Bell's condition and the state of his aircraft.

The He111 crew feathered Jordan's stricken engine and operated the extinguisher system. Acknowledging the impossibility of achieving their objective, they jettisoned the bombs. Home lay many miles away but Jordan hoped good fortune would favour a single-engined sea crossing to reach another airfield on the continent, where Amberger could receive medical treatment. For now, they could only render first aid and make him as comfortable as possible as they laboured eastwards. For a few minutes it seemed as if the doughty Heinkel was rising to the challenge but then the temperature gauge for the remaining engine began to rise, indicating damage to the cooling system. Then, abruptly, the motor stopped. Jordan and his Gruppenkommandeur conferred swiftly. Baling out was possible for three of them, but poor Amberger was in no condition to jump and stood little chance of survival. A crash-landing in darkness on unknown terrain was tantamount to suicide. Their best option was to glide to the enemy coast and attempt a smooth ditching just offshore. If they were successful, the plane might float for long enough for them to evacuate Amberger. Trimming their tattered machine into the role of reluctant glider, they made the most of every metre of altitude.

Not that many miles away Duke-Woolley was wrestling with a desperately unstable Blenheim; not only was it flying on just one engine, but it had suffered damage to its wings and control surfaces. Duke-Woolley was annoyed that their opponent could only be claimed as a probable, despite the hundreds of expended rounds. On the positive side, Bell's wounds were not as severe as first feared. It had been an amazingly close call. The hail of bullets tearing through the Blenheim's floor had narrowly missed the gunner himself, but two impacted into his parachute pack slapping it violently into his face. In the darkness and confusion, poor Bell could be forgiven for at first thinking he was more seriously wounded. Descending towards Collyweston, Duke-Woolley nursed the aircraft into its final approach. Inwardly he prayed that the port Mercury would not falter at a critical altitude and that the control cables would hold despite the stresses placed on them through compensating for the loss of the starboard engine. Crossing the airfield boundary, the battered Blenheim touched down in what was perhaps not the best landing of Duke-Woolley's career – and it was then that the aileron control snapped. A few seconds earlier, and they would have created their own funeral pyre.

Jordan, meanwhile, could see the coastline, clearly delineated by silvered surf, and the sea looked blessedly calm as 5J+DM approached for its final landing just offshore in the shallows of Blakeney Creek. Their airmanship was superb and they settled the bomber so smoothly that most, if not all, of the Perspex panelling in the Heinkel's nose was unbroken. As the He111 lost momentum, the crew moved swiftly to assist Amberger from the gently settling aircraft, and then clambered out, supporting the wounded gunner. Waves were breaking on a beach a few hundred yards away but they felt it was an achievable swimming distance and, still helping Amberger, they made for the shore. Fortunately the sea conditions were sympathetic and they soon felt sand beneath their feet and struggled upright, carrying Amberger between them. Cold and bedraggled, they found shelter in the lee of a beached fishing craft until a small party of armed civilians appeared, perhaps members of the Local Defence Volunteers (later known as the Home Guard). Jordan noticed the inadequacy of their rifles – 'probably for bird-shooting' – but he was in no position to argue. Proffering his reversed pistol as a sign of surrender, he conveyed the need for urgent medical attention and the 'civilians' hastened away, giving Jordan the impression they were pleased to avoid any trouble.

Research by Bob Collis indicates that the first people to encounter the German crew were actually auxiliary coastguards. In fact, they had left their First World War-vintage rifle and its five precious rounds in their small hut at the land end of the 'peninsula' – apparently they were tired of lugging it back and forth on their nightly patrol of the coastline! About an hour elapsed before some soldiers and an officer from the Royal Norfolk Regiment reached the survivors with a stretcher. One of the soldiers later told Bob that they felt the Germans should carry their own casualty and that, when they refused, they were 'persuaded' at bayonet point to do so.

Sand is no easy surface over which to convey a stretcher but the airmen now carried their wounded comrade as gently as possible to a military field station about 2 miles from the beach. Here there occurred a coincidence reminding Ulrich Jordan of happier days when the competition between Britain and Germany avoided bloodshed. Himself an avid rower, Jordan recognised the army chaplain at the field station as the cox of the British eight-oar boat that had beaten his own club craft in the 1936 Olympics. It was, indeed, a small world – and Jordan now faced over six years' imprisonment to reflect on the matter. Karl Amberger was taken to Cromer Hospital, where he was 'segregated' and placed under guard away from the other patients. Ironically he returned home before Jordan and was back in Germany before the end of the year as part of a prisoner exchange programme.

Pictured as prisoners of war in Canada are officers from KG4, several of whose He111s were shot down on 19 June 1940. Oberleutnant Jordan is the front row, second from left; Major von Massenbach sits in the centre of the front row. Leutnant Backhaus, on the far left of the back row, was on 5J+FP which ditched in Palm Bay, Margate. Oberleutnant von Arnim, third from the left in the back row, escaped from 5J+AM at Six Mile Bottom, while Leutnant Simon, in the centre of the back row, was from 5J+GA, which was shot down over Chelmsford. (*Karl-Heinz Koch via Chris Goss*)

The Heinkel had served its crew well but finally succumbed to the ravages of the sea, although not before many pieces were seized as souvenirs. For many years odd pieces appeared on the beach nearby, serving as reminders of the courage shown by the eight combatants concerned.

Blenheim L1458, YP-S, flown by Sergeant Alan Close, disintegrated on impact near Church Lane in the village of Terrington St Clement, Norfolk. Wreckage was scattered for hundreds of yards and the remains of the pilot were found in the debris. Laurence Karasek struggled out of the falling fighter and parachuted safely to earth. He required only minor medical attention. Tragically he would only survive for a few weeks: he perished in a flying accident on 25 September 1940 when 23 Squadron Blenheim IF L8369, YP-B, stalled and crashed near Stourbridge, killing all on board.

Raymond Duke-Woolley was delighted to learn that his probable had been confirmed, and was promised as a trophy the flying boots worn by Gruppenkommandeur Major Dietrich Freiherr von Massenbach. To his disappointment they never materialised, although the clock from Heinkel 111 5J+DM provided many decades of punctual service.

The N&SAM also houses various artefacts, including an Iron Cross, from another incident that occurred in daylight on Wednesday, 21 August 1940, during the Battle of Britain. Poor weather that day precluded large-scale attacks but the Luftwaffe was in a spiteful mood and, taking advantage of the cloud cover, launched some 200 separate raids. These comprised many singleton sorties that were more suited to the prevailing weather conditions, and one of these involved a lone Dornier 17Z-3 from 2/KG2. Coded U5+FK, its call letter F had naturally given rise to the nickname 'Fritz'. Lifting away from the turf at Epinoy that cloud-laden morning, those on board might be forgiven for suffering some apprehension. Their unit had lost five aircraft in just over five days, and units elsewhere had sustained even higher casualties. They were right to be nervous – Fritz was now flying towards its own footnote on the pages of history. Piloting the aircraft was Leutnant Heinz Ermecke. Also on board was Sonderführer Kurt Rasche, an experienced war correspondent attached to 2/KG2; he had flown with the crew before, and this time was planning to submit an account of the day's

Leutnant Heinz Ermecke wearing his Iron Cross, the semi-molten remains of which were found in the Dornier's burnt debris. (*Bob Collis*)

Sonderführer Kurt Rasche was attached to 2/KG2 as a war correspondent but never returned to file his copy. (*Kurt Rasche via Chris Goss*)

events. Rasche had hoped the adverse weather conditions would prevent flying, thereby allowing another social foray into the nearby town of Arras, an activity much more to his liking. Unfortunately, even with the clouds at only 300m, Fritz was ordered to fly. Manning the guns and radio and undertaking other duties as necessary were two NCOs, Unteroffiziers Goetz-Dieter Wolf and Heinz Hermsen. Breaking through one layer of cloud, the Do17 climbed through another to emerge in brilliant summer sunshine over a sparkling cloudscape stretching for miles. Pleasant as this might be, it made for challenging navigation to their target, the RAF aerodrome at Wyton, near Huntingdon. When Ermecke judged the aircraft to be over the appropriate area of England, he descended. Beneath the clouds he discovered only sea, so continued at the same altitude until crossing the East Anglian coast. All the crew were searching for their objective, to administer another blow to the RAF.

Earlier that month the Luftwaffe had commenced its assault on RAF airfields, particularly fighter bases, as a precursor to the invasion. Somewhat over-optimistically, the Luftwaffe Commander-in-Chief Hermann Goering had boasted about destroying the RAF in only 'four days'. He would ultimately blame everyone but himself for the humiliating failure to achieve his aims. Air-crews under his command strode buoyantly forward in the early days and at first seemed to be making progress. Indeed, they did – but interference from Goering would ultimately contribute to their defeat and already the RAF was proving a tougher than anticipated adversary. Radar, aiding the deployment of British fighters, increased the effectiveness of seriously limited resources, and to the German air-crews it seemed as if the RAF had inexhaustible reserves.

Finding an airfield with a distinctively large hangar, the crew decided it was a suitable target, Wyton or not. Turning back, they flew steadily over the aerodrome and released the first of their bombs. Puzzled by the lack of explosions, they banked round for a second run and released the remaining bombs – but again saw no blasts. This was hardly the dramatic result required for Rasche, but a close reconnaissance of the enemy airbase might make good copy and so Ermecke took the Dornier even lower. Then came the cry of alarm dreaded by all Luftwaffe bomber crews: 'Spitfire!'

Although the Dornier had sneaked in using cloud cover, this concealed nothing from radar and controllers had already alerted 242 Hurricane Squadron at RAF Coltishall in Norfolk to the presence of the intruder. Commanded by the legendary legless hero Douglas Bader, the squadron contained many exuberant Canadians with a powerful esprit de corps truly reflecting the squadron motto, 'Toujours prêt' (Always ready). Proving the point, three Hurricanes from Blue Flight had already been scrambled and were climbing over the beautiful cathedral city of Norwich, not that they had time to admire what little they glimpsed through the clouds. In charge of the vic was 24-year-old Flight Lieutenant George Powell-Sheddon. A graduate of the prestigious Wellington College, George had transferred to the RAF in 1935 from the Royal Military Academy for 'the sons of military men and the more respectable classes', and made the junior service his career. He had served in the Middle East before returning to the UK and 242 Squadron in July 1940. Flying Blue Two was 26-year-old Canadian Pilot Officer John B. Latta, whose pre-war predilections as a salmon fisherman were far removed from military discipline. Hours spent seeking such swift-moving quarry had given him a keen eye, patience and persistence, but the excitement of flying tempted him to join the RAF on a short service commission in 1939. Today he was hoping this career would help him catch even bigger fish. He already had two Me109s to his credit, both shot down during the débâcle that was the Battle of France, but he knew that any hostile radar contact roaming so far north was almost certainly an enemy bomber. Completing the trio as Blue Three was a serving Royal Navy officer, Sub-Lieutenant Richard E. Gardner. He had enlisted in the Fleet Air Arm during 1939 but since June 1940 had been on loan from Britain's senior service to help make up the shortfall in RAF fighter pilots. Gardner had already proved his value by destroying a Heinkel 111, caught while protecting a convoy on 9 July. His victim now languished on the seabed some 15 miles off Britain's most easterly point at Lowestoft. Now he had another opportunity as radar tracked the approaching raider and Blue Flight was guided towards it. The hunt was on.

The Form F Combat Reports submitted by Powell-Sheddon and Gardner offer graphic accounts of the next few minutes. Powell-Sheddon wrote:

Do215 (or Do17). At 1200 Blue Section ordered to patrol Norwich. Over Norwich at 1210 hours then given vector 190 followed by a vector of 240. I sighted enemy aircraft at 1214 going at about 200mph on a course of 270° magnetic. I observed black crosses on fuselage. Dark coloured painted. Enemy aircraft was flying in cumulus cloud fairly near the base of them. Enemy turned left into a cloudbank. I took a deflection shot just before she disappeared into cloud. I followed her through the cloud and sighted the enemy aircraft on far side of it. The enemy was still turning to the left and diving slightly out of the cloud. I closed to about 100 yards or 150 yards and gave enemy another burst from beam to stern. I observed no effect of my fire as he opened up all guns on me. Enemy appeared to be using cannon and two machine-guns from rear and underneath. Enemy fire was heavy and he was using tracer bullets. The effect of enemy's fire made me break off attack to the right. As I did this Blue Two and Three came in from port and from underneath.

On making my third attack on the enemy's starboard beam I could not open fire owing to the extremely close proximity of Blue Three. Smoke and flames were pouring from the fuselage and port engine. All enemy's firing had ceased. Enemy aircraft which was losing height was approaching a village. I saw two of the crew bale out . . .

Gardner's account has the odd inconsistency – for example, in the colour of the enemy's fuselage – and is enlivened by the nautical terminology one might expect, but it too details the drama of the engagement:

8 miles west of Harleston . . . enemy aircraft was sighted by the whole section just off the port bow. We were flying between two layers of intermittent cloud (8/10) at 3000 feet. Enemy aircraft on sighting us dived in a left-handed spiral showing the white crosses on his fuselage. Blue One got in a burst before the enemy aircraft reached the cloud. Blue Two and myself dived through the cloud after him. As I came out of the cloud I found Blue One attacking again and I was unable to open fire. The enemy aircraft opened a very heavy fire on Blue One as he, Blue One, closed in and broke away to the right. I opened fire at 250 yards and concentrated on his port engine which caught alight. I then transferred my fire to his fuselage, which also burst into flames after 7 seconds of fire, closed to 20 yards. I stopped firing and followed the enemy aircraft . . . electric sights were very satisfactory as the attack was from the port quarter and showed up well against the dark background of the countryside below . . .

John Latta's account is in similar vein. Following Gardner closely, he hurtled from the cloud to find himself only 100 yards behind and below the diving Dornier. Swiftly manoeuvring his Hurricane, Latta allowed 25° deflection and unleashed a 6-second blast into the enemy aircraft. Scourged by the fighters, the Do17 fought back valiantly but with little effect. The ferocious return fire that forced Blue One to break away had missed his machine and the only damage sustained was torn fabric in the tail plane and a dent in its spar, inflicted not by bullets but by pieces ripped away from the Dornier by the fire from Blue One's own guns. Gardner's aircraft sustained nothing more than a slight covering of oil from the stricken bomber. All return fire had ceased as the burning bomber trailed ever lower.

Unknown to the British pilots, the first ferocious attack on Fritz had sealed its fate. Machine-gun bullets sliced through the cockpit shattering instruments and causing the signal flares to explode. Ermecke was hit, and Wolf was convinced this initial attack had killed the pilot. Despite serious burns to his hands, Wolf grasped his machine-gun and fought back. Rasche, probably less skilled, had grabbed the port machine-gun and fired as more tracers flashed by and others ripped into the flight deck. He felt strikes on his legs just as the signal flares stored on the flight deck exploded and the cockpit filled up with flames. Terrified, he instinctively groped through the blaze for the red emergency release on the aircraft door. In a nightmare world of acrid, blinding smoke and more flames, he fumbled for the elusive handle. Then came a blast of air, but not from beneath – the cockpit cover had vanished. Rasche was now denied immediate salvation as the Dornier surged upwards and threw him back into the flames. Then, just as abruptly, it tilted sharply forward and threw him clear again.

The attack had taken Hermsen totally by surprise. His position in the radio compartment faced aft, and he suddenly realised something was happening in the cockpit behind him. Even as he turned, flames erupted within the cabin but his role now was to man one of their rearward-firing MG15 machine-guns. That Powell-Sheddon thought himself subject to 'cannon and two machine-guns from rear and underneath' is testimony to the determination of Wolf and Hermsen. Seeing one of the Hurricanes break off its attack apparently trailing smoke, the radio operator was convinced it had been hit and he continued calling in attacks through the intercom. Then he realised there had been no answer from Ermecke. A momentary lull in the battle gave him another opportunity to contact others in the crew. Again, there was no answer. Glancing back through a gap in the smoke, he noticed the entry hatch had been jettisoned, but just as he moved to clamber over his seat and escape, the Hurricanes struck again. Hermsen had no alternative but to tug hard on the

Unteroffizier Heinz Hermsen was hauled at high speed out of the stricken Dornier still clutching the cockpit roof, not his parachute ripcord. (*Heinz Hermsen via Chris Goss*)

emergency release for the cockpit roof. He did not even have time to let go of the handle and was whipped out of Fritz still grasping the canopy and not his parachute release. Letting go of the cockpit cover, he grabbed his ripcord and pulled. Barely had the parachute snapped open than Hermsen hit English soil, winded but alive.

Such dramatic scenes were commonplace over more southern counties but this battle created tremendous excitement in rural Norfolk. 'It was a thrilling fight,' one eyewitness told a local reporter, who related how 'Crowds of people, realising the fight was nearly over, came out into the streets while the Dornier was still overhead and cheered the three Hurricanes, each of which did a "victory roll".' Mr J.R. Aldridge, then 17 years old and living at Pulham St Mary, recalled:

I had left Bungay Grammar School in July 1940 and was at home waiting to take up my first job in September. Most of us 16/17-year-olds at the time were infatuated with the RAF and all the publicity and propaganda which surrounded their deeds, and were longing for the time when we would be able to join for air-crew training. The Battle of Britain was, of course, at its height but all the action was further south and seemed to pass us by apart from the odd, single bombing raid . . . You can imagine that it was quite exciting on 21 August to see the Dornier 17 proceeding towards the air station just below cloud at about 3,000 feet. I stood up in the relative safety of a ditch and watched as he proceeded on

A sketch by aviation enthusiast Frank C. Clarke depicts the Dornier under attack. (*Bob Collis*)

his bombing run in a westerly direction and released his bombs, which to me appeared like a string of sausages. They fell, as I recall, in a field between the old hangar and the Pulham–Rudhall road and I do not think any exploded. As the aircraft turned to head east again, three Hurricanes appeared from the Norwich direction and were soon on his tail . . .

Burning fiercely, the Dornier swung downwards in a wide spiral as members of the crew baled out. Seeing a parachute, 14-year-old Ian Daniels grabbed his father's LDV rifle as he and his mother Ada ran from their home in Chancel Farm, Weybread, to greet their uninvited guests. Rasche, lying wounded in a meadow, first heard dogs then a woman's voice calling, 'remain lying, we'll help you'. Able to understand her, he was convinced she had spoken in German, but became frightened of the boy wielding a weapon and pleaded for mercy. Ian's mother, perhaps thinking how she would want to see her own son treated in such a situation, soon eased the young airman's anxiety. Fortunately Rasche was not seriously wounded and first aid was soon followed by the inevitable cup of tea before the authorities took him away under military escort in a Civil Defence ambulance. Wolf and Hermsen were soon captured by pitchfork-wielding farm workers, who would clearly take no nonsense.

The abandoned bomber was now heading directly for the country town of Harleston in Norfolk. Whether Ermecke was dead or badly wounded is unknown, but onlookers thought the aircraft behaved as if the pilot were alive. Flashing over the rooftops on the town's outskirts, the blazing Dornier missed Harleston's clock tower by no more than 50 feet. Gladys Snowling was in the street with her baby daughter, and never forgot the sight of the aircraft, wreathed in flames, its pilot visible inside the burning cockpit. She was convinced he remained there to try to prevent his machine falling in the town. Other eyewitnesses also felt the pilot deliberately stayed on board to avoid their community. Several pieces, including one of the machine-guns, fell away from the stricken aircraft. It just cleared houses in Starston village but clipped an oak tree beyond and dropped hard and fast into a meadow. Slithering at speed on its belly, the aircraft mowed down and killed two ponies that had earlier been grazing in the tranquillity of the countryside. The aircraft then seemed to catapult into a nearby wood, where it exploded in a great erupting fireball of fuel and flames. Men of the Home Guard raced to the scene and one unsubstantiated account handed down locally describes how a sergeant with a particular hatred for the enemy would not allow his men to approach the cockpit section even though the pilot could be seen amid the flames.

The charred and mutilated remains of Heinz Ermecke, aged only 20, were later recovered from the debris, and one of the searchers picked up his semi-molten Iron Cross from the

The carcass of a Bramo 323 engine guarded by RAF personnel. The airman smoking a cigarette was punished for smoking on duty following this picture's appearance in the *Eastern Daily Press*. The air intelligence report noted that the aircraft carried additional armour, and an external bomb rack capable of carrying a 500kg bomb was identified. (*Via Bob Collis*)

ashes. As with many wartime crashes, souvenirs were much sought after and the site attracted many sightseers, as J.R. Aldridge continued: 'I remember running back to our house and getting into the car with my father and heading towards the column of smoke. It was quite a sight on the road with cars, cycles, even a pony and trap heading towards Starston.' The trouble was that with so many souvenir hunters, there was a risk of losing valuable military intelligence that might perhaps be gleaned from the wreckage. Guards were mounted while the press sought stories and photographs that then had to pass the censor's scrutiny. A picture published in the *Eastern Daily Press* passed the censor but apparently earned censure for an unfortunate guard. Portrayed standing near one of the Bramo 323 radial engines, he was caught on camera with a cigarette in hand, 'smoking on duty'. In reality, the Intelligence Branch was getting more examples of enemy aircraft than it could handle and the report on U5+FK merely noted: 'What appeared to be an external bomb rack was found which would be suitable for [a] 500kg bomb. Armour-plate additional to normal was found on this aircraft.' This latter point might account for the amount of punishment Fritz absorbed. There was no mention of extra armament beyond the normal six 7.9mm MG15 machine-guns. Trophies from the Dornier were spirited away into many households, and Martin Smith of Diss inherited another Iron Cross from his father, who said it was 'retrieved' from one of the surviving crew members. Martin also remembers his father saying how the captured enemy airmen were taken to Pulham and confined in a building close to one of their own unexploded bombs, which was thought to have a delayed-action fuse. Kurt Rasche later recalled being taken to the airfield they had just bombed. He was given immediate medical attention and treated very cordially, despite the presence of unexploded ordnance. The commanding officer even lent the wounded German a set of pyjamas and the prisoner was allowed to learn why their bombs had not detonated. It seems Goetz-Dieter Wolf had failed to arm them!

The Iron Cross now in the Norfolk and Suffolk Aviation Museum came from a Mr Baldwin, who found it at the scene of the crash in 1940. Eager for more details, members of the N&SAM mounted a search of the crash-site during the 1970s (and on several later occasions). Numerous fragments were picked from the field and adjoining woodland undergrowth, owned at the time of the crash by the Lomb-Taylor family. Publicity about the finds reminded Doris Baldwin of her own family heirloom relating to the incident, and she duly offered her Iron Cross to the museum. Bob Collis felt the medal should first be offered to the family of Heinz Ermecke. Contact was eventually established with his sister, Gisela Falke, through former KG2 flier Heinz Möllenbrook, who was himself shot down during the Battle of Britain. Plans were made for him to collect the medal in 1997, but in a generous gesture Gisela Falke decided the medal should be displayed at Flixton in honour of the courage of her beloved brother. Today he lies buried with some five thousand of his comrades in the German Military Cemetery at Cannock Chase near Birmingham. She sent a photograph of him to accompany the exhibit, and a copy was given to Doris Baldwin, who cried when she saw the young pilot's image. 'The first thing I thought when I saw it was that it could have been one of my sons,' she said. In a moving ceremony attended by Heinz Möllenbrook and Doris

Above: Doris Baldwin holds Ermecke's Iron Cross on the day of its presentation to the Norfolk & Suffolk Aviation Museum.
Right: Bob Collis, Heinz Möllenbrook and Doris Baldwin at Flixton. The 446BG Memorial is in the background. (*Bob Collis*)

Baldwin on Sunday 31 August 1997, Bob accepted the medal on behalf of the museum. Fritz was the only enemy aircraft brought down in Norfolk during the Battle of Britain, and it might have remained as little more than a footnote to that epic conflict had Bob not felt strongly that the medal represented so much more. Speaking during the presentation, he paid tribute to the fallen airman and the museum's German guest:

> There's no doubt that Heinz Ermecke would have been extremely proud to wear his Iron Cross, as any serviceman would be to wear a similar decoration . . . his family must have mourned his passing . . . but he was a serviceman and he died serving his country. I do not think that the politics of the Second World War have any bearing on Herr Möllenbrook's visit today. If you wanted to make an analogy between the two pilots, Heinz Ermecke came to Britain as an enemy of our country in 1940 and was killed . . . Heinz Möllenbrook was very fortunate to survive as a prisoner of war. Fifty-seven years later he's come back to Britain as a friend, to pay his respects to his comrades who did not return. We look forward to adding the Iron Cross to the display so that our visitors can see it and read its story . . .

Another Dornier story that features in the museum reflects a different aspect of Britain's defences. The events in question occurred only three days after the loss of the unfortunate Fritz.

Warner Steward pictured while serving in Burma. (*Warner Steward via Bob Collis*)

They had the enemy in range. Without hesitation, the aptly named and very confident Londoner Lieutenant Ernie Battle roared his command to the waiting gunners. An instant later the first salvo of 3in shells blasted away from 3 Section, 243 (Heavy) Anti-Aircraft Battery. Peering through his telescopic viewfinder, Corporal Warner Steward saw shells exploding by the Dornier, then the distinct flash of a strike on its port engine. Within moments the aircraft faltered, then started falling. Around Warner, cheering erupted among the jubilant gunners.

Almost 20,000 feet overhead, 26-year-old Oberleutnant Joachim-Heinrich Hellmers did not see the muzzle flashes. His position as navigator was on the starboard side of the Do17Z's cockpit. He was too busy concentrating on his maps and the course they required for Coventry. Their bombs were intended for engine factories in that heartland of British precision engineering and manufacturing. The blast as shells bracketed the aircraft took him completely by surprise.

Oberleutnant Joachim-Heinrich Hellmers, a Staffelkapitan with Stab/KG2, found the weather worse than predicted. (*Joachim-Heinrich Hellmers via Goss/Collis*)

It was Friday 23 August, and the day had commenced far too soon for Corporal Steward and his gun crew with yet another dawn stand-to on Red Alert with little chance of action. As on many previous occasions, the only likely excitement would be tracking yet another lost brylcreem boy. It made the gun crew feel as if they were stranded and forgotten in the Cambridgeshire countryside as the war passed them by. Not once since the outbreak of war a full year earlier had their guns been used in anger. Before the war they had practised, polished and trained in their Territorial Army Drill Hall on All Saints Green, Norwich. Honed and ready, the Norfolk lads bonded with their brash officer from London and he knew exactly how to handle his somewhat bucolic band of brothers. Sonny Gudgeon, Tom Widdows, Bill Ayres and the rest of the boys felt as frustrated as he did. Now, stuck on a road junction off the A505 towards the village of Thriplow, their role was to protect the nearby fighter aerodrome of Duxford, from where Spitfires, Hurricanes and Blenheims had been doing battle. Today was comparatively quiet but Ernie Battle always liked to keep his boys busy and had persuaded his seniors to allow 243 (Heavy) Anti-Aircraft Battery to perform a special function which was about to play a vital role, and one that would increase in importance as AA gunnery developed. Many years later Warner recalled:

There was one aspect of the engagement on 23 August 1940 that was kept very much under wraps at the time. It was, in my experience, one of the first occasions that the fledgling radar (then called Radio Direction Finding) took part in targeting a hostile aircraft for the guns. Radar for AA guns was then in prototype form and served mainly for 'early warning'. It could detect incoming aircraft and give the direction and range but not, at this stage, either height or angle, both of which were, of course, essential to gunnery. However, the policy was to train selected operators on it where possible and one such set of equipment, together with its demonstration team, had been 'dumped' on the Thriplow site, to which personnel from various units in the area were ferried daily for training . . . Lieutenant Ernest Battle was always anxious to use anything available to extend our usefulness, and persuaded the demonstration team to turn out with us during alerts and transmit any data via a field telephone. On this particular occasion it worked well. The radar team located the aircraft in the clouds, the bearing data was bawled to us and we converted it to a rate of course change so that the guns and command post were constantly pointing towards the unseen target. We fed in a provisional height of 20,000 feet, being the cloud ceiling given us by the Met boys. As soon as the Dornier reached a break in the cloud, it was 'Target Seen' and the shells were on their way in a split second before it could change course . . . The most unusual factor in this engagement was that, when the alarm sounded, we were diverted by Operations to face a bearing heading inland, i.e. towards Royston. Normally we would face the coast as the direction from which trouble might be expected. Then the old Mark One gun-laying radar located a target and we were slowly directed by it south-west, south and then south-east . . .

In fact the Do17 had been tagged as 'Raid 22' and was being tracked by the main radar defence system as it approached the English coast. Once again inclement weather – heavy clouds over northern France and southern England – enforced a respite and prevented large-scale attacks by the Luftwaffe. On the airfield at St Leger near Cambrai, Staffelkapitan Hellmers, on the staff of KG2, had prepared a series of nuisance raids, armed reconnaissance sorties, intended to probe British defences. He would lead a small force set to depart at 30-minute intervals, thus keeping what he hoped were tired and weary defenders on their toes while using cloud cover to his advantage. As his Dornier departed the French coast near Cap Gris Nez, Hellmers observed the weather to be worse than predicted but it kept his aircraft concealed within clouds as it crossed into British airspace, flying to the east of London. But being hidden also meant being unable to see. With his navigation handicapped, Hellmers sought visual references to confirm wind speed and direction. As the bomber dipped beneath the clouds, he took some bearings and was just working out their course when the flight engineer Paul Seidel reported an aerodrome below with bombers parked on it.

Far below, there was frantic activity on 'B' Site. A year of uneventful frustration had just ended. The morning's preparations simply had to produce a result. Ernie had chalked up figures for the gunners giving wind speed and direction plus barometric pressures, from the information provided by the RAF's daily meteorological report. He had pre-set the Kerrison

Predictor. This early electro-mechanical computer required a team of six operators and used the pre-set data plus estimates of the target's speed, bearing and course, combined with the velocity and direction of the shell. In theory this mixture of pre-set and hot data entry predicted a point in the skies where the target and projectile would meet. In theory. Supporting the Predictor was a visual height-finder operated by three men who called out the target's height. The two guns themselves were each served by an NCO and eight men. All were ready and waiting for the approaching aircraft to come within range.

Studying the sky through his graduated sighting telescope, Warner had a grandstand view and suddenly saw the aircraft emerge between clouds. It was tiny in the viewfinder – he noted twin tails and the slim fuselage of a 'flying pencil' but it was too far away to determine any markings confirming it as hostile. Warner was surprised when Ernie Battle shouted 'Engage', but he presumed Operations had given his officer confirmation of the target as an enemy. Even so, Warner half expected a cry of 'Target out of range' from his number four. Instead, with little movement on the traversal handles, a shout of 'Fuse 15' was given (the maximum fuse setting), giving barely enough time before the target escaped. Two salvoes barked into the heavens before Battle gave the command 'Cease fire', slightly too late to prevent a final round from being fired. Only five shells were used in all. 'Cease fire' usually meant that the target was out of range or that the fighters being scrambled from Duxford were at risk. With no sign of RAF activity, it was up to the accuracy of 243 Battery – and Warner flushed with exhilaration when he saw the momentary flash of an explosion on the Dornier's port engine as it passed from right to left in his lens. The aircraft climbed for a moment into the sanctuary of cloud cover but then reappeared falling steeply away on its port wing, dropping fast but still under control. All around him, gunners cheered, waved and shouted 'We've got it!'

On board the stricken aircraft, the crew members remained well disciplined. Oberfeldwebel Günther Wagner was an experienced pilot and reacted swiftly by pulling up to regain cloud cover, but even as he did so, the fire in their port engine overwhelmed the extinguisher system. There was also damage to the tail unit, and Wagner was obliged to compensate for the loss of power and check the controls. Hellmers' considerations about Coventry vanished; now all they needed was a course for home. The engine was still burning so Wagner now adopted a risky course of action, dropping the Dornier into a steep dive, side-slipping vigorously to port, in an effort to extinguish the flames before the fuel tanks ignited or the aircraft broke up. For some 200 stomach-wrenching metres the Dornier sliced steeply earthwards, but then Wagner's gamble paid off. The fierce draught finally withered the flames engulfing the engine and Wagner levelled out. The aircraft now faced a long haul home on one engine, mirroring a similar achievement some days earlier when British Hurricanes had badly damaged their aircraft. This time, hopes of a repeat performance evaporated when Wagner felt power failing on the starboard engine and realised that it too must have been damaged by shrapnel. His instruments confirmed this unhappy diagnosis as the rpm counter faltered. Hellmers made a decision. Ten 50kg bombs intended for Coventry now tumbled away to fall harmlessly on open farmland near the village of Babraham. The bombs did not explode, so caused neither casualties nor much damage.

Watching the Dornier dragging away eastwards, Warner saw a stream of tracer shells lance up from a 40mm Bofors site at Whittlesford and he felt sure one of the shells struck the bomber's rear fuselage. Still shedding altitude, the aircraft was finally lost from view behind some trees over towards Cambridge.

The British defences still had not finished with the Dornier and somewhere between Babraham and the Suffolk hamlet of Ousden a well-aimed burst of .303in machine-gun fire inflicted further damage. There were strikes on the port wing root, several rounds hit the already feathered port propeller and one bullet passed through the left-hand side of the cockpit but caused no injuries. It was now almost 0930 and their descent had taken them some 25 miles from Duxford in a valiant but futile effort to reach home. Their task now became one of selecting a field suitable for settling some 6 tons of bomber, landing wheels up, at nearly 100mph. Choosing what appeared to be an empty meadow, Wagner nurtured the aircraft in a wide circle over Ousden and commenced his approach. The clover field, known locally as the High Sevens, bordered Spring Wood close to Lodge Farm near the Suffolk village of Wickhambrook. Unfortunately the field was not entirely empty, but even if Wagner did see the obstacle, it was too late. Skimming over the hedgerow, he slithered the machine in and put their fate into the hands of providence. Skidding and bouncing across the clover, the aircraft smashed into an agricultural disc roller left out by the farmer. The bomber slewed round and slid the last few feet backwards, facing the way it had come in. The impact with the roller might even have helped because the aircraft stopped short of trees that would have torn it and its crew apart. In the uncanny silence that followed their rough arrival, the crew were amazed to find themselves unscathed and the Dornier relatively intact. With this in mind, they knew their duty was to destroy it and, grabbing the detonators carried for this eventuality, they swiftly evacuated the machine. Hellmers was intensely annoyed when his incendiary failed to ignite. Paul Siedel, the flight engineer, dropped his into a hole in the wing but, as he slid back off the main plane and dropped clear, the incendiary device popped free and rolled out behind him. It also failed to detonate and the approach of would-be captors put an end to further efforts.

Having seen the Dornier obviously preparing to crash-land, Mr F.G. Mison, the Ousden air raid patrol parish organiser, had immediately alerted the police at Dalham. His later report timed the aircraft's arrival at 0930, although he mistakenly identified the aircraft as a Dornier 215. It was an easy mistake to make, as the two types were almost indistinguishable. In fact, the crew were first 'captured' by local gamekeeper Lewis Frith, a part-time member of the West Suffolk Constabulary whose pitchfork and dutiful gundog were not really required. Approaching warily, Lewis tapped the pockets of the nearest German, gesturing for the surrender of the airman's pistol, which was promptly handed over. Lewis was later commended for his role in their capture and awarded £5 by his employer, Mr Griffith-Woollard. By now a party of soldiers had arrived and apparently sought to impose a more military manner on the proceedings. In classic Dad's Army style, the Home Guard officer hastened across to demand that the airmen hand over everything from their pockets – cigarettes, money, photographs – and then their flying suits. These were all conceded without fuss but the over-enthusiastic officer seemingly overlooked Hellmers's pistol. Some moments elapsed before Hellmers, who spoke fluent English, enquired of the officer whether he, Hellmers, would have any use for the weapon in a POW camp! This officerly oversight caused great merriment among the man's (in)subordinates as the embarrassed officer now demanded a weapon already peacefully volunteered. In fact, the entire event was somewhat light-hearted. One local, Alfred Hicks, recorded in his diary the 'great excitement in the village', and further noted how the airmen all seemed very intelligent 'university types'. In the now more relaxed atmosphere, Hellmers, Wagner, Seidel and the radio operator Feldwebel Albert Dietel shared out chocolate and peppermints from their rations, while the British soldiers obtained tea and cigarettes for their prisoners. Hellmers, peacefully sharing a cigarette in the shade of a stout English oak, quietly contemplated the absurdity of war. Soon a bus appeared and the Dornier crew began their journey into captivity in Canada, while their Dornier, now a prize of war, began working for the opposition.

Strangely, British intelligence records do not record the arrival of Dornier 17 U5+EA and scant interest appears to have been shown in it. The *Bury Free Press and Post* of 31 August 1940 briefly reported the incident, noting that 'all four Germans spoke English'. It went on: 'One interesting point was a little red, white and blue ring, painted on one wing and bearing a date. This was a hole where repair had obviously been made to the fabric and was possibly a memento of a previous clash with British fighters.' However, even now the aircraft had sustained little damage and within hours a recovery crew from 54 Maintenance Unit had arrived to dismantle the Dornier for new duties.

Exhibiting captured enemy aircraft was a practice carried out by both sides and U5+EA embarked on a propaganda tour of towns and cities in eastern England, raising money for the

The Do17 being dismantled at Wickhambrook. Note the grass placed over the national insignia to avoid unwelcome attention from both the RAF and the Luftwaffe. (*Frank Harber family*)

On High Sevens Field the engine cowlings are opened as personnel from 54MU begin removing the engines. (*Frank Harber family*)

One casualty of the crash-landing was this unlucky rabbit. Note the flak damage to the fuselage and cockpit. (*Via Chris Goss*)

Great excitement in Eaton Park, Norwich, as members of the public crowd round the captured Dornier. Note the port engine is feathered. (*Via Bob Collis*)

Spitfire Fund. After removing the engines, the men from 54MU managed to lower the undercarriage for better mobility on tour and the aircraft attracted much interest during its travels, as John Ward, later a prominent member of the N&SAM, remembered. The aircraft was to be displayed in Eaton Park, Norwich, but a young John, spotting it on an RAF 'Queen Mary' trailer parked by the City Hall, was unable to curb his excitement and clambered up for a closer look. He was just peering into the cockpit, and might have proceeded further than simply looking, but he was seen and shooed away. One enduring memory was 'the beautiful engineering that had gone into building the aircraft'.

It is known that the Dornier proved an attraction elsewhere in the eastern counties. So there may well be other souvenirs in Suffolk that were 'liberated' from this well-travelled veteran. Beautiful though the engineering might have been, the aircraft was not destined to survive its tour and was subsequently broken up for scrap. A few oddments of the Do17 survived and the gunners of 243 (Heavy) AA were each delighted to receive a polished 7.9mm machine-gun casing taken from one of the aircraft's ammunition panniers. Some

A fragment of aviation history. Is this all that remains of Do17 U5+EA? (*Bob Collis*)

months later an even larger trophy turned up via their HQ at Stradishall in the form of a tail-fin swastika claimed to be from U5+EA. The team from 243 had been slightly disgruntled at being obliged to share the honours for their kill with the Whittlesford Light AA unit but all the gunners involved received a Commendation from the 2nd AA Division on Battery Orders. The 243 swastika soon proudly surmounted the unit's canteen hut for the duration of their UK duties. When they left Duxford, the swastika went to Steward and Patterson's brewery in Norwich, because many of the territorials had been recruited from the brewery's ranks and their CO, Major Peter Finch, was a director of the company. The swastika's subsequent fate is unknown. The only positively identified surviving souvenir from the aircraft's 'beautiful engineering' is a tiny manufacturer's plate marked 'Dornier-Werke G.m.b.H. Friedrichshafen a. B.' and inscribed R1011 with a component serial number.

Warner also kept his own souvenir as his army career continued. Soon after downing the Dornier, he was posted for training as a radar team leader and later returned to 243 Battery for service in North Africa as a radar sergeant. Success in this role led to further selection for training on 'newer and more sophisticated equipment' and he concluded his war in Burma occupying a brigade staff post. Despite these achievements, Warner always thought fondly of 243 (Heavy) AA Battery, remarking that he had 'never encountered such a splendid team as the Norwich territorial boys'.

The fascination for wartime aviation memorabilia continues to this day and some go to tremendous lengths to unearth – often quite literally – artefacts representing a swastika story. One such enthusiast is Chief Technician Pete Stanley, curator of the RAF Wyton Pathfinder Museum. Pete was intrigued by the possibility that there may be some wreckage extant from a Junkers 88A-1, F1+CP of Kampfgeschwader 76, which had been attacked by a night-fighter over Birmingham. It crashed near Hitchin in Hertfordshire, and RAF records suggested that the engines and other wreckage might still be buried where it fell. Enthused

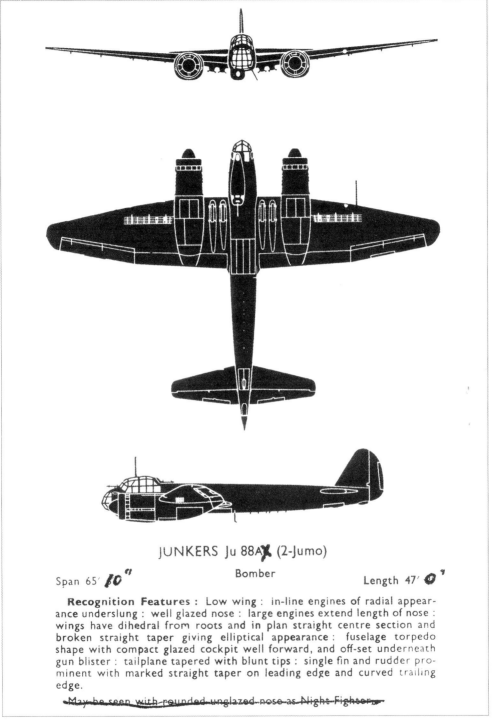

JUNKERS Ju 88A⚡ (2-Jumo)

Span 65' *10"*

Bomber

Length 47' *0"*

Recognition Features : Low wing : in-line engines of radial appearance underslung : well glazed nose : large engines extend length of nose : wings have dihedral from roots and in plan straight centre section and broken straight taper giving elliptical appearance : fuselage torpedo shape with compact glazed cockpit well forward, and off-set underneath gun blister : tailplane tapered with blunt tips : single fin and rudder prominent with marked straight taper on leading edge and curved trailing edge.

~~May be seen with rounded unglazed nose as Night Fighters.~~

A wartime aircraft recognition silhouette of the Junkers 88, one of Germany's most potent and versatile aircraft. Note the contemporary corrections, perhaps made by an enthusiastic member of the Air Training Corps.

by the prospect of a major recovery, Pete now devoted countless hours to pinpointing the crash-site and fleshing out the story. His efforts found him plodding along numerous winding lanes and tracks in villages to the south of Hitchin where there still existed vast tracts of farmland, despite the suburban developments encroaching from nearby Luton and Stevenage. Detailed locations for crash-sites are not always found in the archives and those that do appear can be inaccurate, so Pete also prospected for local accounts. With detective-like determination, he narrowed the area to a few fields on Prestonhills Farm, where he tried to match the contemporary landscape with a grainy wartime picture taken the day after the crash and showing a small wood in the background. Surprisingly, the topography had changed little, and the picture plus local anecdotes and official records focused his attention on a particular field. He hoped his metal detector might find proof, and began pacing the field with rapid sweeps of the detector. A few minutes later came the first bleep, triggered, to his satisfaction, by a tiny piece of twisted aluminium. This initial discovery was soon followed by further fragments and confirmation came when he unearthed a small component identification plate engraved in German. This was clearly the site, but were the engines still buried here? His metal detector was unsuitable for working at depth so a subsequent trip saw Pete armed with an ex-military Forster magnetometer capable of detecting engines or bombs buried at depths of 15–20 feet. Carefully setting the controls, he traversed the crash-site and was thrilled when the needle swung over to register very powerful signals. Carefully criss-crossing the spot, he obtained consistent signal strength over key points and felt confident he had now located the main point of impact and that substantial remains of the Junkers 88 lay beneath the surface of this innocuous-looking field.

Pete now pursued the practical aspects of recovering the lost bomber, while simultaneously following new lines of research, hoping that both elements would combine to reveal the aircraft's flight into history. He knew a mechanical digger would be essential but there was paperwork to do before he could contact any plant-hire companies. First, the landowner's written consent was gained, thus allowing the Ministry of Defence to issue a licence for the recovery of Junkers 88, Werke-nr. 4199. Once Pete had obtained all the necessary documentation, he began planning the excavations, and soon organised a team of fellow enthusiasts. Gathering on site after the 1990 harvest, he briefed both the team and the digger driver. Their first action was to scrape away the topsoil and set it aside for re-use when they had concluded the recovery. This reduced the risk of earth contaminated by aviation fuel appearing on the surface and affecting crop growth. Within minutes, a dark stain appeared in the sub-soil, clearly illustrating the extent of the original crater. A few inches further down and the machine revealed large sections of shattered airframe, followed by more interesting and easily recognisable items such as oxygen bottles and a complete wing-mounted, external bomb rack, still fitted with stabilisers. This and many other finds bore superbly preserved paintwork showing colour tones in grey and blue. Setting aside larger items and sifting through the spoil for smaller finds, they were elated by the condition and quantity of the wreckage being recovered. The excitement increased when the first Jumo 211 was revealed at a depth of some 12 feet. Studying the power-plant, Pete determined it was the port engine

The first engine recovered from some 12 feet down bore evidence of flak and fire damage. (*Pete Stanley*)

and saw evidence of fire and combat damage. The engine also served to orientate the angle of crash, and by working out the dimensions of a Ju88, the recovery of the first engine helped pinpoint the starboard motor. To the team's delight, this was intact and still bore its stencilled serial numbers, manufacturer's labels and a Mercedes Benz engine badge. Buried still deeper were the propeller boss and two smashed propeller blades. Pete could already envisage their finds in a museum where, with a pictorial storyboard, they would make splendid exhibits, but even as the team's activities drew to a close, he knew there were many elements of the story still unresolved. His research now needed to keep pace with the restoration and display of parts from the aircraft.

Exhaustive studies in the Public Record Office (now the National Archives), plus strenuous networking among the aviation fraternity, eventually produced results just as enthralling as the excavations. A turning-point came when a letter arrived from former Obergefreiter Willihad Vogt, the Bordeschütze on board the aircraft. Fortunately Willi's memory was excellent and Pete soon had a clear picture of the events of the night of 9/10 April 1941, when the Luftwaffe targeted Fort Dunlop. This massive, 350,000-sq. ft tyre-manufacturing factory at Erdington in Birmingham produced tyres and other rubber products for the British war effort, and its destruction would hinder the mobility of vehicles and aircraft alike. The aircraft assigned to Willi and his crew had already completed forty-five operations against Britain and seen action on fifteen sorties against North African convoys. The crew were also veterans, with Unteroffizier Heinz Kircher as pilot, Feldwebel Fritz Stahn as Bombeschutz, and Unteroffizier Hans Kellner as Bordfunker. They were based at Creil near Paris but on this occasion, to increase their effective range and allow them to find a more suitable route to their target, a refuelling stop was planned. The day before the mission found them staging through the Luftwaffe base at Leuwarden in the Netherlands. Leaving Leuwarden, their journey across eastern England to the Midlands proved uneventful and they were approaching Birmingham when they were pounced on by what Willi thought was a Bristol Beaufighter. Fire from the British night-fighter raked their port wing and Kircher, hoping to evade their assailant, flung the Ju88 into a steep, spiralling dive. His efforts succeeded but the initial attack had seriously damaged the left engine and they had no alternative but to jettison their load of twenty 50kg bombs and head homewards. The Jumo 211 was a robustly constructed twelve-cylinder inverted V-12 engine capable of absorbing considerable punishment but this time the port engine had sustained terminal damage. Kircher was also struggling to control the aircraft because of the damage to the left wing, and their predicament rapidly worsened as the other engine's temperature soared. With his eyes on the remorselessly climbing gauge, Kircher kept them airborne for some 20 minutes after the attack, until the overheated Jumo finally caught fire. Their fate sealed, the crew decided to bale out. One of Willi's tasks was to operate the emergency release mechanism for the rear exit. Quickly checking his own parachute, Willi released the hatch. The chill night air blasted into the cockpit as, without further ado, Willi dropped away into the darkness. His departure was almost copy-book and his parachute functioned perfectly – he could only hope his comrades would escape as easily, as the Ju88 continued flying on a south-easterly heading. Descending towards the dark, featureless landscape beneath, Willi was unable to ascertain details of the terrain until it was too late and he had the misfortune to fall heavily into the grasping branches of a large tree. This abruptly arrested his descent but he badly injured his knee-cap and would later learn of damage to his kidneys. Releasing himself from the entangled parachute, he clambered painfully to earth, but the injury to his knee prevented any prospect of travelling, and he felt he had no chance of escaping his enemies. It had just gone 0230 so he decided to wait until daybreak before seeking assistance. As dawn eventually shifted shadows into substance, Willi limped across country until, just after 0700, he emerged on to the Harlington–Sharpenhoe road and waved down the first vehicle he saw.

Joe West was driving his chum Jack Peppiatt to work at Vauxhall's airfield when both were startled by the appearance of the German aviator. Braking swiftly to a standstill, the two workers warily approached him. At this moment, there was an incident that might have had disastrous consequences. As Willi held out his pistol, Joe, a former rugby player, suddenly feared that he was going to shoot and so administered a swift blow that knocked Willi to the ground. In later years Willi frequently protested that he had been offering his gun as a gesture of surrender but the burly workman was taking no chances. Following this incident, Willi's welcome at the police house in Harlington was rather more civilised. PC

The Ju88 crew as prisoners of war in Monteith, Canada. On the far left is Willihad 'Hadi' Vogt, beside Heinz Kircher. Next to him is Hans Kellner, while Fritz Stahn is ninth in from the left, at the back. (*Pete Stanley*)

Goodhall, acting upon orders to be hospitable, cooked his guest a fine breakfast of eggs and bacon. His appetite sated, Willi was taken for hospital treatment and then escorted to an interrogation centre in Leicester. During this journey he was befriended by some RAF personnel who chivalrously provided him with currency, chocolate and even a few cigarettes. Willi's war was over and he was initially held in a prisoner-of-war camp near Bury in Lancashire. There he was delighted to meet up with the rest of his crew, before all were eventually shipped to Liverpool for a trans-Atlantic convoy and captivity in a Canadian POW camp for the duration.

Heinz Kircher also landed in trees at the southernmost corner of King's Walden deer park in Hertfordshire. Uninjured, the pilot was soon striding boldly and rather noisily along the road to Whitwell. Shouting in German, he passed one cottage whose occupants had been awoken by the crash; perhaps wisely, they remained quietly within their dwelling while the pilot passed by. A few minutes later the German reappeared but the householder, now bolstered by the presence of his shotgun, still felt discretion was the better part of valour and decided not to confront Kircher, who continued walking away from Whitwell along the Lilley Bottom Road. Here he encountered Colonel Harrison, who was not intimidated at all and duly took the 'loud and arrogant' German into captivity.

Guarded by two police constables, a smouldering pile of debris is all that remains of the Ju88. (*via Pete Stanley*)

Unteroffizier Kellner was a more compliant captive. Having walked into the village of Harlington in Bedfordshire, he greeted Special Police Sergeant Adams by throwing up his arms and calling 'Kamerad'. In very broken English Kellner explained how his machine had crashed some half-mile distant and stressed that he had discarded his pistol. Gesturing and grimacing, the German also conveyed the point about an injury to his ankle and seemed relieved that his ordeal was over. Feldwebel Fritz Stahn, also suffering some minor injuries, was caught near Streatley. With all four crewmen accounted for, little official interest was shown by the British authorities in the crater containing the remains of their Ju88. Willi Vogt's parachute was pulled from its tree by J. Hall and W. Brown, both members of the Home Guard, whose families probably welcomed the material, German or not. Several weeks later the cockpit canopy, complete with its integral MG15 machine-gun, was found in woodland near Shefford. Thereafter the fate of the aircraft slipped into obscurity until Pete Stanley commenced his investigations some fifty years later.

However, even with the recovery complete, Pete still had many unanswered questions, not least of which was who had downed the Ju88? Surprisingly Willi Vogt wrote to Pete expressing how much he wanted to meet and shake hands with his former adversary, who he now credited with saving his life! True, he had spent six years in captivity but, a few weeks after the loss of F1+CP, KG76 had found itself embroiled in the merciless campaign on the Russian front and there were few survivors among his companions. The savage treatment of

Staples and Parkin with their all-black Boulton Paul Defiant N3479 being readied for another sortie. The Defiant served in an interim role pending the arrival of more suitable types equipped with AI (Air Interception) radar. (*via Pete Stanley*)

German prisoners saw many perish in captivity and countless others disappeared without trace; comparatively few emerged from behind the Iron Curtain in the 1940s and 1950s. In contrast, Willi found himself released from Canada in 1946 and returned home to rebuild his life and his nation. Had the British night-fighter missed, Willi's chances of surviving the war would have been very slim indeed.

Facing the challenge of linking two aircraft in time and space on a black night over Birmingham, Pete again visited the National Archives in Kew. He set about checking every squadron operational record book for units operating on the night of 9/10 April 1941. During the following months Pete's options dwindled to just two, with the more likely being an encounter report filed by the pilot of a Boulton Paul Defiant, serial N3479, from 151 Squadron at Wittering. Sergeant Lionel Staples described attacking a 'Dornier' over Birmingham. Setting aside the inadequacies in aircraft

Sergeant Lionel Staples thought his victim was a Dornier 17. (*via Pete Stanley*)

Sergeant Parkin in his Sidcot suit poses with a pet. (*via Pete Stanley*)

recognition by both air-crews, Pete felt the time, the description of events and Staples' time of landing all matched. Convinced he now had his man, Pete's next task was to trace whether Staples had survived the war and might still be around. Setting off for the local library, Pete painstakingly went through the UK's entire series of telephone directories and returned with a list of 'Staples' that would have been a credit to any genealogist. Even the most dedicated researcher needs some help from Lady Luck and Pete's efforts were suitably blessed – his second phone call found him speaking to a very surprised Lionel Staples, who well remembered the encounter.

Taking off from Wittering, Staples and his gunner Sergeant Parkin set course to intercept the enemy raiders now wreaking havoc in the Midlands. It was a clear moonlit night and evidence of the Germans' efforts soon became visible. Amid the weaving searchlights the flashes of bursting bombs and burgeoning flames testified to the battle raging in the heart of their homeland. Down there, men, women and children were suffering and the Defiant's crew wanted to punish the perpetrators. Lacking radar, they headed towards the target, knowing that the bombers would be more concentrated there, and the Defiant thundered in, guns primed, crew vigilant. Scanning the night sky, Staples spotted the merest shadow of another aircraft on his starboard side but could not clearly discern its identity. None the less, he told Parkin to align his four .303in machine-guns and felt the turret traverse as he closed in. That the aircraft was an enemy seemed obvious but proper recognition eluded him and he guessed it was a Dornier 17. Edging up from astern on the enemy's port quarter, he carefully reduced range but kept himself in the shadows until they were alongside and below, hidden, he hoped, from its crew's view by the bomber's own port wing. It was impossible to miss. Now! Parkin fired. A bright rippling of bullet strikes flashed into the engine and ran along the port wing as the bomber, reacting like an ambushed horse, reared over into a steep, twisting dive. Pushing his joystick hard over and down, Staples followed it but Parkin found it impossible to train his turret and sights on the fleeing bomber. With snapping bursts of gunfire they harried their prey as both machines hurtled earthwards, lower and lower, but the pursuit proved inconclusive. Staples, realising they had chased the enemy almost into the deadly cables of the city's barrage balloons, now broke off the attack. Climbing warily to a safer altitude, he set course for home unaware of subsequent events until the phone call from Pete Stanley nearly fifty years later.

The casualties and damage inflicted upon communities in and around Birmingham that night were ghastly. Taking advantage of good visibility, and using radio beam technology (even though this was increasingly handicapped by British countermeasures), some 237 bombers rained 285 tonnes of high explosives on the city. In addition, around 40,000 incendiary bombs showered into the devastated structures igniting the inflammable interiors. We can only imagine the terror of trapped victims as the flames closed in, and it was a scene repeated many times over as countless fires raged in the city centre and surrounding districts. Serious damage was inflicted on key railway targets, including Saltley Wagon Works and Birmingham East goods station. The Rover car company's plant was hit and flames from gas-holders in Saltley and Nechells and the Windsor Street Gasworks illuminated the skyline. The city's suffering was visible for miles. Bombs tore through the roof of the Prince of Wales theatre in Broad Street and devastated the interior but fortunately there was no performance in progress and there were no casualties. Elsewhere, seven churches were destroyed or damaged, including St Philip's Cathedral, and serious damage was done to gas, electricity and water systems, the latter creating a water shortage that only exacerbated the defenders' woes as fire hoses lacked pressure or ran dry. Beyond the material damage, 237 men, women and children perished in this attack and in another raid the following night. Many more were injured and countless scars were inflicted on the fabric and people of the communities in Britain's industrial heartland.

This was one of the Luftwaffe's largest air raids on Britain and it proved very successful. They lost only 8 aircraft – less than 2 per cent – of the 480 participating in attacks not just on Birmingham but on Newcastle, Tynemouth, South Shields and elsewhere in the north-east and other regions. However, the Luftwaffe's ability to mount such powerful assaults would shortly be diluted by the demands of the Eastern Front, and Willi Vogt certainly realised that, somewhat ironically, he owed his own survival to Lionel Staples. Willi hoped the former RAF fighter pilot would be willing to meet and shake hands with his former adversary. Many souls had suffered grievously in those dark, distant days but this simple gesture would symbolise the bonds of friendship that had since developed between Britain and Germany. Pete Stanley, whose efforts had made such a meeting possible, would be delighted to act as an intermediary.

In 1976 Willi had returned to Harlington and shaken hands with Joe West and Jack Peppiatt on the precise spot where Joe's greeting had been somewhat pugilistic because of the misunderstanding over Willi's pistol. For Willi, the meeting with Lionel would be the chance he wanted to kindle friendship from the embers of war, and in its own small way would represent the desire for an abiding peace between the two nations.

Pete duly arranged the meeting and it occurred in the RAF museum at Hendon, fifty years to the day since their first encounter. The two former airmen shook hands and embraced. There followed a lively discussion about the events of five decades earlier and, thanks to Hendon's hospitality, Willi was allowed inside the museum's Ju88. This was the first time he had even seen one since his hasty exit from F1+CP, and he was particularly interested to see the fascinating display of artefacts from his own fallen aircraft – the surviving fragments from its flight into history. Pete's research had corrected a published account that listed a different aircraft and crew for the crash. The following day, both airmen visited the crash-site, accompanied by journalists, and that afternoon Pete had arranged a 'top table' lunch for his

Left: Former foes but now old comrades, Willi Vogt and Lionel Parkin share memories while visiting the RAF Museum. (*Pete Stanley*)

Above: The once powerful Jumo engine, wrecked in action, in the Perch Rock collection. (*Pete Stanley*)

two guests in the Sergeants' Mess at RAF Henlow. The bond between Lionel and Willi formed during their initial meeting endured until Lionel's death some years later.

Items from the Ju88 were loaned to museums and parts are now exhibited at the RAF Wyton Pathfinder Museum where Pete acts as curator. Sadly the superbly preserved starboard Jumo was stolen while on temporary display outside the Booker Aircraft Museum in Buckinghamshire, but the fire-damaged port engine can still be seen in the Perch Rock collection on Merseyside. Pete still regularly contacts Willi Vogt, who numbers among the dwindling numbers of Second World War veterans whose misdirected courage had seen them serve under the swastika.

The word swastika comes from a Sanskrit term meaning good luck or good fortune. Adopted by the National Socialist German Workers' Party, its crooked form soon became the embodiment of evil. Any association with good fortune vanished and the swastika now represents oppression and some of the worst atrocities ever to result from man's inhumanity to man. Only in defeat could it be used beneficially – a swastika from a downed enemy aircraft often served as an important morale booster for those fighting against what it represented. Even fifty years later, those involved in aviation archaeology understand this sentiment. The recovery of the mangled remains of this debased symbol from beneath the soil of a nation it sought to subjugate honours not only those who brought about its demise but also acknowledges the misplaced heroism of German air-crews. One such swastika is exhibited by the N&SAM. Retrieving it from a crash-site in Suffolk, the museum's

Bob Collis points to the swastika still discernible on the remains of the Dornier's tail fin – a broken symbol of a broken tyranny that sought world domination. (*Bob Collis*)

investigations also corrected the official records and added names to the grave-marker of four enemy airmen. They had grown up in a nation bereft of any stable democracy and suffering from the crippling war reparations imposed by the victorious powers following the First World War. These circumstances created a seedbed in which the perverted ideologies of the Nazis took root and flourished, and the consequences convulsed the world into another war. This crew and countless others perished in the ensuing conflict, but the fate of these four individuals was rescued from historical anonymity by the dedication of researchers and aviation archaeologists.

By 13 May 1943 even the most ardent Nazis admitted the possibility of defeat but any public comment to this effect earned Hitler's swift and vicious retribution. In reality, the Axis troops were already on the point of surrender in North Africa. Churchill and Roosevelt were meeting at the Trident Conference in Washington to determine the date for opening a second front in France. The remorseless Russian advance was under way and Japan's treacherous leadership had tasted defeat in the Aleutians and elsewhere. Goering's much-vaunted Luftwaffe would increasingly diminish into an ever-weakening defensive force as it faced the relentless advance of increasing Allied air power. Only against the hapless inmates of the Warsaw ghetto was it operating virtually unchallenged. Over Britain the Luftwaffe saw mounting losses for diminishing returns, but for the attacks planned that Thursday night, 13 May, it could at least claim to be striking legitimate military objectives.

Several such targets lay within the town boundaries of Chelmsford in Essex. Regarded as the birthplace of radio, the town contained a number of Marconi factories busily producing radio communications equipment for the British armed forces. Elsewhere the Hoffman Manufacturing Company made ball-bearings in their New Street facility and Crompton-Parkinson produced electric motors for a variety of military applications. These and other industrial targets made the town a key objective for Luftwaffe tacticians but they were no longer capable of the mass assaults seen during 1940–1. However, the headquarters of Luftflotte 3 and its subordinate bomber groups still managed to muster some eighty-five aircraft to attack the town. In addition to losses and the drain on resources imposed by having to fight on several fronts at once, the Luftwaffe's power had been further diluted by a lack of investment resulting from the 'certainty' of victory in 1940. Development of new aircraft had slowed and those new machines that eventually emerged, including the remarkable Me262 jet fighter, were too little, too late. Meanwhile German aeronautical designers and engineers stretched the capabilities of existing concepts to the maximum. The Dornier 217, which had its origins in the Dornier 17, was a heavier, longer-range variant initially proposed by Dornier in 1937, but its development had been delayed owing to the Luftwaffe's obsession with dive-bombers. To meet the required specification, Dornier attempted to incorporate this capability into what was essentially a heavy bomber, and months of development time were squandered pursuing this pointless objective. Allied intelligence used various methods of tracking the development of German aircraft but one of the most basic was the interpretation of evidence from the remains of enemy aircraft brought down over the UK. They tracked the new Dornier 217E series but initially overlooked the first example of the upgraded Do217K series because destruction of the first example to fall on British soil was so complete that it lay unknown for many decades. British archives state that the first specimen of this new Dornier sub-series was shot down over the mainland by a Mosquito of 85 Squadron during the night of 9 July 1943 but aviation archaeology in Suffolk was to set the record straight several decades later.

When the raid on Chelmsford was being planned, KG2, still operating the Do217E, had recently received the new Dornier 217K-1 and so used both types in battle that night. The Do217K-1's redesigned cockpit gave a speed improvement of some 20mph and it also boasted increased power from twin BMW 801D engines. Operationally it was hoped these features would reduce losses, but the British defences were now so advanced that the later mark fared little better in combat than its predecessors. That night German losses amounted to four machines, two of which fell in the sea. One mine-carrying Ju88 from 1/KG6 crash-landed in a cornfield at Great Barton in Suffolk and its crew were captured. The other airmen, far less fortunate, were simply listed as missing and it would be many years before wreckologists determined the fate of one of the missing crews from the 'Holzhammer' Geschwader. The name derived from the unit's emblem emblazoned on its machines – a clenched fist clutching a mallet, poised to strike. Had they known it, the airmen of KG2 and the other units involved had struck a serious blow against British industry in Chelmsford and matters might have been much worse but for a navigational blunder.

Bombs began tumbling into the British town at 0145 hours, with Dorniers from KG2 among the force leaders. Some 15 minutes into the raid, a parachute mine exploded over the electronics test department and storage facilities on the Marconi site in Broomfield Road. Sensitive apparatus was destroyed and production output was delayed for several weeks. Fires were also started at the Hoffman Ball and Roller Works and in the Crompton-Parkinson factory. More seriously, bombs falling on the bus station, the YMCA and in residential areas saw casualties increase to 46 killed with 226 injured. Further lives were undoubtedly spared because many bombers scattered their ordnance further north in the Suffolk countryside around Ipswich. Bob Collis has studied this attack and believes the raiders mistook the similarly shaped Stour Estuary for the Blackwater Estuary 20 miles further south. Between 0200 and 0300 hours 94 high-explosive bombs, 11 parachute mines and over 1,300 incendiary devices dropped into twenty-one parishes. Fortunately most of the bombs fell harmlessly on farmland and the only lives lost were those of some cows burnt in their blazing byre at Charsfield.

Of the KG2 casualties, one fell to the guns of Sergeants R.L. Watts and J. Whewell of 157 Squadron, whose Mosquito attacked it at 0215 off the Suffolk coast at Southwold. The clatter of cannon fire and four sharp stabs of tracer set the Dornier's starboard engine on fire at 10,000 feet. Moments later a patch of burning fuel on the sea's surface marked its passing. Five minutes earlier, and some 25 miles further south, the gunners of light Anti-Aircraft Gun Site 2 had scored a direct hit on another Dornier. The aircraft immediately plummeted from 8,000 feet and exploded in a sugar beet field known locally as Bullock Meadow, just off East Lane on Red House Farm.

The following morning dispirited personnel from KG2 noted three aircraft and their crews as *vermisste* – missing. The resulting submission to Luftflotte 3's General Quartermaster 6 Department of Records noted the losses of Do217E-4 U5+BK of 2 Staffel, work number 4368, and two of the more modern Do217K-1s, U5+IM of 4 Staffel, work number 4420, and U5+CP of 2 Staffel, work number 4526. Families were notified that their loved ones were 'missing after a mission over England', and the war moved on. Meanwhile, on the other side of the English Channel, RAF intelligence officers from Air Intelligence 2(g) were poking about on the edge of a still-smoking crater. Measuring about 6 feet deep and some 20 feet in diameter, the hole was surrounded by clods of earth and debris, much of which had been volcanically ejected in a subsidiary explosion earlier that morning when the local fire service started playing their hoses into the wreckage. Cold water intended to douse the flames apparently triggered a blast that blew earth and fragments of the fallen aircraft for some distance, and the fire service personnel were lucky not to sustain any injuries. A search for survivors was soon called off when grisly evidence of the crew's fate was found amid the wreckage. Robert Simper, a local lad, was watching with other equally inquisitive children when one of them picked up a 'wig', only to discover it was a mass of human hair with a scalp still attached! This and the grim scattering of additional human remains were gathered, but the absence of documents or identification tags meant that no names could be forwarded through the Red Cross. The destruction of the bomber was so comprehensive that RAF Intelligence Report 7/101 simply stated:

> This aircraft crashed on 14th May 1943 at 02:15 hours at Bawdsey, near Ipswich. Map Ref number 8038. The aircraft dived almost vertically into the ground from about 8,000 feet. It was completely destroyed, and most of the wreckage is buried in a very large crater. It is believed that the aircraft received a direct hit by A/A fire. No identification markings could be traced, but some portions of wing were marked 3387. The little wreckage still on the surface showed nothing new, and this was probably a standard Do217 of sub-series E-2 or E-4.

Had the RAF known the true identity of this aircraft, greater effort might have been expended in recovering the wreckage. Instead, the officers departed, taking only a few pieces back to RAF Martlesham Heath, and left the local authorities with the grim chore of tidying up and burying what had been found of the airmen on board. A funeral was arranged and a single casket containing all that had been found of the four fliers was interred in the nearby church of St Mary. According their enemies full military honours, personnel from RAF Bawdsey attended the service. The RAF had taken over Bawdsey Manor, the Victorian stately home of the Quilter family. Built by Sir Cuthbert Quilter between 1886 and 1910, the house was to enter the history books through its association with the RAF and the development of radar. In 1935 it was chosen as a research and development establishment for RDF (radio direction finding), which later became known as radar. Research had commenced at nearby Orfordness and Robert Watson-Watt took over as Superintendent when RAF Bawdsey was set up. The first RDF training school was created at Bawdsey and the first Chain Home RDF station became operational in 1937. Interestingly the British Army also worked at Bawdsey developing a gun-laying radar enabling anti-aircraft guns to track the target and fire in poor visibility. The station undoubtedly tracked enemy raiders during the night of 13/14 May and the AA fire proved devastatingly effective against the Dornier whose crew were now being buried. One of those attending the service was Edward Lipscombe, who later recalled: 'The local verger was also the station coalman and on the day of the service he arrived at the church wearing only a cassock as his official vestment. But as this was rather on the short side, it allowed a large pair of coal-begrimed boots to be seen, while further up his legs could be seen the lengths of string holding up his trouser bottoms!'

For the next nineteen years the remains of the four comrades in arms rested beneath a simple marker, which was inscribed, incorrectly, with the words 'Four unknown German sailors 14.5.43'. During the 1960s the Deutschen Soldatenfriedhof was consecrated at Cannock Chase in Staffordshire and became the main cemetery for German war dead, and some 5,000 casualties were re-interred in this heather-clad heath in the heart of England. On 17 September 1962 the remains of the men from the Bawdsey bomber were exhumed and reburied in Block 9, Row 5, Grave 29, still listed as 'unknown'. This state of anonymity

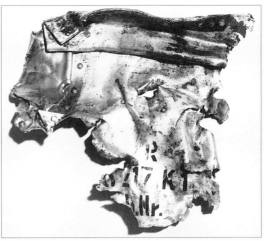

Left: Excavations on Red House Farm recovered much – but not all – of the aircraft before the weather closed in and turned the site into a quagmire. (*Bob Collis*)

Above: A fragment of history. Careful recovery and subsequent cleaning can identify parts or reveal important data, as discovered on this piece of the Dornier. (*Via Bob Collis*)

would have prevailed but for the crash-site investigations by Bob Collis and a team of aviation wreckologists from the N&SAM.

In October 1980 the land where the bomber had fallen was once more awaiting the ploughman's touch before commencing another season of growth. This year, however, the landowners, J.W. Mann (Farms) Ltd, generously consented to a site investigation. James Mann remembered the crash and how the aircraft 'had exploded upon impact . . . although nothing is visible now of the crater'. His son Peter, currently farming the land, also supported the site survey and potential recovery of wreckage. Within minutes of commencing their search, the team's metal detectors were chattering busily over the sprinkling of small metal fragments in the stubble. Soon the searchers had a focal area where even stronger signals were being emitted, signifying larger items lying beneath the surface. They set to work with their spades and their first significant find was an engine cylinder shorn from one of the BMW 801s. Fred Graham, the local gamekeeper, had commented how the aircraft hit the ground and must have gone 'right down to hell'. Bob Collis felt there was no need to go quite that far, and hoped that a standard JCB would have sufficient reach. On 19 October the team reconvened, now armed with a bright yellow JCB and a driver grateful for his cab as the steady drizzle deteriorated into a downpour. Soon the machine was gouging through the mire as the team members busily sifted and sorted each soggy spillage of spoil on to an ever-growing heap. With the aircraft's identity still unknown, it was essential not to overlook any clues in the wreckage now being unearthed. A close scrutiny was maintained over the crater and the JCB's pace adjusted accordingly. As the machine shifted ever more debris, one observant enthusiast spotted the crumpled but recognisable outline of a swastika, its form just discernible on the remains of the mud-caked starboard tailfin and rudder. Careful exhumation ensued and the trophy was then gently cleaned to reveal more clearly the swastika's outline and the number 4526 painted in white. On another part of the same empennage were the letters 'CP', also in white. Further confirmation came as a section of concertinaed aluminium was carefully prised apart to reveal black stencilling reading 'Do 217 K Masch 4526'. Beyond any doubt, the team had discovered the remains of the first Do217K to fall on British soil and they could now correct the history books. More importantly, perhaps the crew could now be named and given proper recognition. The N&SAM team enthusiasm's was not dampened by the rain turning the site into a quagmire but the wet conditions did hamper further effective recovery, so the excavation was brought to an end.

A young man in uniform. The true fate of 22-year-old Herbert Voss was lost for many decades until aviation archaeologists and researchers pieced together the facts. (*Via Bob Collis*)

A fine study of a Dornier 217 from KG2 in flight, taken from a companion aircraft. (*Via Bob Collis*)

During the following weeks, months and years, Bob busily networked the aviation fraternity, adding to the information already gathered. The renowned Air Britain researcher Richard Bateson studied Luftwaffe loss listings in the General Quartermaster returns, and there, on 14 May 1943, was Do217K-1 U5+CP number 4526, listed as '100% loss, location and cause unknown'. The Luftwaffe war graves historian Stephen Burns confirmed the crew's last resting-place. Gradually the loose strands of history were woven together and names could now be linked to the aircraft. The pilot was 23-year-old Leutnant Richard Ludwig from Freiwaldau in the Sudetenland. His observer, Unteroffizier Joseph Wilhelm Roseman, was two years younger and came from Osnabruck. Unteroffizier Herbert Erich August Voss, the radio operator, was 22 and came from Quitzobel/Perleberg, being one year the junior of the Dornier's gunner, Unteroffizier Andreas Weber from Baden Bei Wien. So devastating had been the Dornier's impact that none could be identified from the remains recovered at the time. Now, at last, their names had come to light. An approach was made to the Volksbund Deutsche Kriegsgräberfürsorge (German War Graves Commission) for a new grave-marker. Initially, they hesitated, unconvinced, but the intervention of former Dornier pilot Heinz Möllenbrook carried the day and in 1997 names, dates of birth and ranks were added to a new stone over Grave 29 at Cannock Chase. Heinz himself visited that summer and placed a

Crew members of the lost Dornier. Their fate was a mystery until aviation archaeology took a hand. (*Via Bob Collis*)

Now a grave-marker honours the crew of Dornier U5+CP as individuals with names and families. (*Via Bob Collis*)

commemorative wreath there honouring all the fallen airmen from the Second World War. Two years later Luftwaffe researcher Ed Clark traced Günter Voss, brother of the radio operator, Herbert Voss. In August 2000 Günter wrote:

> After 57 years of uncertainty, I now get to know, through your researches, the ultimate fate of my brother Herbert Voss. The last information I got about my brother's destiny was 1943 – 'Missing after a mission over England'. Since this time we didn't get any further information. Perhaps the separation of Germany was one reason for this. My residence is in the east of Germany and the East regime at that time didn't have any interests for the clearing up of destinies of former German soldiers. We thank you very much for the detailed explanation about the crash, the place and the grave. The documents will have a place of honour in our house. After so many years of uncertainty, it is a gratifying to know that there are people in England who have the courage and energy after such a terrible war to find out about the destinies of German soldiers and pass those results on to their relations.

Enclosed with the letter was a portrait of Herbert, and another picture of him with his crew, four young airmen smiling in the evening sunshine. Theirs was a story of service beneath the swastika. The symbol may have been dishonoured, but one cannot discredit the courage of the men whose swastika stories represent such wasted heroism.

CHAPTER THREE

Lest We Forget

The Second World War drew many nations into conflict and countless individual combatants and non-combatants alike perished. An accurate figure is impossible to express but some sources show over 62 million lives lost – each a person both loved and loving. Many more were scarred, physically or emotionally, for the rest of their lives. We of later generations owe our liberty to those who fought for the Allied cause. It is impossible to capture the accounts of all who contributed to that freedom, and authors are frequently obliged to select one to represent the many. I hope the story of Sergeant Maurice Raes will serve to honour the men of one of the smaller countries to take on Hitler's might – brave little Belgium.

Invaded on 10 May 1940, Belgium was rapidly overwhelmed by the German superiority in numbers of men and material. Their daring use of parachute and glider forces, most notably against Fort Eben Emael, stunned the Allies. Thought to be impregnable, the fort succumbed in less than two days after gliders swept silently in under cover of the pre-dawn's semi-darkness. Elsewhere the German strategy outwitted the Allies and the débâcle climaxed in the miracle of Dunkirk but, heroic though this was, the overall defeat was humiliating at both national and personal levels. For many Belgians, this was compounded by the embarrassment of King Leopold's capitulation on 28 May without informing either his own government or its allies of his intentions. The bitterness of this bungling failure left many Belgian nationals determined to continue the struggle and restore their nation's honour.

One such man was Maurice Raes. Born in Mons, Belgium, on 17 June 1921, Maurice was the eldest son of a blacksmith who fought in the Belgian Army during the First World War and met his future wife when serving near Mons. Maurice developed into a handsome young man, whose sense of humour and mischievous spirit endeared him even to the victims of his many practical jokes. His younger brother was the frequent victim of such pranks but the boys bonded well and were a credit to their parents. Maurice was a fine young athlete, and sprinting absorbed the energy and enthusiasm of his competitive character. A slightly more studious side evinced itself in an interest in philately but this dwindled when time devoted to the track saw him training at least three nights a week. His efforts paid dividends and his proud parents were delighted with the numerous trophies he won during school competitions. He and his

Looking very serious and older than his years, Maurice Raes demonstrates that the garb of a 1940s Belgian aviator had changed little from fliers in the First World War. (*Via Cynrik De Decker*)

brother also joined a local bicycle-touring group and the pair enjoyed many excursions into the surrounding countryside. For Maurice, the physical effort of cycling proved more attractive than the mechanical effort required to maintain his machine and he invariably relied on his younger brother for routine maintenance and repair. Speeding unfettered along country lanes, Maurice was exhilarated by the wind in his face and might have embraced motorcycling but, perhaps, for the mechanical side of things. Instead his spirits soared skywards towards the exciting world of aviation. In the Air Force, his energy and enthusiasm for speed might be assuaged and, after all, they had mechanics to look after the aeroplanes.

Maurice's thinking may have been slightly fanciful but he also realised the need for serious endeavours as a pilot. That German bombers might soon darken the heavens had become all too evident with the increasingly aggressive nature of their Nazi neighbours. The outbreak of war prompted a decision and Maurice quit secondary school to enrol for three years in the Army, which then included the Air Regiments of the Aeronautique Militaire. His initial army training took place at Zellik with the inevitable 'square-bashing' and indoctrination into basic military attitudes. Surviving these rigours, Maurice was part of the 82nd Promotion and moved on to the next stage at Wevelghem. It was an excited and enthusiastic young aviator who returned to Mons on leave. The family shared his stories of aeronautical adventures and encouraged his eagerness to move forward with his training, perhaps even to pilot one of the new British-designed Hawker Hurricane fighters now being manufactured under licence in Belgium. The 'phoney war' had already seen these aircraft in action, although it might be argued that intercepting a Dornier 17 with three *unarmed* Hurricanes was a pointless farce – which turned into a tragedy when one of the Hurricanes was shot down, killing its young pilot, Second Lieutenant Xavier Henrard. Belatedly the Belgian authorities now decided to arm their aircraft against such eventualities. Perhaps they had hoped that their unarmed interceptions demonstrated their capability for interception without provoking the situation and risking Belgium's declared position of strict neutrality. If so, such political naivety would be rudely shattered by events on 10 May 1940.

Frustratingly for Maurice, he was still under training when the massive German assault was launched. Like almost everyone else that morning, the Aeronautique Militaire was caught napping. Most of its aircraft, including many precious Hurricanes, were destroyed on the ground and the pitifully few that went into action were almost annihilated. The Hurricanes were too few, and the outmoded Fairey Battles and Gloster Gladiators, plus an assortment of other machines, were soon wiped from the skies by the superior Me109s.

Amid the chaos of a rapidly collapsing kingdom, it was decided to evacuate the flying school and its pupils via Marseilles to Oujda in Morocco, where the French, still Allies, had control. Here the swiftly emerging political fault lines following the fall of France soon made the position of those supporting the British untenable as French forces in the region supported the Vichy government. Not wishing to play any part for the Axis powers, Maurice considered his options. A return to occupied Belgium was out – his opinion of the Nazis made this impossible. He could head for the Belgian Congo to escape, but it would be impossible to continue the fight from there. Should he go to England, perhaps?

In a manner that is still rather mysterious, Maurice managed to reach the United

Maurice poses in the Moroccan sunshine at Oujda with a Potez 25 biplane that would likewise not have been out of place on an aerodrome during the First World War. Some 87 variants of the aircraft were built during a production run exceeding 3,500. (*Via Cynrik De Decker*)

Maurice with another Potez 25 at Oujda. The type served with several air forces and was flown in combat during 1935 by the Chinese against the invading Japanese and by the Ethiopians against Italian forces. (*Via Cynrik De Decker*)

A tousle-headed Maurice pictured with Spitfire 'Yaunde'. The Yaunde are a tribe from south central Cameroon but whether this was the intended connection is unknown. (*Via Cynrik De Decker*)

Kingdom on 5 August 1940 with a cadre of other would-be and current aviators, all eager to combat the fascist power now subjugating their beloved Belgium. In fact the initial trickle of airmen would become a stream, enabling the formation of a whole squadron of Belgian nationals. Meanwhile, Maurice, like many others, began to enhance his English language skills as he continued his flying training with the RAF. The inability of many students to have participated in Belgium's '18-day war' was undoubtedly a source of shame to some and evoked in many others a determination to enter the fray. Now they would be given the chance. A short stay at RAF Tenby in Wales, to be taught, among other things, basic English, only increased Maurice's frustration because he had already accumulated 25 hours of flying under instruction and 30 hours solo. For good reason, however, the RAF insisted on improving the English language skills of its foreign pilots, and it was 23 November 1940 before Maurice finally became airborne at RAF Odiham in the humble Miles Magister basic trainer under the tutelage of instructor G. Dieu. Almost a month later Maurice took the tiny trainer aloft for his first RAF solo. Training continued for several months and Maurice had risen from 'average' to 'above average' by the time he completed his training in January 1942. This improvement came about when the young aviator graduated from the Magister to its larger and more powerful brother, the Miles Master. This stepping-stone then allowed him into the cockpit of a Hurricane. Only a few years earlier this had been the choice of the Aeronautique Militaire and the Belgian aviation industry for indigenous manufacturing, but already the type was outmoded for front-line operations in Europe and Maurice cast covetous eyes towards the sleeker Spitfire. Indeed, no one could have given the young pilot a better gift that Christmas season of 1941 than his first flight in a Spitfire on 29 December. He made a further 16 flights in January and added 14 more in February to make him very conversant with the characteristics of this already legendary aircraft, although, as time would tell, Maurice still had more to learn.

The Spitfire Mk IIs used by 53 Operational Training Unit and the Fighter Training School were somewhat weary specimens, but by now the Belgian Air Force in exile was progressing from feeding pilots into existing RAF squadrons (primarily 609 and 131) to establishing a unit of its own. There were now enough fully trained Belgian pilots and ground-crews available to enable this historic and morale-boosting step to be taken. To accompany the formation of 350 Squadron at Valley on Anglesey on 13 November 1941, leaflets were dropped over occupied Belgium

Maurice relaxes in the somewhat spartan surroundings of his quarters. (*Via Cynrik De Decker*)

Maurice put his mishap with the Spitfire down to his own inexperience. (*Via Cynrik De Decker*)

announcing the establishment of the 'Belgische jachtvliegtuigen escadrille in Engeland'. The new unit's motto, 'Belgae Gallorum fortissimi' was taken from an account in Julius Caesar's *De Bello Gallico*, in which he acknowledged the courage of the Belgians: 'Of all the inhabitants of Gaul, the Belgians were the bravest.' The squadron was soon operational on convoy patrols over the Irish Sea plus mounting the odd scramble. In February 1942 it moved to Atcham and an enthusiastic Maurice Raes arrived the following month. His debut on the squadron's more powerful Spitfire Vb was an inauspicious occasion because he bent it after leaving the runway, noting dismally in his log-book that this was down to his own inexperience. Additional training for fledgling pilots was part of the squadron's routine and Maurice overcame his anxiety with 30 further flights during April and May without mishap, including an introduction to formation flying.

In April 350 Squadron took a step closer to the likelihood of combat when it moved to Debden as part of 11 Group. On 4 June 1942 Maurice Raes took off for his first operational sortie, and his formation cocked a snoot at the enemy coastline before returning. It was an exhilarated Blue Two who touched down safely at Debden. The next day he participated in a fighter sweep seeking to taunt German fighters into combat. Their lack of reaction proved disappointing and Maurice had to wait for his first taste of action. On 12 June he undertook a

Wartime romances were risky. The identity of the young lady with Maurice is unknown. (*Via Cynrik De Decker*)

more mundane but essential maritime activity when his B Flight, commanded by Jean Easter, was assigned to cover a convoy off the east coast. There would be no weekend respite because orders were posted for two similar sorties the next morning, Saturday.

That day Raes was allocated a rather special Spitfire although there was little about its appearance to suggest it was anything out of the ordinary. It carried typical military markings, all camouflaged in waves of dark green and dark sea grey, with the fuselage code MN-R and the serial number W3446. One distinctively unmilitary feature was the name 'Jennifer' painted below the cockpit, and Maurice wondered about its origins.

This machine had been ordered as a Mk I but developments of the Spitfire frequently saw orders being amended. Contract B19713/39 was altered to produce some machines as Mk Va and Mk Vb versions, fitted with a new variant of the Rolls-Royce Merlin engine, the more powerful Series 45. This gave improved performance to help pilots cope with the newer models of the Messerschmitt 109, in the continuing contest of technological leapfrog between the belligerent powers. When Maurice entered combat, the Germans had already outclassed the Spitfire V with their superb Focke-Wulf 190, but the leapfrogging would continue as the Spitfire's capabilities were further extended. Jennifer was the 1,845th model built under contract at Eastleigh. After a test flight on 4 July 1941, she was delivered to 5 Maintenance Unit to undergo the latest operational modifications required by the RAF.

Allocated on 20 July 1941 to 54 Squadron at Hornchurch, she resided only briefly with that unit but did see combat and was credited with a 'probable' victory over an Me109 on 25 July near St Omer, when flown by Flying Officer E.F.J. Charles. She was then transferred to 403 'City of Calgary' Squadron, Royal Canadian Air Force. Indeed, Jennifer already had a Canadian heritage because she was a 'Presentation' aircraft.

In the desperate days of 1940 the plight of the beleaguered British triggered a flurry of sympathetic activity to support the nation with additional funds for the fighting forces. One aspect of this was the Spitfire Fund. Organised and supported by Lord Beaverbrook, the Minister of Aircraft Production, the Spitfire Fund encouraged people from all walks of life in the UK and British Commonwealth countries to raise £5,000 to purchase a Spitfire. In reality, this was less than half the cost of each aircraft but the idea burgeoned and the Spitfire's already legendary status stirred tremendous activity as communities and organisations were inspired to generate funds to buy 'their' Spitfire. In all, some 1,500 Spitfires were funded in this way and became Presentation aircraft, and many proudly carried into combat the names chosen by or linked to their sponsor.

That Jennifer was a Presentation machine is known, but less clear is the connection between the name on her fuselage and the man who funded her. Businessman and newspaper publisher John Wilson McConnell, one of Canada's greatest philanthropists, was contacted by Lord Beaverbrook, a fellow Canadian, with a request to help finance pilot training and the provision of aircraft. Beaverbrook was delighted with the response in August 1940 when McConnell cabled to confirm his donation: 'As an expression of unbounded admiration and gratitude for the heroic work of the Royal Air Force and, after consultation with the Canadian Government, I wish to place at your disposal and for employment at your discretion, £1,000,000 for the most vital immediate air force needs.' Both Hurricanes and Spitfires were duly funded, and the media merrily announced the creation of 'McConnell's Squadron'. This was abhorrent to the unassuming Canadian who immediately distanced himself from the idea, largely because he preferred his many charitable activities to remain secret. Confirming the amazing sum of money, McConnell emphasised that the provision of aircraft must not indicate any association with him personally, and stressed that it had not been his idea. Jennifer was an innocuous name, and no direct association with Mr McConnell has been found, but her service with the Canadian 403 Squadron was again brief because she moved to Air Service Training on 29 August 1941 and did not emerge from that establishment until April 1942.

Air Service Training Ltd was part of the government-sponsored Civilian Repair Organisation, and one of its functions was the repair and overhaul of Spitfires. Jennifer was only one of 3,400 machines to receive attention from the AST during the Second World War, and the refurbished machine was released to 81 Squadron at Ouston on 20 April 1942. However, her tenure there was again brief and she departed for 72 Squadron at Biggin Hill on 1 May. Poor Jennifer seems something of a gypsy because she barely paused with 72 Squadron before moving on to 350 Squadron at Debden on 20 May 1942, where she and Maurice merged for his sorties on 13 June.

Landing after the morning convoy patrol, Maurice clambered from the cockpit and sought relief and refreshment while Jennifer was checked and refuelled. He was one of a pair ordered to patrol over the convoy again that afternoon. It was a dismal evening over Norwich. Low clouds squeezed the skyline creating a gloomy, grey atmosphere that suited the city's mood. Norwich was still counting the cost of air raids in April that had devastated several parts of that magnificent historical city and, although the British press proclaimed this Baedeker attack a failure for missing the '3 Star' buildings (those of historical interest noted in the Baedeker Guide), bombs falling in residential areas and elsewhere had killed 162 people and injured nearly 600 more. The preceding lack of enemy air activity had lulled some into a sense of complacency, but following the April attack the city was still jittery and the wailing of the air-raid sirens sent many scurrying for shelter. This time the crash alarm (meaning raiders imminent) convinced many doubters but others had no time or were disinclined to take cover. The sound of aero-engines was already over the city.

Sixteen-year-old Donald 'Donny' Stowers was at home at 142 Sprowston Road when the crash alarm sounded, and he hurried to check the skies overhead from the front bay window. The clouds clung almost to ground level but above Marshall's shop and from the direction of Mousehold Heath he heard the noise of a low-flying aircraft. He knew instantly it was in serious trouble. Instead of a strong, steady engine tone, there was a series of bangs and splutterings. He was craning skywards when suddenly a Spitfire flashed into view, plunging earthwards. Barely clearing the rooftops, the fighter plummeted to oblivion behind the buildings opposite Donny's home. In those few heart-stopping seconds he became aware of small pieces from the blast clattering down on to the roof tiles. Racing across the road, he was sure he was first on the scene. The aircraft had almost vanished and flames sizzled from a deep crater. If the pilot were still on board, he clearly stood no chance of survival but his parachute might have drifted to earth elsewhere, unseen because of the low cloud.

Walking home from work, 14-year-old Kathleen Ellis and her chum had no time to take cover. The aircraft that spun from the cloud base seemed to be heading straight for them and both girls ran in fear of their lives as the machine exploded nearby. Russell George Nichols, then in the Home Guard, later recalled what happened:

> I was upstairs in Spencer Street. The steam crash hooters sounded. I heard a plane diving, I looked out of the open window and saw the Spitfire diving and spinning . . . breaking up. It hit the ground in the grounds of the slaughter-house. I grabbed my tin hat and ran down Branford Hill and out on to the Sprowston Road, which was littered with pieces of aluminium, to the slaughter-house. The rest of the plane was a raging inferno. There was no hope of getting the pilot out as the heat was far too hot. I saw the pilot burnt. I am afraid the pilot was cremated but mercifully it was a quick end . . .

Russell departed when the authorities arrived and traffic on Sprowston Road was halted to clear the scattered wreckage.

Young Ray Corke was an Air Training Corps cadet at the time and had a very inquisitive nature when it came to do with aircraft. He had taken cover in the family's Anderson shelter in the yard when he heard the aircraft's engine scream and a 'terrific bang' about 100 yards away. He knew immediately what had happened and raced across the neighbouring gardens to reach the scene. Strangely Ray does not recall any fire but remembers the Spitfire embedded up to its cockpit; the wheels were missing and its wings and tail had been torn off. The cockpit canopy was missing and he could see the dead pilot still in the cockpit; he had ginger hair.

Many others saw or heard the crash and visited the scene but their accounts are contradictory. Donny Stowers remembered 'a blackened object with its legs bent up' being carried on a stretcher to a waiting RAF ambulance. Others had more fleeting and less grisly recollections. 'I heard the aircraft coming down and got under the table,' recalled Mrs L. Brooks, who was anxious for her sister living at 120 Sprowston Road, almost exactly where the aircraft had crashed. Luckily her sister was unscathed, if shaken, but Miss Cornwell, living on the opposite side at no. 157, lamented the loss of her rabbit which had presumably died of fright or shock. Roy Butler stated: 'As I recall, the plane had nose-dived almost vertically and gone between two buildings only a few feet apart and demolished a garage or shed before burying itself several feet in the ground. The buildings concerned stood on the corner of Lawson Road and Sprowston Road. No one will ever know if the pilot managed to guide his stricken plane into that small gap, or if it was sheer luck that it missed the buildings. If it was the pilot's skill that avoided a catastrophe, then his bravery deserves some recognition.'

Autumn leaves sprinkle the grave of Maurice Raes in the field of honour at Pelouse d'Evere, Brussels. (*Via Cynrik De Decker*)

After the afternoon's convoy patrol Maurice Raes had become separated from his companion. Crossing the coast, he faced appalling weather conditions as he set course and descended towards Debden. Clouds swirled around his cockpit as he concentrated on his instrument flying panel with its essential artificial horizon. His existence depended on this and the other instruments. Many a pilot had perished because he lost confidence in their guidance; as doubt set in, doubting pilots would become confused, and start correcting for imaginary errors of attitude, and in so doing, created them. The potential for the deception of the senses was well known but in such circumstances hard to deny; it was an almighty act of faith to trust the bank and turn indicator and the artificial horizon. They could only hope the sky was empty.

It is unlikely that Maurice even saw the barrage balloon cable, but Jennifer's impact with that taut,

On 10 October 2006, following a campaign championed by Dennis Tye, Maurice Raes' nieces, Michelle and Denise, unveiled a plaque commemorating the young pilot at the entrance to Maurice Raes Close in Norwich. RAF veterans, current members of the Belgian Air Force, local dignitaries, including Mayor Felicity Hartley, and several eyewitnesses to the tragedy also attended the ceremony.

treacherous steel hawser must have been terrifying. Tethering the unseen balloon high overhead, it was intended as a deterrent to enemy bombers. Now it had caught Maurice, perhaps tearing away vital controls or striking the propeller and engine causing massive damage. Even if the actual damage was slight, the impact would have thrown the Spitfire out of control, tumbling the gyroscopes and rendering useless the instruments for blind flying. Perhaps Maurice grasped the knob to jettison his canopy and was trying to jump out. We can only guess at what was in his mind. But it was too late. The last thing the young man from Mons saw was a spinning, kaleidoscopic swirl of buildings in a city peopled by those he had come to defend, people seeking to liberate Belgium.

Sixty-four years on Belgium is a free nation at the heart of a new Europe, one built over the bloodshed of battles fought by a generation now physically fading but whose spirit should be honoured and from whom the torch of freedom should be taken and treasured.

One citizen seeking to ensure that the city of Norwich perpetuates the memory of that brave young pilot is Dennis Tye, who has successfully lobbied for a cul-de-sac in a new housing development to be named in tribute. Maurice Raes Close now stands on the precise point where poor Maurice perished, just four days short of his 21st birthday. He will never be forgotten.

CHAPTER FOUR

Lost Wings

A ny modern army needs fuel and during the Second World War the planned invasion of Europe presented logistics personnel with numerous problems regarding the supply of petrol, particularly where rapidly advancing ground forces over-stretched their supply lines. In September 1943 a new method of shipping gasoline by air was proposed and trials took place of a British-designed aircraft interior roller-conveyor for quick expulsion of fuel cans. Dropping by parachute, the jerry-cans would be contained in specially designed wicker panniers to cushion their landing. In order to evaluate the effectiveness of this system, trials took place with the Polish Armoured Division during Exercise Link in East Anglia.

The Douglas C-47 was one of the most enduring aircraft in aviation history. Numerous examples are still active worldwide yet its history also encompasses aviation archaeology. C-47A serial 42-23479 was lost on 27 September 1943 after only 271 hours recorded flight time. (*Martin Bowman*)

Both USAAF and RAF air-crews took part, flying an aircraft that was familiar to and favoured by both services, the ubiquitous C-47 Skytrain, known in RAF parlance as the Dakota. Developed by the Douglas Aircraft Corporation from their successful pre-war civilian DC-2 and DC-3 airliner series, the C-47 was an extension of one of the most successful designs in aviation history.

Six air-crews took part in Exercise Link, three from the RAF and three from the USAAF. One of the latter came from 43 Troop Carrier Squadron, 315 Troop Carrier Group (TCG), based at Aldermaston. The navigator was Second Lieutenant Peter J. Pfeiffer, who had gained his cherished wings after graduating from Navigation School during December 1942. The wings themselves were made from sterling silver, bearing a winged globe with a circumnavigational track to denote his new craft. Following graduation, Peter was sent to Mobile, Alabama, where he joined a replacement crew destined for 315 TCG. None of the men milling around at Mobile had met before but Peter soon teamed up with Flight Officer Richard Vance as pilot and Second Lieutenant Robert W. Drew as co-pilot. Attending to the intricacies of the radio was Sergeant Oren H. Kelley, while the engineering aspects of their machine were the responsibility of Sergeant William F. Patterson. Their introductions were barely over before movement orders were received ordering them to a C-47 equipped with ferry tanks and a cargo that hardly seemed crucial to the war effort – a shipment of bicycles! In reality, this humble mode of transport predominated on most airbases in England and probably saved a fortune in terms of man-hours. Their orders were to fly the southern route to Brazil then over the south Atlantic and northwards to Morocco. The final stage took them across Land's End to Aldermaston. Tired from their travels, the crew were surprised to find the airfield somewhat bereft of machines and soon learned that they had, in a sense, passed by their unit while en route. Most of the 315 TCG were in North Africa supporting the operations that would result in ultimate victory for the Allies in the region, as they finally evicted the Axis Powers from Africa after years when the combatants had drifted to and fro across the desert like its wind-blown sands.

For Vance's crew, now with 43 Troop Carrier Squadron, matters were more mundane and a humdrum series of duties saw their C-47 slogging the length and breadth of the UK, lugging cargo and ferrying personnel. Their most exciting activity saw them in northern England conducting trials with their C-47 hauling the large British Horsa glider. The USAAF were testing the combination and the usual C-47 crew carried additional observers to monitor technical data including engine temperatures and fuel consumption under varying conditions. Satisfied with the results, the C-47 and Horsa pairing was cleared for operational use. The Vance crew returned to Aldermaston but soon responded to the demand for crews to participate in the petrol-dropping trials. Receiving movement orders from Major C.O. Braden, they took the recently overhauled C-47, serial 42-23479, north to RAF Fulbeck in Lincolnshire before journeying south again to join the other participating air-crews at Snailwell in Suffolk.

As the day wore on, the request for resupplying the Polish Armoured Division did not materialise when anticipated and the C-47 crews warily observed the steady deterioration in

Navigator Peter Pfeiffer and his new wife Lenore pictured on their wedding day in 1942, before he left for the dangers of operations overseas. (*Peter Pfeiffer*)

the prevailing weather conditions. Acknowledging the importance of these trials, the RAF had several observers present, including Wing Commander H. Burton who had been one of the organisers of Exercise Link at Transport Command HQ. Also observing the trials was Squadron Leader P.B. Robinson, whose experience as a pilot and, later, as controller at an RAF sector Fighter Operations Room, saw him viewing the preliminaries for the drop with increasing concern. In his opinion the delay in requesting supplies allowed more time for preparation but it was not wisely used. It had been envisaged that the first sortie to be flown would be at about 1400 hours but several more hours had now elapsed without any request for fuel coming in. At 1815 hours Robinson heard RAF Flying Control query the viability of air-to-ground communication and one of the American pilots suggested trials with the C-47's radio. He returned 15 minutes later saying such communication was possible, but apparently no procedure was agreed for doing so, nor was any radio transmission recall code agreed. Robinson also noted that none of the pilots appeared to have any experience of night supply dropping and his anxiety increased as the weather conditions continued to worsen as night fell. At last the signal for fuel replenishment was received and final preparations commenced. The pilots and navigators were driven from the dispersal area to a briefing given by the RAF Flying Control officer in the control tower. He advised them of the runway in use, frequencies for local radio beacons (known as pundits), night-flying regulations and updated local weather conditions, which were patently dismal. Following this the air-crews returned to the dispersal area, where Wing Commander Leigh-Smith gave them a more detailed briefing on features for the dropping zone (DZ). He pointed out the location, their expected height above mean sea level and the signal lights they would see. The minimum height for the drop was given as 600 feet – any lower, and the parachutes had insufficient time to deploy. Squadron Leader Robinson listened attentively, his apprehensions about the weather unassuaged. Not having attended all the briefings, he could only assume he had missed a short-range forecast showing some improvement. However, he remained a very worried man.

Meanwhile, Wing Commander Burton had departed by car for the DZ some 30 miles away, accompanied by Group Captain Homer from RAF Netheravon and Major Hilary of Transport Command. It would take the aircraft far less time to reach the DZ, as Peter Pfeiffer plotted his course. The weather conditions still comprised low cloud and drizzle, with the wind at 290°, gusting to 15mph in the east. There was a risk of icing above 8,000 feet in a cold front on the east coast, but they should remain well below this level, flying through thick clouds that trailed their petticoats down to only 200 feet in places. With the USAAF crew were five British army personnel who would handle and dispatch the petrol panniers. Senior among them was 36-year-old Captain William Boyce RAOC from Hove in Sussex. His senior NCO was Sergeant John S. Wells of the RASC, a 24-year-old from Radford, Coventry, who was accompanied by three more RASC soldiers: Lance Corporal James T. Barnes, aged 22, from Bolton in Lancashire, and Privates Tom Lord Parker, aged 24, another Lancashire lad from Burnley, and Cyril Stoodley, aged 21, from Chard in Somerset.

At 2245 hours the C-47 departed for the DZ. As the aircraft cleared Snailwell, Wing Commander Burton was arriving at the DZ, where he contacted the RAF Air Adviser to the army, Squadron Leader White. Soldiers laid out the ground equipment ahead of the arrival of Vance's aircraft, expected at 2300 hours. Precisely on time the drone of a C-47 was heard approaching very low, but this caused no concern because of the intended dropping altitude of only 600 feet. Unfortunately the cloud base was now much lower, and the stage was set for a tragedy.

Watching the aircraft's navigation lights, Burton saw the plane bank away to make another run. He thought it 'went very close to the ground in a gentle dive and, from the DZ, it appeared that it almost went down to ground level although this may have been an optical illusion'. As the C-47 overflew the DZ for a second time, its lights were hazed in cloud and Burton estimated its altitude as '300–400 feet'. The aircraft disappeared and the sound of its engines faded until, some 4 minutes later, it was observed flying west to east, north of the DZ. An Aldis lamp was flashed and the C-47 again overflew the DZ but whether it was responding to the signal is uncertain. Burton now suggested to Squadron Leader White that on the next run the aircraft should be signalled by lamp ordering it to return to Snailwell, 'as the cloud base was too low to allow the parachutes to open before reaching the ground, and therefore nothing could be gained by risking the aircraft further'.

Burton watched the aircraft leave the DZ and presumed it would circle for another run, during which it should see the cancellation signal. It was now heading south and began a turn to port. As it came through 90° of the turn, it suddenly swooped earthwards, almost into the treetops, before commencing a shallow climb. The darkness concealed its silhouette but its troubles were broadcast by the screech of engines and the peculiar angle of its lights – 'a conglomeration of the red port light, white tail light and starboard green light was then seen'. The anguish of the twin Pratt & Whitney R-1830-92s echoed over the countryside as they screamed for every vestige of power. With the C-47's nose angling heavenwards, the engines gave their all but could not prevent the machine being drawn inexorably earthwards. The end of the struggle came with the crump of impact and the distant flowering of flames in the darkness. Fed by the aircraft's own fuel and the petrol containers it carried, the fire's ferocity burst into a surging demoniacal dance, visible for miles and reflected in grotesque patterns on the cloud base. Watching from the DZ, onlookers could only pray for the poor souls on board.

With such a short trip to the DZ, Peter Pfeiffer had had no navigational concerns, and having given Vance the course to steer, he went forward and stood between the two pilots. Kelley and Patterson, also with little to do, had gone aft into the forward section of the cargo area to observe the drop. Further movement was restricted because they literally had to crawl over the cargo to move around the fuselage. Initially unaware of the grim conditions outside, the British handlers were preparing for the drop, but as they approached the DZ the aircraft was squeezed lower and lower by the decreasing cloud base and they were now below the required dropping altitude. The DZ itself was indicated by a line of lights formed into an arrow, and as the aircraft flew over Vance saw the green light signalling them to drop but the aircraft was too low for the parachutes to deploy. Hoping to find a patch where the cloud base was higher, Vance powered the C-47 into a left turn to circle for another run at 650 feet.

Approaching the DZ again, he saw nothing but impenetrable cloud. No lights were seen and he banked away to run in 50 feet lower. Again, nothing. Four passes were made, each 50 feet lower than the one before, but no further lights were seen. On their fourth run the lights became visible but the aircraft was again too low. Frustrated by events, Vance entered another climbing port turn. As he banked, he felt the aircraft give a sudden jerk and the nose pitched upwards into a partial stall. Slamming the throttles open and pushing the control column forward, he fought to regain level flight. As he wrestled with the controls, he heard an ominous rumble and clatter from the fuselage and realised the cargo had shifted, either released prematurely or broken loose. For a few moments he gained some vestige of response but it was not enough to prevent the aircraft from mushing earthwards. Now, with the engines at full throttle, the propellers clawed desperately for grip, like a man sliding off an icy roof. Vance needed altitude to effect a recovery and give time to re-stow the loose cargo. But with all the weight sliding aft, the straining engines were overwhelmed and could not counteract the impossible angle of attack on the stalled aerofoil with disastrous loss of lift. Inevitably the C-47 stalled again and this time slid off on its port wing. Vance fought valiantly until the very end but he stood no chance at such a low altitude.

Peter felt the aircraft falling and held on as best he could. His next recollection was of pain and fire. Wherever he was, it was burning. He was also unable to stand up. Gaining leverage on part of the structure, he hauled himself painfully upright. Close by, flames were devouring the crumpled cargo area and surging greedily towards him. Visible nearby was an opening and he readied himself to fall forward and attempt to roll out. At that moment someone shouted 'Don't jump!' and in an instant Polish soldiers were carrying him clear of the conflagration. As they placed him safely on the ground, Peter told them anxiously about the others still inside but although human forms were discernible in the flames, they were clearly beyond help and the onlookers could only hope that death had been mercifully instantaneous.

The force of the impact had torn the pilot's seat from its mountings and Vance was thrown through the instrument panel and windscreen. Astonishingly he was still alive, although badly lacerated and in shock. The Polish troops also rescued co-pilot Drew but found no other survivors. Those saved were swiftly transported to the RAF hospital in Ely, where Peter's broken leg was set in a cast, Drew was treated for severe burns on one leg and Vance's extensive facial injuries were attended to. After this initial treatment, they were transferred to an American hospital where it was discovered that Peter's compound fractures had not been set correctly before being encased in plaster. He now needed further painful remedial work. Peter had also realised that, in the chaos of the crash, he had lost his coveted navigator's wings. He regretted their loss but as he commenced what would be six long months of treatment, he knew he was one of the lucky ones, lost wings or not.

As with any military exercise, one purpose was to learn about problems and implement corrections before real combat situations arose. Seven lives had been lost in these trials and the initial report from the Aircraft Accident Classification Committee was rejected by Colonel L.R. Garrison from HQ VIII Air Support Command, who returned it for further investigation because the committee had 'not sufficiently investigated incidents which it appears may have contributed to the accident'. The committee had correctly concluded that prematurely untying the load preparatory to the drop was the major cause of the accident. Better communication between the flight deck and the loadmaster was essential so the load would not be untied until the drop was certain. Similar incidents had occurred previously but no preventative measures had been forthcoming. The committee also found the weather to be a major factor. While Garrison accepted these points, he questioned why the aircraft had been dispatched in weather that was clearly unsuitable for the experiment. Details of the briefing given to the crews were also sought and it was evident that the arrangements for communications were inadequate for both visual signals at the DZ and for radio traffic. He further questioned the wisdom of sending out a pilot with no night dropping experience on such a stormy night.

Other official documents were more mundane. On 19 September 1943 Mr W. Osborne of 3 Bircham Tofts near King's Lynn signed an Army Air Force Form 17, 'Damage to Property Certificate', stating: 'I hereby agree that the landing on my premises . . . of Army Airplane No. 42-23479 . . . caused the following estimated damage, ½ ton of sugar beet, £2.0.0." In fact the damage could have been much worse. The aircraft had fallen close to a row of houses, and the cockpit itself ended up in the garden of the house occupied by Frank and Lily Wadsworth. They and other residents were evacuated while the crew of an RAF fire tender from Bircham Newton fought the blaze. Their appliance proved inadequate for dealing with so much blazing gasoline and the corporal in charge soon phoned for the Hunstanton fire brigade. Pilot Officer Cyril V. Jones from Bircham Newton ordered the RAF vehicle to protect civilian property until the National Fire Service arrived. Drawing water from a nearby pond, the NFS and RAF then coordinated to douse the flames while search parties continued to check the surrounding land seeking any survivors who might have jumped or been thrown out. None was found. As the ashes of the aircraft settled, the fire crews stood by in case of further combustion, while RAF orderlies removed the charred remains of the casualties and local residents were allowed home.

For security reasons, the people of Bircham Tofts were not given any details of the crash and the story soon spread that there had been no survivors. In subsequent years Frank Wadsworth continued to find evidence of the tragedy in his garden, including an engine plate bearing the Pratt & Whitney eagle logo but showing manufacture had been sub-contracted to Chevrolet. More poignantly, he also unearthed a pair of silver wings that had been worn by one of the crew on board. These were eventually given to his daughter Pauline, who was born after the war. She was fascinated by the story and later became determined to discover the facts behind the finds.

Believing that all involved had perished, Pauline's curiosity was revived when the British Society for Psychical Research made enquiries about plane crashes in the area. Her own investigations took a more conventional line, including contact with the author. I was able to tell her that, contrary to local legend, not all on board had perished, and the survivors might just possibly still be alive, thus rendering redundant any spiritual involvement. The Imperial War Museum at Duxford identified the wings as those worn by a navigator, and gave Pauline

Dedicated research by Pauline Fisher led to the return of Peter Pfeiffer's silver wings, found in her parents' garden. (*Pauline Fisher*)

Patriot Peter Pfeiffer beneath the superimposed image of the wings he lost in the C-47 fuel trials tragedy. (*Peter Pfeiffer*)

details for the 315TCG Association. Contacting them, Pauline was both amazed and delighted to discover that navigator Peter Pfeiffer had survived and was now living in Maryland. The 315TCG Association asked Peter for permission to release his phone number to Pauline, and finally she was able to speak to the owner of the lost wings that had been in her family's possession for some fifty years. She felt it was only fitting to reunite them with their rightful owner, who had earned them and worn them with such pride. Peter was delighted and, prompted by Pauline's interest, he arranged a pilgrimage to the crash-site but the horrific events of 11 September 2001 overwhelmed his plans. As he recalled: 'I had spent my career in Military Airlift, and I am sure they now had greater priorities than hauling a retired officer.' However, the correspondence between Pauline and Peter burgeoned into friendship – a greater reward than she could ever have imagined when she commenced her research. Peter still lives in Joppa, Maryland, but has never forgotten the night his wings were lost in a Norfolk garden. To this day he feels that seven lives were needlessly sacrificed. He believes that at least some of them might have been saved had they simply carried water or some other non-flammable liquid for the trials. It is to be hoped that lessons were learned so that their lives were not given in vain.

CHAPTER FIVE

No Particular Courage

'Shooting a line' was RAF parlance for exaggeration, and was frowned upon by those whose heroism was hidden behind masks of modesty, irreverent humour and self-deprecation. One such was navigator Harold D. Church, who later recorded his dramatic experiences in novel format as a tribute to his fellow airmen. Initially he wrote them in the third person, but after reading the story I strongly encouraged him to revert to a first-person narrative. Harold felt he had 'no particular courage' and was reluctant to follow my advice because he didn't want to be misrepresented as a 'line-shooter'. He was only persuaded to do so in the end because the story honours those of his crew who did not survive. The work is dedicated to the memory of his fallen comrades and others who have since faded, in respect for the men that they were.

My role in his story has been that of research assistant, adding background detail to the narrative where Harold's own records were incomplete. The words 'no particular courage' are Harold's. I think he and his men had a very special courage, and I am convinced you will agree when you read Harold's story, which was originally penned in the 1990s.

* * *

We did not know, we could not know, that within two hours some of us would die, violently. Statistically, we were aware that there was at least a 5 per cent chance we would not return that night, or any other such night, but we refused to admit it, even to ourselves. A one in twenty chance tonight did not necessarily mean a certainty by twenty such nights. It happened to others, so we persuaded ourselves; we believed, or pretended to believe, we were immune, even though, privately, most of us were scared of what lay ahead. Even if we had known, there was little any one of us could do, except report sick, and it was too late for that now. It would be unthinkable to desert comrades with whom work and pleasure had been shared. Besides, any action deliberately taken to avoid participation would result in disgrace. Last month, one friend, a flight sergeant, suffering from extreme stress, had asked to be relieved of any more operational flying. The letters LMF (lack of moral fibre) had been duly entered in his service book and he had been reduced to the ranks and sent elsewhere, and was

Harold D. Church enlisted and then fell in love. The war would separate him from Olive for a long time but he was luckier than many of his comrades and contemporaries, for whom the separation from loved ones was permanent. (*Harold D. Church*)

Waiting for the night, a clutch of Lancasters slumber at Fiskerton. (*Via Martin Bowman*)

now probably cleaning lavatories or whitewashing coal. It was harsh treatment for such a person, a volunteer, as we all were, who was genuinely at the end of his tether, but possibly advisable in order to attempt to ensure that expensive training was not wasted. Fortunately such action was necessary only for a few. It is surprising how much value is attached to self-esteem. What was it that Shakespeare wrote, in *Hamlet*? 'This above all: to thine own self be true, And it must follow, as the night the day, Thou canst not then be false to any man.' If we had opted out, we would remember and be ashamed of ourselves for the rest of our lives.

Fourteen colleagues had failed to return one night last week. We had raised our glasses and toasted 'Absent Friends', then those friends had been replaced almost immediately by new crews, who would soon become friends, even if only for a short time. Such was life – and death – in the autumn of 1943 on a Lancaster bomber base. No. 49 Squadron, based at Fiskerton, a few miles east of Lincoln, was one of many in 5 Group, regarded by many, and certainly by the crews themselves, as the elite of Bomber Command. Their isolated bases were scattered over the flat Lincolnshire countryside. No. 49 Squadron's brick buildings, Nissen huts, control tower, three hangars, bomb dumps and all the other necessities had been erected hastily, and three concrete runways laid down in the usual 'A' pattern. Over a thousand airmen and members of the Women's Auxiliary Air Force (WAAFs), of all ranks from lowly aircraftmen to group captain, had moved in some months ago from their previous base at Scampton, an established pre-war aerodrome. The grass runways at Scampton were unsuitable

The WAAFs were an essential part of the RAF. Here Leading Aircraftwoman Lilian Yule tows Lancaster DV238 at Fiskerton in the summer of 1943. (*Via Martin Bowman*)

for heavy bombers, particularly when they were fully loaded on take-off. The people adapted quickly to their new base. Even though they missed Scampton's many facilities, and complained endlessly about the war, Adolf Hitler, the rations, the basic accommodation and the mud, they still set to work and cheerfully got on with their jobs. The squadron consisted of sixteen aircraft divided between two flights, A and B, usually with a few spares, both in men and machines.

Unlike most bomber squadrons, here painted emblems of blondes or bombs on the fuselages were scorned. This squadron was above such fripperies; the Lancasters flew unadorned, their crews proud of their individuality. Only the RAF roundels, the squadron identification letters (EA) and the individual aircraft letters were displayed. Nothing else was necessary. If questioned, though, they would have had to admit that the lack of emblems was based on pure superstition. Earlier in the war a few crews on the squadron had had their aircraft decorated with emblems and it so happened that they were the ones that failed to return. So the commanding officer, or someone else in authority, had decreed that such adornments were not welcome. Many airmen were superstitious, and a large number of them carried mascots on their operations.

Our crew of seven stood by the huge undercarriage of their Lancaster, 'E-Easy', their flies open, ready for the ritual urination before climbing into the aircraft's dark and narrow interior. As well as fulfilling a superstitious need, this was a very practical thing to do, as there would be no other reasonable opportunity for several hours. True, there was the Elsan (the chemical urinal) but there was little time to use that.

The stars twinkled brightly in the early November sky; mist lay like a silver carpet on the damp grass; the dope on the wings and fuselage contributed to the unmistakable and evocative smell of a wartime airfield at night, one that cannot be described to those who have not experienced it. The heightened awareness of the senses augmented the sights, sounds and smells to produce a feeling of excitement and adventure. This feeling was a natural one for young men. Some of our crew were still teenagers: one of us was 18 and another 23. (His friends sometimes called the latter 'granddad'!) Older men (over 30 years of age) were often considered unsuitable for the job, and they usually had more sense than to volunteer for flying duties, even though they did get paid an extra shilling or so a day as flying pay. Was it by reason of their youth or their hairstyle that RAF air-crews were nicknamed the 'Brylcreem Boys' by some in the other armed services?

Norman Carfoot was our pilot. A flight lieutenant by the age of 21, he had already completed almost 2,000 hours' flying, most of them on Sunderlands patrolling the Atlantic, searching for enemy submarines. He had become bored with this comparatively mundane life, and had requested a transfer to Bomber Command. A burly young man, he had the confidence and deep respect of his crew, who would willingly accompany him to hell and back – and often did. The aircraft he piloted did not just land; they floated down on to the runway and kissed the ground lightly. Norman's magnificent moustache was the envy of many air-crews. Why did they still have mere down on their upper lips when they had tried so hard to grow something to twirl? All they could do to be different was to leave undone the top button of their tunic or battle-dress. This method of 'cocking a snook' at authority became a tradition in Bomber Command. Sergeant 'Jock' Mason, the flight engineer, was a typical Scot, dour, down-to-earth, good at his job and reliable. He had reached the ripe old age of 22. He had been an engineer with a reputable British motor manufacturer before volunteering for air-crew, and spent many of his non-duty hours fussing around the aircraft's engines with the mechanics.

I, Harold Church (Harry to all my RAF friends), was the navigator; aged 21, I was born and bred in Hemsby, Norfolk. I was able to boast, quite modestly of course, that I had never been lost in the air. I neglected to mention that on one occasion I had got lost in Lincoln after drinking a few pints!

The bomb-aimer, Flight Sergeant Steve Putnam, aged 21, was a Canadian from Winnipeg, who had almost completed his pilot's training in Canada when he was advised to transfer to a bomb-aimers' course. He spent most of his time in the nose of the aircraft and always carried an empty milk bottle, in case he needed to urinate. That particular part of his anatomy which relieved the need became stuck in it on one occasion, during a long flight, much to the glee of the rest of the crew.

Sergeant Hank Woods, a Londoner, was the wireless operator. He was 20, and dated a different girl every night of the week when he was not flying, and wrote letters to several others. His line-shooting to his colleagues consisted of boasting about his many conquests. His line-shooting to some of his conquests followed a different pattern. He would sit in the Mess, writing to one of his 'popsies', as airmen usually called their girlfriends, pretending to

Pilot Norman Carfoot pictured in his parents' garden at Burton on Trent around the time of his 21st birthday. (*Iris H. Shuttleworth*)

be flying over Germany while he wrote, and professing his undying love and hopes to see her in the not-too-distant future, should he survive the current operation! Hank could send and receive Morse code messages at well over twenty words per minute.

Flight Sergeant Dave List, the rear gunner, aged 21, came from Newcastle. He didn't have a 'Geordie' accent, though, as his home town was the Newcastle in Australia. He had volunteered to travel halfway round the world for the purpose of sitting, cramped and cold, despite the electrically heated suit, in the most exposed, most lonely and most dangerous part of the aeroplane. He called himself a fatalist, taking the view that, if his time *was* up, he would not survive. While maintaining there was little purpose in searching the skies for enemy aircraft for his own sake, he assured the rest of the crew that he would keep a keen look-out in case he could save their lives! Was he serious, or was he indulging in an Aussie leg-pull? On the assumption that the latter was the case, the rest of the crew had made a point of thanking him effusively when he announced that generous concession! Dave was an excellent gunner, having qualified with high marks on his particular course, which included instant aircraft recognition as well as gunnery.

Sergeant Wilf Marson, the mid-upper gunner, was the baby of the crew at just 18 years old, having falsified his age in order to volunteer at the age of 17. Amused by the initials of his position in the aircraft, he told his friends that he must be a MUG to sit there for hours, searching the skies for something to shoot at. His home was only a few miles north of Lincoln. He always carried an old Home Guard helmet with him on operations, which he carefully tied around his groin. Many air-crew members particularly feared two fates: burning to death and suffering damage to the 'family jewels'. Wilf was determined to avoid the latter if at all possible. He was the joker of the crew. Small and wiry, he smoked an enormous pipe and had an imaginary dog, a figment of his fertile imagination. He 'walked' it around the perimeter, to the pub and even took it on the train to Lincoln, talking to it, and praising or scolding its behaviour. Many a spectator was puzzled, to say the least. Wilf called this 'dog' Fido, named after the fog dispersal system recently installed on either side of the main runway. FIDO – an acronym for Fog, Intensive, Dispersal Operation – consisted of a system of pipes along which petrol, mixed with methane, was pumped in foggy weather. When ignited, the flames from the regularly spaced holes in the pipes helped to clear the fog over and near the runway, so that planes from the squadron and others in the vicinity, or even those based in Yorkshire or Norfolk, could land reasonably safely. However, it was only 'reasonably safe', because the glare from the flames and the turbulence they caused provided considerable problems for pilots who were already tired from an operation over enemy territory. Our squadron was the first to have the FIDO system, and the crew of E-Easy were the first to test it, late one afternoon in October. This honour, if so it could be called, was a source of great pride to Wilf, although we were almost certainly chosen because Norman was the most experienced pilot on the squadron. On the first night testing, fire engines raced over from Lincoln, thinking the buildings were on fire. No one had told them about the practice burn. FIDO was very expensive on fuel; nearly 200,000 gallons of petrol could be consumed in one burn, and petrol was generally in very short supply. Nevertheless, the system undoubtedly saved many aircraft and the lives of their crews from the Lincolnshire fogs. War is an expensive business!

This was the seventeenth 'op' for most of the crew, although the great majority of them had been undertaken with another squadron, before being posted to this special one. 'Op', short for operation, sounded more casual, less ostentatious, than the American 'mission'. They had only thirteen more to do after this one to complete their tour. Completing a tour was not a simple exercise; towards the end of 1943 few crews managed to complete thirty operations over enemy territory. However, they did have the privilege of a week's leave every month or so. If they were lucky, and the weather was suitable, the tour could be completed in four to six months. Then they would be entitled to a long rest, probably as instructors, before beginning another tour. Needless to say, the completion of those thirty operations provided a reason for great celebration, both by and for the fortunate crew. Unfortunately many crews did not complete a tour at the same time; some individuals missed operations for one reason or another, and then had to function as a replacement with another crew.

E-Easy JB305 was an almost new Lancaster, only weeks old. It had been delivered to the squadron by a young female pilot. Many aircraft were flown to the operating squadrons by young women of the Air Transport Auxiliary, who, by reason of their sex, were not allowed to fly on operations. I, for one, felt envious and quite inadequate when seeing these slips of girls piloting huge aircraft so competently. At Elementary Flying Training School, more than a year ago, I had learned to fly a Tiger Moth. I was allowed to go solo after 10 hours of instruction, but after that memorable flight, which lasted about 15 minutes, I tried to land about 6 feet above the ground! The Tiger Moth had inelegantly bounced and bounced again, before coming to rest close to a hedge on the perimeter fence with a damaged undercarriage. I was not particularly popular with the instructor. I liked to think that I was chosen for the navigators' course because of my good examination marks and ability in that occupation, rather than because of any lack of promise as a trainee pilot. After all, I *had* managed to fly once without the help and advice of an instructor.

The commanding officer, Wing Commander A.A. Adams DFC, inevitably known as 'Triple A', enjoyed flying E-Easy and usually did so when he selected himself for operations. When 'Wingco' was not flying, Norman welcomed the opportunity to take over what he liked to think of as his 'own' aircraft, for night-flying exercises as well as operations. Our previous regular Lancaster, 'F-Freddie', had been written off, full of bullet and shrapnel holes and with one engine damaged beyond repair, on a previous op. Even with the aircraft in that condition, Norman had landed with his usual skill and aplomb. Lancasters were marvellous aircraft, but they did differ in performance. While F-Freddie had been a bit of a beast, slow to climb and slow to turn, E-Easy was a delight, with a ceiling of 22,000 feet fully loaded, and a top speed of almost 200 knots unloaded. The average life of a Lancaster on operations was, in those days, about forty hours.

The briefing had been held that afternoon, and was attended by all fourteen crews nominated for the operation. The number of aircraft involved depended on the demands of Group Headquarters, the number of serviceable aircraft and the number of crews available.

Therefore it was only on rare occasions that all the squadron's Lancasters were involved in a particular operation. When the target was announced by the wing commander as Dusseldorf, there were hearty groans. The Rhine/Ruhr Valley, known by air-crew as 'Happy Valley', was not a popular destination, being well guarded by anti-aircraft batteries, searchlights and fighters. 'Short, sharp and shitty' was the pithy description given to these trips by the air-crews. Together with all the other information necessary, we were given tracks to follow, expected wind velocities, and known searchlight and flak sites, and were advised of predicted cloud cover. The briefings always ended with 'Synchronise your watches, gentlemen; the time is now —.'

After the briefing the navigators stayed to complete their plotting of tracks and establish the first course to follow, based on the predicted wind velocity supplied by the met. officer. Later, they would need to obtain fixes on their actual position over the ground, calculate the actual wind speed and direction and work out the new compass course to take. This information would then be passed to the pilot over the intercom. Individual preparations were made by all other members of the air-crew. It was ironic that many of the ground staff would already have a good idea of the target area for tonight; the amount of petrol put in the tanks to ensure that the maximum bomb-load was carried gave them a vital clue. Just 500–600 gallons, with a consumption rate of about a gallon a mile, meant a short trip, and there was only one realistic destination: 'Happy Valley'. Many of the ops recently had been concentrated in that area, and they were the most dreaded targets, along with the 'big city', as Berlin was known. Then came the kitting-out; helmet, oxygen mask, flying boots, jackets, parachute harnesses and 'Mae Wests' were donned and parachutes issued. Valuables and all form of identification were handed in or put in lockers.

We were then ready for transport to the dispersed hard-standings. We were usually driven out by a pretty young blonde WAAF called Vi, who was always very quiet on such occasions, though usually happy and talkative, particularly when she collected us on our return. Climbing the steps behind the wing on the starboard side, we made our way along the narrow fuselage, made clumsy by our accoutrements. We who were stationed at the fore climbed laboriously over the main spar, while the rear and mid-upper gunners settled themselves for an uncomfortable journey. The four mighty Merlin engines were started; one by one they coughed, spluttered and roared into life. The necessary checks were made to ensure all was well. At a signal the aircraft taxied out of its dispersal bay, leading the rest of the squadron aircraft towards the main runway. When we reached the runway, we waited for the 'take-off' signal and then the engines howled at full throttle as E-Easy sped towards the far hedge. Becoming airborne was always a tricky business with a full load of bombs and with only two or three minutes between each aircraft taking off. Three weeks ago one Lanc had failed to lift off, with disastrous consequences for all the crew as well as the plane itself. Fortunately the bombs had not exploded. Tonight we had about 14,000lbs of bombs slung under the Lanc, consisting of two 'cookies' and several smaller bombs and incendiaries. No doubt the ground-crew had inscribed the cookies with short and impolite messages addressed to Mr A. Hitler.

Once airborne, the usual drills were followed. The undercarriage was retracted and a course set. We climbed steadily, westwards first to gain height, then eastwards, for the rendezvous over Skegness. Some 589 bombers, mainly Lancasters and Halifaxes, were operational that evening, all on the same course, flying without exterior lights along a corridor some 20 miles long, 2 miles wide, and at heights between 16,000 and 22,000 feet. On previous operations there had been many near-misses and some had no doubt collided, but it was a calculated risk; certainly it was preferable to the use of navigation lights or straying from the main stream, where a ponderous bomber could be easily picked off by an enemy fighter. There was safety in numbers; the enemy could not attack all the aircraft at once! It was a grim fact that those singled out for special attention seldom returned to base, and those that did return usually bore scars. Landings with only three engines functioning were not unusual, while shell holes in the wings were commonplace.

After crossing the coast, the air-gunners tested their Brownings with a short burst, to ensure efficiency and readiness. The following exchange would be typical:

'Navigator to pilot – course 097 – airspeed 185 knots – on track.'
'Pilot to navigator – thank-you – changing course, now, to 097, at 185 knots.'

'Enemy coast ahead' announced the bomb-aimer over the intercom and then we were over hostile territory, not that we had been particularly safe from fighter attention over the North Sea. Now we would have searchlights and flak to deal with too. We were becoming used to this, gaining more and more confidence with each op, but we knew we could not afford to become over-confident or careless. I remembered the first one; after the target had been confirmed and the time of take-off approached, I had felt very unwell and had almost persuaded myself that I was unfit to fly, that I would be a danger to the rest of the crew and ought really to report sick. It had taken a great deal of will-power to convince myself that I was not really ill, just scared stiff. After that, it had been a bit easier. The waiting was the problem; once in the aircraft, all the crew members had their specific tasks to perform and involvement with the job in hand left little time to think of other things.

At a pre-arranged point, a further change of course was made; the track to the target usually entailed at least two such manoeuvres in an attempt to confuse the enemy as to the target. A further minor course correction was necessary, arising from a glance at the H2S and my subsequent calculations of wind speed and direction. The H2S was a blessing; this navigational aid had been developed quite recently and our squadron, often known as the 'try it out squadron', was one of the first to use it. Pulses from the transmitter beneath the aircraft were reflected back to the aircraft from the surface below, whether or not there was cloud. The nature of those surfaces was displayed on a cathode ray tube above the navigator's table; towns and water below could be distinguished by the difference in shades from light grey to black. Dead reckoning, using the Mercator's chart, was still essential, but this new aid was very valuable in obtaining a fix. However, we and the boffins did not then know that German fighters could home in on the H2S, having already salvaged and painstakingly reconstructed one from a crashed bomber. Had it been known, or suspected, air-crew would not have been at all keen to use it anywhere near the target! On later raids the navigators would make sure it was switched off before the bombing run began. The 'Gee' set, its predecessor, was still installed and could be useful, but it was limited in range because it relied on synchronised radio signals from England, which could be jammed by the Germans, while astro-navigation, using major stars to obtain bearings, could not give an accurate fix. The wireless operator, too, had to maintain silence, except in case of dire emergency, as Morse-code signals would be picked up and homed in on by the enemy.

Then came the first attack. 'Enemy fighter to port,' called Dave, and his Browning guns began to chatter spitefully at the intruder in their air space. Wilf's joined in, and the enemy broke off to choose another target. The two gunners had sent a twin-engined German fighter, a Ju88, spiralling down in flames on one trip, much to their delight and the relief of all. Most operations were like this. Enemy fighters were often spotted, but there was no point in attracting attention unless they attacked. Some did attack and were either driven off or broke off the engagement for some reason. Such attacks had sometimes resulted in minor damage to the aircraft, but so far none of the members of our crew had been injured and Wilf's helmet had been superfluous. On two or three occasions anti-aircraft fire had torn jagged holes in the wings, but the overworked, dedicated and efficient ground-crew were adept at such repairs, so that the damaged aeroplane was quickly made serviceable again.

'Window', the aluminium strips that confounded enemy radar, were ejected and then, spot on the ETA, the target loomed ahead. It could hardly be missed. Myriad searchlights probed the night sky and occasionally an aircraft was caught in the interlocking beams. A blazing bomber spiralled down in flames, while another suddenly exploded. The crew of that one did not have time to suffer. Innocuous-looking but deadly white puffs, like balls of cotton-wool, blossomed around us: as expected in 'Happy Valley', the flak was heavy tonight. The cotton-wool puffs were close now and E-Easy rocked, as if in protesting at the intrusion. Then began the run-in, straight and level. Now came the really hairy half-minute or so.

After the bomb-aimer had released the load, the aircraft would leap, owing to the sudden loss of weight, but it would be necessary for the pilot to stay as straight and level as possible until the camera had done its job. The resultant photographs would indicate the accuracy of the bombing and also give valuable information as to probable damage when they were analysed by the experts. For that reason Bomber Command pilots had been recently instructed that they must not weave over the target.

'Bomb-aimer to pilot, left, left – steady, right, – steady . . . steady . . . bombs gone.'

Simultaneously, and before I could enter that fact and the time in my log-book, we were coned by searchlights. The interior of E-Easy was starkly illuminated. All air-crews dreaded being caught by the lights as the operators rarely allowed their victims to elude them. Anti-aircraft shells or a night-fighter's bullets would soon target them, and all too few returned to base to tell the tale. Norman threw the aircraft into a dive, turning violently to port at the same time. The searchlights pursued E-Easy relentlessly and the flak increased in intensity. The aircraft shuddered like a wounded beast as the anti-aircraft shells exploded; in the harsh light it was obvious that the starboard wing had been damaged. The flak stopped suddenly, but the crew knew the likely consequence. Sure enough, Dave announced, almost conversationally, 'Ju88 to starboard – dive, dive'. The gunners' Brownings burst into action. But they were already diving. Norman fought for control. Then came disaster; our gunners' fire had no effect on this occasion. I escaped death by inches as tracer bullets appeared lazily across my vision from left to right. This illusion of laziness was caused by the fact that tracers were regularly spaced among the equally deadly other bullets in order to help the gunner direct and correct his fire.

The port wing burst into flames. Jock made valiant efforts to divert the fuel supply to a different wing-tank. Norman's calm voice was heard over the intercom, checking the well-being of the crew. No reply came from the wireless operator, but we others reported in, one by one. Seconds only had passed, but already it was obvious there would be no bacon and egg tonight after landing and debriefing. As the op was an early evening one, that treasured meal in wartime Britain, always keenly anticipated, was due on our return, rather than before the trip. Often on a long operation, perhaps of eight hours in duration, crews were served with a meal beforehand. Some air-crew were unkind enough to suggest that by serving the meal after the operation, a saving of rations was very likely.

(Taking into consideration the time of the attack and other factors, research into the Abschussliste (Claims listings) indicates that Lancaster JB305 was most likely hit by Oberfeldwebel Erich Becher of 2 Nachtjagdgeschwader 6, who claimed four victories before his own death in aerial combat on 24 February 1944.)

Inevitably, the dreaded 'Abracadabra, Jump, Jump' order was issued, calmly, by the pilot. 'Skipper, I can't get out,' called Dave from the rear turret. 'The navigator will come to help you,' said Norman reassuringly, as if such a minor problem would soon be solved. I drew the blackout curtain behind me, and was about to move when Dave announced, 'I'm OK now, skipper'. I could not help my vast relief that I would not now have to struggle to the rear of the blazing aircraft. Relief turned to shock as I looked to my left and saw the wireless operator, or what remained of him. The bullets that had passed across the navigator's table had not missed Hank, who was now quite unrecognisable. The shock was even greater in that I had never before seen a dead body, even one that had passed away peacefully. By this time Norman had managed to pull the Lanc out of its steep dive in order to enable his crew to bale out. Had he been unable to do so, our evacuation would have been almost impossible. I quickly reported Hank's fate, clipped on my parachute, removed my oxygen mask and moved to the escape hatch in the nose. As I passed Norman, still fighting the controls in order to keep the aircraft as steady as possible, my pilot, skipper, friend and colleague briefly took one hand from the controls and waved goodbye. 'Greater love has no man . . .' – we both knew that Norman had no chance of survival. If he relinquished the controls, E-Easy would spin violently. The hundreds of gallons in the tanks would probably cause a major explosion

Caterpillar Club
Certificate of Membership

W/O. H. D. CHURCH

is a member of the **CATERPILLAR CLUB**
having saved his life by parachute.

SIGNED ....
HON. SEC. EUROPEAN DIVISION.

Having saved his life by parachute, Harold became a member of the Caterpillar Club. He still treasures his membership card from the Irvin Parachute Company. (*Harold D. Church*)

at any second. Even if, by some miracle, he managed to reach the hatch, it would not have provided him with a means of escape; he had often joked about it: 'I've tried out the hatch for size and I'm far too fat for it to be any use to me', or words to that effect.

Reaching the nose, I saw that the hatch had been removed and Steve and Jock had gone. Now it was my turn. E-Easy was now burning fiercely. I dived out. At that height the temperature was far below freezing point and my oxygen supply was non-existent.

It was inadvisable to use the ripcord on the chest parachute too soon, in case the aircraft exploded immediately, and it was necessary to fall towards breathable air and a warmer temperature as quickly as possible, but it was also important to avoid blacking out before pulling the D-ring. The few seconds' delay in my doing so was certainly not from force of habit. I had not had this experience previously and sincerely hoped I would never repeat it. As the chute opened several seconds later, I saw our aircraft, below and in front, plunging earthwards in a ball of flame. A minute or two earlier I had escaped death by inches, now I had survived by seconds – but I had thoughts only for Norman, Hank and any others of those close friends who could not escape the inferno.

I drifted down. The quietness now was almost unbelievable, entirely free from the barely perceptible sounds that are not even registered in the brain in what is thought of as total silence, on a quiet night in the countryside or on a deserted mountain. Not only was it an enormous contrast from what had just happened, but it was also a silence I had never before experienced. It was all so peaceful and, in spite of my predicament, almost relaxing. The fall seemed unending; it must have taken at least 30 minutes. Then I saw clouds below and suddenly, with no warning, I just stopped, standing upright! The chute collapsed around and on me.

'Now I know where I am,' came the thought. 'I am at the Pearly Gates, and at any moment St Peter will greet me.' However, as I came to my senses, which no doubt had been partly befuddled by lack of oxygen, I realised what had happened. The cloud was actually a ground mist, the same type of mist we had left behind such a short time ago. I had landed gently in a ploughed field. So much for the warning that landing by parachute was similar to jumping off a high wall. As I gathered up my parachute I also gathered my wits, deciding what to do next. Fortunately I was wearing the new type of flying boots, with laced shoes on the feet to which the legs were attached; so many others had lost the old type while baling out. In order to avoid attracting attention I cut off the tops with the knife provided, then tore off my navigator's brevet and insignia of rank. A nearby straw-stack offered a hiding place for the parachute, harness and Mae West; I ripped the chute into several pieces and pushed them under the straw, retaining one small piece. I knew that I had torn the parachute so that it could not be used by the enemy, but had no idea why I kept a piece of it. This was no time to think of mementoes, and I wasn't a sentimental type! Then I sat by the stack for a few minutes, deciding what to do.

Orientating myself by the Pole star, I trudged south, hoping to find a copse or wood to hide in until any probable search had been called off. However, after a few hundred paces I climbed over a low bank and found myself on a narrow road, along which I walked. By now the moon was shining brightly and I was able to identify what looked like a village ahead. Deciding to bypass it, I prepared to take to the fields again, but before I could do so, heard footfalls and a man's voice called 'Gute nacht'. Although a few German phrases were posted in the Mess for such an eventuality, I now wished I had learned to speak the language better. However, the meaning was obvious, so I returned the greeting as best I could. One small hurdle had been surmounted. Jumping another bank, I crossed another field, and – my luck was in – saw trees ahead. Approaching, I found it was indeed a small wood in the corner of the field. I entered, pushing my way through bracken and bushes, and sat down. I would wait until midnight, when all should be fairly quiet, before resuming the journey. Looking at my navigator's Omega watch, I could see well enough that the time was 2125. 'What a lot has happened in a few hours,' I muttered to myself. A favourite quip among air-crew was 'Join the Navy and see the world; join the Air Force and see the next'. Well, I hadn't done that – not yet, but I thought again of my friends, who had so recently died. Hank was dead and Norman could not possibly have survived; of the other four, how many had been as fortunate as I?

I had 2½ hours to wait, to think and to plan my next moves. Thinking came first. My mother and father and my popsie would not, in their wildest dreams, believe the situation in which I found myself. They did not even know I was on operations, as I had deliberately not told them. Why should they worry unnecessarily? There would be time to tell them when I had finished the tour of thirty ops. Now I wondered whether it would have been better to have mentioned it when I was last on leave: tomorrow Mum and Dad would receive a telegram saying, 'I regret to inform you that your son is missing in action', or words to that effect. Any additional platitudes in the letter that would follow could not disguise the fact and could not be of much comfort to them. Had they known that I was on ops, would they have been better prepared? How long would they have to wait before finding out that I was still alive? Would it be on my arrival in a neutral country, after escaping, or would it be after I had been captured? The latter I knew was a possibility, even a probability, but I had to be positive. I thought ruefully, 'In a few days' time I should have been on a week's leave'. Such leaves were not usually postponed, except in emergency. In fact, the welcome breaks were sometimes advanced, especially when a crew due for leave failed to return from an op.

Now it was vital to think constructively. To the north and west were the rivers Rhine and Ruhr. Bridges would be guarded and I could swim only the two lengths of the pool compulsory for air-crew. I had never fancied the possibility of ditching in the sea, even though it would entitle me to membership of the exclusive Goldfish Club. I could never fathom why such a short distance as two lengths had been chosen as the qualification; such limited ability would not help in the North Sea, or even in crossing a river, particularly if fully clothed. If I had failed the swimming test, would I have failed my air-crew training? But at least I had qualified for the Caterpillar Club – the other exclusive organisation for men who had parachuted to safety.

To the north and west, too, would be German troops, thousands and thousands of them, and they would be very unfriendly. Eastwards would not be a rational direction to take, so south to Switzerland seemed to be the best bet. After all, it was only some 300–400 miles to that sanctuary, albeit with the Alps to cross on the last part of the journey! My mind made up, planning came next. Knowing I would not be far from Dusseldorf, I would first travel eastwards, through the less populated uplands of Westphalia, before striking southwards towards Mannheim. I knew the location of many German towns and cities well enough from the charts I had so often studied and worked from. Surely I could jump a goods train travelling south in the direction of Basle. If I did manage to reach Switzerland, I would probably be interned for the duration of the war. I could not help thinking of that possibility as a bonus, in that I would then be freed from the dangers of my chosen wartime occupation. No, that was not the right way to think; my first duty was to escape from Germany and its occupied countries and the second priority was to return to England. Nevertheless, internment remained an attractive proposition, and certainly an additional incentive in my attempt to leave Germany. Checking my watch, recently synchronised and correct to the second (which was necessary for astro-navigation), I began the journey. Before I left I ate some chocolate from my emergency rations and a pep pill, to keep me wakeful. Resolutely I set off, planning to walk for an hour and then rest for ten minutes, and continue this pattern until I became so tired I had to rest up properly. Although the moonlight helped, the first hour's journey seemed interminable. I stumbled over the unfamiliar ground, and caught sight of two army patrols before finding a dry ditch in which to rest. After ten minutes or so I rose to continue the journey and began to feel hungry. I spotted a farmhouse with outbuildings ahead; stealthily approaching, I saw a shed. Could there be chickens? A hen's egg would not go amiss. There *were* chickens and there were eggs. I took two eggs, feeling rather guilty; it was stealing and I had not been brought up to do that. The journey continued and by now I realised I had a long, long way to go to reach freedom. A running stream provided a much-needed drink. The pattern of walking and resting continued.

At about 0200 I rested for longer, this time burrowing into the base of a stack of straw, and ate the two raw eggs, ruefully contrasting them with the eggs and bacon I should have had hours ago. Although weary, I could not sleep or even doze, as the tablet was still taking effect, so I set out again. About half an hour later I stumbled on a railway line running north to south. I had intended to walk much further eastwards but this looked promising. If I could find an upward incline, a goods train might pass slowly and I could perhaps jump on a passing truck. After all, it happened in films, where it looked quite easy! I walked southwards along the line. Then I saw a bridge spanning the railway, with what seemed to be a minor road approaching it. Another idea surfaced; perhaps I could stand on the bridge and drop on to a slow-moving goods train. I had seen that in films, too. But as I began to make my way to the centre of the bridge, I quickly realised it had not been a wise decision.

'Halt, who goes there?' were not the words actually spoken, but the commanding tone made the meaning quite clear. I turned to run, but the sound of a shot dissuaded me and I halted. I had been lucky on three occasions – to avoid death four times in a few hours was too much to hope for. Two soldiers approached, rifles at the ready. One soldier appeared elderly, the other young, in the light of the torch that one held.

'Englander terror-flieger,' the older man declared. 'Schweinhund,' said the younger. Unwisely, I retorted, 'Hitler ist scheisen-hausen' – one of the very few phrases of German that I knew, even though I couldn't spell the words! For my pains I received a spiteful blow on my knee from the butt of the youth's rifle; the natives were not at all friendly and it seemed that my all-too-brief attempt at escape was over, at least for the time being. It was difficult to realise that I had been captured – or 'in the bag' in RAF slang.

I was taken to a nearby anti-aircraft site; there I was instructed to stand in the corner, like a naughty schoolboy, I thought, and was searched, somewhat perfunctorily. My pep pills, emergency rations and maps were taken from me, but I was allowed to retain my wristwatch. Then I was motioned to sit on a narrow wooden bench, while a spotty-faced young German soldier sat facing me, revolver in hand. After some time I was escorted outside the hut to relieve myself, then it was back to the bench. A mug of hot ersatz coffee, made from acorns, was put before me; I was very thirsty and drank it gratefully. 'If this is a sample of their coffee,' I thought, 'they are sadly lacking in taste.' No food was offered, so, hungry, lonely and somewhat depressed, I stretched myself out on the bench and eventually dozed off, sleeping fitfully. In the morning, at about 0700, I was prodded and given another mug of the unpalatable brew, with two pieces of bread sparsely covered with margarine. The bread that I was used to eating was usually white, sometimes brown, but this was almost black. It was my first experience of black rye bread. It tasted unpleasant but I ate it hungrily, wondering again that German troops had to put up with that sort of fare. What's more, they seemed to almost enjoy the food and drink that they had before them. Breakfast over, and with no opportunity even to wash, I was escorted outside by two soldiers; I was then pushed into a small closed vehicle and driven off, I knew not where. On reaching the chosen destination, evidently a police station, I was escorted into a cell and left there for an hour or two before being searched again. No one spoke to me, which I thought rather unfriendly; on this occasion my watch was taken from me, which was also unfriendly. I was given a receipt, which seemed incongruous, and meant nothing, although I retained it. This search was very rigorous; all possible hiding-places on my body were explored, which I found most embarrassing. However, the miniature compass, concealed within the top button of my tunic, was not discovered. This was not because the searchers did not attempt to unscrew the button, but because it had been fitted with a left-hand thread! Obviously, previous shot-down air-crews had been searched and the hidden compasses discovered, and somehow that information had found its way back to Britain. Subsequently intelligence officers had decided to change the thread, rather than choose another hiding-place. Such was the methodical and almost predictable nature of my captors, who could hardly be said to be endowed with the gift of lateral thinking. I was then left alone in the cell. It contained nothing but a bucket in one corner, which I used during the hours of waiting, not knowing what would happen next. During the day I was given a bowl of soup; it tasted like boiled, sour cabbage, which was probably what it was. I ate it hungrily, with real appreciation of its quantity but not its quality. In the evening, after darkness had fallen, I was taken to a railway station and put in a guard's van, accompanied by an armed soldier I guessed to be about 40 years old. The train clattered through the night and I dozed on the straw, which had been so generously provided. I had no idea of the time, which was of little consequence anyway. My companion did not communicate with me; it would not have helped had he done so, unless, of course he spoke English, and even had he done so, it was certain that the conversation would not have been stimulating. My custodian did not sleep, but sat, revolver in hand, watching me. I became hungry and thirsty, then very hungry and very thirsty. Eventually the train came to a stop and I emerged with my guard on the platform of a large station. The sign read 'Frankfurt um Mainz', and I thought ruefully, 'Well, at least I am travelling towards Switzerland, but the circumstances are not as I would have wished.' Next I was bundled unceremoniously into a small covered lorry and taken, unfed, unwashed and unshaven, to the infamous interrogation centre known as the Dulagluft, at Oberurall, nearby.

The cell to which I was taken was about 7 feet long by 5 feet wide. There were no windows, but a bare bulb hung from the ceiling to provide constant light. The door had a spy-hole and an aperture near the bottom, a little larger than a letter-box opening. The cell contained a narrow wooden bunk, a straw palliasse, a rough grey and tattered army blanket and an uncovered bucket in the corner. The door was locked and I was left alone. Eventually the inevitable bowl of soup, a spoon and a mug of ersatz coffee were pushed through the door aperture. By now I was prepared to eat, and almost enjoy, anything edible, and was just beginning to find out what true hunger is like. Most healthy people profess to be hungry when they have had no food for several hours, while deprivation for a day seems to be an ordeal. Real hunger, approaching starvation, is a state where the sufferer can think of nothing else but food. A humble, dry crust becomes a mouth-watering feast; the mind is entirely focused on food and drink; nothing else matters, not even family, friends or bodily comfort. Energy is dissipated. I had by no means reached that state, yet. I lay on the bunk and eventually slept. Some time later, I had no way of telling how much later, I awoke in the artificial light, sweating profusely. I removed my now dirty tunic, then off came my trousers and shirt, but I continued to perspire freely. Eventually, tired out, I slept, but probably not for long. I awoke again in a very cold atmosphere, chilled to the bone. I put on shirt, trousers and tunic, wrapped myself in the blanket and again, eventually, fell asleep. The heat was then reintroduced and the pattern continued, it seemed for ever. The alternating hot and cold temperatures continued for days; I later learned it was five. At the time it seemed like weeks. Occasionally, and it seemed irregularly, a mug of coffee, a bowl of turnip soup or a slice of black bread, would appear through the door's aperture; sometimes cabbage or potato soup was presented as a change in the menu. I soon learned that the bowl and mug had to be pushed back through the door aperture if they were to be replenished. On occasions, too, I was taken along a corridor, with no natural light and lined by similar cell doors, to a lavatory at the end, and guarded while I attended to the needs of my bowels. It provided a crumb of comfort that I did not have to use the bucket in the cell. No words were ever spoken to me. This, then, was the softening-up process, about which we had been warned at various lectures, it seemed so very long ago. The 'sweat-box' method had been mentioned, but no words could ever prepare you for the actual experience. However, the knowledge helped a little to prepare me for what was to follow, although the thought that others had endured the same treatment was of little consolation. That the cell had been occupied previously was evident from the word 'Greetings' scratched on the plain brick wall above the bed, probably using the handle of the spoon. I was cheered to know that someone had retained his sense of humour. I decided to add my own message, which read, eventually, 'Harry was here'. It took a long time to scratch this, my first and only attempt at graffiti. However, there was plenty of time, not only to deface the wall, but also to think and to review my twenty-one years of life.

Until the beginning of the war, in September 1939, my life had been unremarkable and unexciting. I still remembered my first trip out of Norfolk, on a Sunday-school outing to Thorpeness, in Suffolk. I recollected a short ride on my uncle's BSA motorcycle and the rabbit-shooting ritual on Saturday afternoons with my father, on which occasions I had learned to fire a twelve-bore shotgun with some success. I thought longingly of the cheery log fire that was always lit in the front room on Sundays during the winter months. On leaving school, I attended a Pitman's business course and obtained a job in a solicitor's office in Great Yarmouth, where I licked stamps, learned how to write wills for clients and picked up the basics of accounting. I began with a salary of £26 – that is, 10 shillings a week, from which I retained a shilling as pocket money. I hoped that I would eventually become a solicitor and earn a princely salary. I had learned ballroom dancing, played tennis, fallen in and out of love three or four times a year, and became widely travelled by means of occasional visits to Norwich, some 20 miles distant, in order to watch Norwich City (the Canaries) play football.

The Second World War began when I was 17 years of age and life began to change drastically. It is said that all humans have three main needs; security, identity and stimulation. I had reasonable security, with savings amounting to nearly 10 pounds, and a strong sense of identity, with caring parents and several good friends; now stimulation was at hand. I joined the newly formed Local Defence Volunteers, later to become the Home Guard, and learnt how to clean and fire a rifle and a Bren machine-gun and how to throw a hand-grenade without blowing myself up. On night patrol I once fired my .303 rifle at a marauding German bomber flying low overhead. Unfortunately, I failed to shoot it down, but the bomber did immediately drop its bombs on a field on the outskirts of the village! No doubt it was a coincidence.

At the age of 18 a decision had to be made. I would soon be called up to join one of His Majesty's services. If I waited until that happened, I would probably be allocated to the Army. While that service might well be more appropriate by reason of my LDF membership, I did not fancy the possibility of being perforated by an enemy bayonet. My father had served in the First World War and had been wounded at Gallipoli. My girlfriend's father had been gassed in France and still suffered greatly from the effects. No, life in the trenches, whether they be muddy or sandy, was not for me if I could help it. I was not at all keen on the Navy, either, with the prospect of a watery grave. My choice was now limited to the Royal Air Force, which I rather fancied, as the girls seemed to prefer that uniform. The problem was how to join that service. If I waited for my call-up, I would probably be allocated to the Army, anyway. The responsible authorities usually seemed to place conscripts in the service they least wished to join, and more often than not to do a job for which they were not suited or qualified. I decided, therefore, to volunteer for flying duties in the RAF, not least because air-crews were even more popular with the girls! Youngsters of my age were being offered the opportunity to join the PNB (Pilot, Navigator, Bomb-aimer) scheme, just being introduced. This began with basic training, during which the candidate would be assessed on his potential ability as a pilot or navigator. Those deemed an unsuitable prospect for either would be expected to follow the appropriate course for a bomb-aimer.

My application was followed by an interview and an initial medical examination in Norwich; subsequent tests at RAF Uxbridge indicated that I was suitable, both physically and mentally, for air-crew and I was given an RAFVR badge to show that I was a 'volunteer reserve' waiting to be summoned. I had not yet learned the serviceman's motto, 'Never volunteer for anything'. I had to wait for over a year, and it seemed interminable. During the waiting period I met a girl called Olive and fell in love for about the seventeenth time. We talked, walked, cycled and danced together, and then came the summons for me to report to Lords' cricket ground, St John's Wood, London, on 6 March 1942 at 1100 hours. An uncle, who was a farmer, gave me a 10-shilling note as a going-away present, and I felt quite rich! On arrival at that illustrious venue, with others of the intake, I was issued with a uniform.

Surprisingly, it fitted quite well! Then I collected various items of underwear and was instructed to parcel up my civilian clothes and post them home. My new comrades and I were then marched (or rather, we attempted a pathetic rendering of that skill) to our abode for the next three weeks, namely some very expensive and exclusive flats in St John's Wood which had been taken over by the RAF. We were there instructed in the art of blanket-folding, with corners at precise right-angles; in cleaning boots until they dazzled the onlooker; and in presenting kit on beds for frequent inspections. Drill, more drill and yet more drill eventually transformed the new intake into a reasonably smart unit, marching in time – well, most of the time. More medical examinations and tests of physical and mental ability were dispersed among the drill periods and parades. 'Haircut, you' became a common, dreaded command from an officer or NCO. Often the offender had just had a haircut, expensive in terms of income, but protests were confined to inaudible comments on the parentage of the issuer of the order. We were 'rookies' then and would not dare to risk disobedience by 'forgetting' the order and hoping to avoid retribution. Lack of money was not accepted as an excuse.

Three times a day, every day, we marched through Regent's Park to the zoo premises, where we were fed, and three times a day we marched back again, for more instruction and more drill. We also learned Morse code, having to pass a test by operating at four words a minute. For all this mental and physical activity we were each presented with the princely sum of 10 shillings and 6 pence a week, with free board and accommodation. We enjoyed the experience of course, although we had not enough money, or time for that matter, to visit central London.

Then the whole squadron was marched to the railway station, where we entrained to Scarborough, to no. 11 ITW (Initial Training Wing). Was it there, or at St John's Wood we were given the white flashes to be inserted in the front of our forage caps, to denote our status as air-crew under training? How proud we were of those flashes. We thoroughly enjoyed our ten to twelve weeks at Scarborough, learning the basics of navigation, aircraft recognition and Morse code at a greater speed. We became very efficient at marching. An improvement in general fitness was ensured by participation in cross-country runs. In spite of the humorous grumbling, most of us enjoyed the runs. It was on the first of these runs of about 5 miles that I discovered my aptitude for that activity. I had become bored with trotting along with the majority, and, taking the view that the sooner I finished, the sooner I could shower and change, I had put on speed and finished well ahead of the rest. Now that this latent ability had been discovered, I began to train properly and soon achieved a reputation for running. I had never been so fit.

We were billeted at the Prince of Wales Hotel. It was there, outside the hotel entrance, that I had done my first, and only, guard duty during my service life. It seemed a pointless exercise and I was glad I had not joined the Army! One evening I went out with a few friends and after a couple of beers each we started 'fishing for submarines' in the ornamental pool across the road from the hotel. I smiled when I remembered how we had then returned to our room and wakened our sleeping friends by asking if they would like to buy a submarine. This generous offer was not accepted; in fact, the replies received were unnecessarily impolite and unprintable. Now, as I lay in my cell in the Dulagluft at Oberurall, I wondered where those friends were now. No doubt many of them had lost their lives. Perhaps others had reached high rank. I reflected that I still had, back at home, a photograph of a group of those friends.

After ITW all those who had passed the course were promoted to Leading Aircraftmen and were transported to Wigtown, by the Solway Firth, to an Elementary Flying Training School (EFTS). A gifted few had managed to fly solo after just 6 or 7 hours of instruction, while rather more were able to do so within the mandatory maximum of 12 hours. Those who ran out of time and were not allowed to fly solo were adjudged to be unsuitable for further pilot training. My solo flight took place after 10 hours of training. I would never forget my first ever flight, with the instructor at the controls. Air experience, it was called. The instructor, a veteran fighter pilot on rest from ops, had flown his Tiger Moth, with its valuable passenger, under the telegraph wires. He threw the aircraft into a spin and looped-the-loop. Strangely enough, I was not even slightly scared, having realised that the pilot had no intention of risking his own valuable life in order to assess his pupil's suitability as a pilot.

The survivors of the course were then sent to Heaton Park, Manchester, for assessment, after which we were to be posted somewhere for further training. Hundreds of aspiring pilots and navigators slept out in lodgings and waited, all day, every day, for weeks. The prospective bomb-aimers, some of whom were possibly destined to train as air-gunners, had gone elsewhere. By this stage I had been informed that I was well suited to continue training as a navigator. Eventually the chaps from my squadron were told we would continue our training in South Africa. Before we had the opportunity to rejoice at our good fortune or bemoan the fact that we would be far away from the action, the posting was rescinded, as all available troopships were required for the North African campaign. I would have liked to go to South Africa, being in no great hurry to endanger the life I was thoroughly enjoying!

After a further short delay, our group of firm friends was posted to 1 Navigation School at Bridgnorth in Shropshire, and we were divided into two flights, A and B. An intensive and demanding course was followed for weeks. It was there that I properly learned the noble art of boxing, although I had done a little as a schoolboy. Our PT instructor was Corporal Arthur Boggis, who, before being called up for service, had been the trainer of Tommy Farr, the British heavyweight champion. Training included long cross-country runs, which were just up my street, so to speak. More importantly, I escaped the boring physical education inflicted on my colleagues. Under the corporal's tutelage I became extremely fit and capable enough to represent the Wing at light welterweight, in competition with an Army team. As my opponent had not had the benefit of my training, I managed to win. In fact, I believe all Corporal Boggis's boxers won. We were very, very fit. However, we were not there for the sole purpose of keeping fit. Our course was difficult and intensive, and included dead-reckoning navigation, meteorology and astro-navigation. The latter involved getting up or staying up to take star shots at unearthly hours of the morning, in order to fix our position on the surface of the planet. We had to identify twenty-two major stars in order to be able to do this. It did seem a bit pointless, as we already knew where we were! At the time, of course, we did not realise that this knowledge and the practice would be of invaluable assistance to many of us during operational sorties.

We did not spend all our time in study and keeping fit at 1 Navigation School. The town was only a mile or so down the hill and contained girls, a dance hall and pubs, the three main interests of most of us. Perhaps not surprisingly, on dance-nights the girls congregated at the dance hall, so we enjoyed giving them the benefit of our company. I was again reminded that the young ladies appeared to be fond of air-crews or potential air-crews, so we had no problem in persuading them to dance with us. Local lads and Army types tended to become a bit annoyed.

Our final examinations were duly taken and we anxiously awaited the results. However, a celebration was in order, whether or not we had passed. Our instructor, a navigator holding the rank of flight lieutenant, took us to town, so that we, in our gratitude, could buy him a drink or three. When he had had his quota, he had gone off and left us to our own devices. We drank more. We drank too much. I often wondered what local people thought when they saw a group of irresponsible young airmen, literally crawling up the hill in single file towards the camp. The corporal at the gate had been understanding enough; perhaps he was used to the experience. Those of each flight who passed the final examinations were then posted for flying training. Those who failed were probably encouraged to train for other air-crew duties. A Flight was posted to Canada and B Flight to North Wales. I was in B Flight and we duly arrived at the airfield at Llandwrog, at the foot of Snowdon. What a silly place to have an airfield for 'sprog' navigators, we thought; what happens in fog? We soon found out. Within a week of our arrival, an Anson that was attempting to land in murky weather ploughed into the lower slopes of the mountain. The Anson, nicknamed the flying greenhouse because of its vast expanse of glass, was an ideal aircraft in which to train navigators. The all-round visibility enabled trainees to map-read more efficiently, which was a vital part of their early training. This period was another very enjoyable part of service life. Most days we were flying over beautiful countryside, not just Wales but also along the west coast of Scotland, using our new-found skills to guide the pilot on given tracks, eventually to arrive back at base. One never-to-be-forgotten sight was the tip of Snowdon just protruding from a layer of white stratocumulus cloud above which the pilot and I were flying. At least, it was an excellent fix, ensuring we were on the right course.

Once this part of the training was over, we trainees had qualified as fully fledged navigators and we were promoted to sergeants or pilot officers and were presented with our wings. The rank allocated appeared to depend on the school attended, the father's profession (rather than job!), the games played and the candidate's accent! Afterwards we were all sent on a week's leave. It took me almost a full day to reach Hemsby in Norfolk, my home village.

B Flight was then posted in its entirety to an operational training unit at RAF Cottesmore, where we began flying in larger aircraft, in our case the twin-engined Wellington, or 'Wimpy', as it was affectionately called. As night flying was of paramount importance, most of this further advanced training was done during the hours of darkness, over all parts of Britain, on flights of several hours' duration. It was at this final stage of training that crewing-up took place. The method of deciding who should fly with whom was largely self-selective. I well remembered how I had teamed up with James, my first pilot, after we had been joint winners of a rifle-shooting competition. They had been good days, too.

Then a further development occurred when we moved to a heavy conversion unit at Wigsley to fly Lancasters for the first time. It was easy enough for most of the crew, who performed the same work in slightly different surroundings, but it was very different and often more difficult for the pilots. It was highly regrettable that James just could not learn to fly a Lanc competently, so he remained with most of the crew to be posted elsewhere. I was sent to 49 Squadron. On arrival, I was informed that Flight Lieutenant Norman Carfoot had accepted me as his navigator, without even asking for my opinion! Apparently, or so it was said, Norman had a habit of getting what he wanted; he was reputed to have an older brother, a group captain no less, at Air Ministry headquarters, who had some influence. So that was how Norman and I had met. Norman did, in fact, tell me, at a later date, that his elder brother worked at HQ, but the rumour of exerted influence was probably unfounded.

So had ended the fun and now I must begin to earn my keep. I chastised myself for being such a fool as to volunteer for air-crew. I would have enjoyed the RAF just as much and in almost complete safety if I had been appointed as a group captain in charge of WAAF welfare. Oh well, perhaps I would have been bored looking after the needs of hundreds of young and attractive women! It was conceivable that such a post was not available anyway, and had it been I might well not have been chosen! Perchance to dream.

In early October Flight Lieutenant Carfoot and his crew were posted to 49 Squadron, and Norman was immediately appointed as the flight commander of A Flight, with half the squadron under his control. Our first op with 49 Squadron had been to Leipzig. There we had had to circle the target twice before finding a gap in the cumulus cloud in order to bomb accurately. On this raid severe icing had reduced our airspeed so much that Jock warned Norman that there was insufficient fuel left to return to base. I recalled my satisfaction when I calculated that RAF Coltishall, a fighter airfield in Norfolk, was a feasible alternative, and the relief we all felt when Norman touched the wheels lightly on the grass runway there. Any fleeting ideas I might have entertained of a brief visit home or a few hours with Olive were soon dispelled. Norman was far too keen and conscientious in ensuring that we arrived back at base by noon the next day, in case we were needed for another exciting evening. Who needs that much excitement? Evidently Norman did!

Back in the Dulagluft at Oberurall I told myself there was no point in dwelling on the past, and it was certainly futile to feel sorry for myself in my present predicament. 'It can only improve', I told myself firmly. On the sixth day I was taken to a small room with a table and told, in English, to sit down. Then I was presented with a form to complete. This form, headed 'Red Cross', was so transparently ingenuous and naïve that it almost cheered me up. It asked for my name, rank and number, and these I filled in as required by the Geneva Convention. Then followed similar requests for my squadron number, its location, the number of aeroplanes, and the names of the squadron commander and commanding officer. I made no attempt to complete this section, in spite of threats that failure to do so would result in no word being sent of my survival to my parents and the Royal Air Force. This then, I thought, was an example of the renowned German efficiency. No further comments were made.

I was then escorted to an adjoining room, well furnished. A very smart German senior SS officer, who had evidently lost one arm, probably in battle, sat behind a large desk, laden with a telephone and some files; a chair had been placed in front of the desk, facing the officer. I correctly saluted the senior officer by standing to attention, as I had no headgear. In perfect English he invited me to sit, and the tone of his voice was very friendly. A cigarette was offered, but politely refused. I noticed that the cigarettes were in a British packet.

'You have given your name, rank and number, but I see you have omitted to complete the rest of the form.'

'Yes, Sir.'

'But this is essential if your family and friends are to know you are safe. Where do you live in England? I know by your accent that you are English.'

'I am authorized to give you my name, rank and number, and no more – Sir.'

This mild exchange continued for a time, with the German trying to glean a few snippets of trivial information in order to progress further, while I knew that I must not give such information.

Gradually his tone became less friendly, and then, following more unanswered questions, very unfriendly.

'You realize that you can be shot as a spy; you have no indication on your tunic that you are a flyer, no brevet or badges of rank. Unless you cooperate, you will be shot, just as one of your comrades is being shot outside, now.' The interrogator moved to the window and gave a signal, which resulted in a number of rifle shots. I might not have been brave enough to withstand this last threat had we not been warned in lectures that such a thing might happen. Even as things were I did not feel at all brave, just depressed, weak, hungry and washed-out. 'Oh well,' I thought hopefully, 'things can only improve.' It was a very optimistic thought.

I was pushed back into my tiny cell, but was incarcerated there for only one more day. I had not washed or shaved or had a change of clothes for more than a week, and I was very glad I was not due to meet a girlfriend immediately; she would certainly not have appreciated the sight or the smell! However, I was not alone. I was escorted to a large room in the building that was already occupied by eight other air-crew, all equally dirty and unshaven. The nine of us must have been the sole survivors from the shot-down aircraft lost on the operation over a week ago. Much to my delight and relief, among them were Jock and Steve. However, my pleasure was soon tempered by grief. During Steve's interrogation he had been told of the deaths of Norman, Hank and Dave, and he was assured that the remaining crew member would soon be found, alive or dead. Steve had actually landed on the roof of the police station in Wuppertal, probably the same one which I had visited briefly. Jock had landed in a street and was saved from a probable lynching by an understandably angry crowd by the intervention of a passing patrol. The bodies of Norman and Hank had been discovered in the crashed and burned-out aircraft, evidently identified by their 'dog-tags', while Dave's body was retrieved from the Rhine. Wilf had not been mentioned. Obviously the German authorities had concluded that Jock, Dave and I were part of Norman's crew, accounting for a total of six of the seven. What had happened to Wilf? It was unlikely, but perhaps he had escaped!

We were then taken outside and photographed, but no one smiled at the photographer! Wearing our best scowls, and in our dirty, scruffy and unshaven state, it would be surprising if such photographs would be of any use in identifying escaping prisoners. Back inside again, each of us was issued with a small cardboard box, by courtesy of the Red Cross. How grateful we were to that wonderful organisation. Each parcel contained a bar of soap, a small towel, a toothbrush and a razor. Two by two, the prisoners were escorted to a basic washroom, where we cleaned ourselves as best we could. Back in our new abode, we were each issued with an enamel mug and a spoon before receiving a welcome meal, even though it did consist of the inevitable stale black rye bread and a bowl of watery vegetable soup! Although we now had time to talk, we knew we had to be very wary of a possible listening device or the presence of a German dressed as a British airman. By unspoken agreement, no squadron numbers or names were mentioned. We did, however, begin the process of 'goon-baiting', which consisted of annoying the enemy guards. We talked of the good food we had had in England, of the certainty of Germany's downfall and anything else that might irritate our hosts. We did hope our conversation was recorded. 'Goon-baiting' seemed to be a way of life for air-crew prisoners, helping to relieve the monotony. The procedure could not have been learned from anyone; it just seemed the natural thing to do!

During the afternoon the nine of us were escorted to the railway station at Frankfurt and bundled into a carriage, escorted by two armed guards. The train, carrying passengers in other carriages, travelled eastward for hours, at first in daylight. We were not in the right frame of mind to appreciate the wonderful scenery. Darkness fell, the train stopped at a station and water was brought. It tasted better than the acorn coffee! Still the train rumbled on, until, during the night, we reached the end of the journey. There were no lights to identify the name of the station, but someone outside shouted 'Leipzig'. Jock, Steve and I remarked ruefully, 'We were over here a couple of weeks ago.'

By this time deprivation of food and drink had begun to befuddle us prisoners. We had little idea of time and distance and were almost in a stupor; even our eyesight was affected. We did vaguely remember being herded into a cattle truck, which was already partly filled with civilians, male and female, young and old. One of the airmen spoke German fairly well and learned that they were Jews, being transported they knew not where. The conditions were most unpleasant for all; the cattle truck itself was not an ideal means of transport and the crowded conditions provided little or no opportunity to sit. The journey seemed never-ending and became more and more uncomfortable as time passed. We airmen were more sorry for the Jews than we were for ourselves and we were certainly sorry enough for ourselves. All things eventually come to an end, and eventually the train stopped. We airmen were selectively removed and then herded, shuffling, along a narrow road with fields on

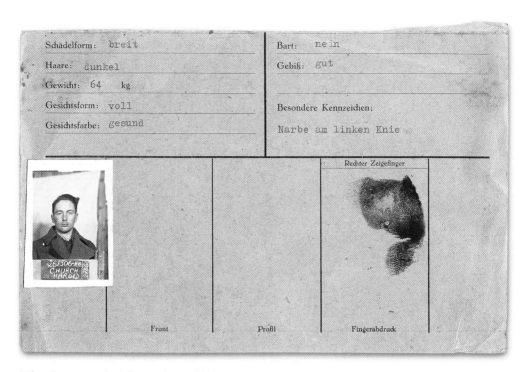

Schädelform: breit	Bart: nein
Haare: dunkel	Gebiß: gut
Gewicht: 64 kg	
Gesichtsform: voll	Besondere Kennzeichen:
Gesichtsfarbe: gesund	Narbe am linken Knie

Rechter Zeigefinger

Front   Profil   Fingerabdruck

When his captors had departed, Harold liberated his POW record card and retains it to this day. (*Harold D. Church*)

either side. Some stumbled and were prodded to their feet to continue. This road continued for several miles until we saw a large rectangular enclosure, fenced with double coils of barbed wire to a height of about 10 feet, with sentry boxes at each corner and others spaced along the sides. The enclosure itself was approximately 200–300 yards square, with a formidable gate at the end of the road, guarded by sentries with rifles. Outside the camp were acres of bare fields on all sides; there were no trees, hedges or vegetation of any kind. We would discover later that nor were there any birds, which always seemed strange. The interior of the camp was similar in that there was no vegetation, just a great number of large wooden huts, grouped in separate compounds, together with a small, detached section containing more solid administrative buildings and German quarters.

Once inside, the nine of us were taken to a brick building, where we were told to strip, then ordered into a room in which there were a number of shower points along the walls. The welcome showers were turned on for far too short a time, but sufficiently long for us to clean ourselves with the aid of the soap provided by the Red Cross. After drying ourselves we dressed, unfortunately having to don again our dirty clothing. Then we were escorted to another room, where our heads were shorn, almost to baldness. We were, by now, so tired, hungry and thirsty that we could not have cared less. Finally, carrying our precious soap, razor, mug and spoon, we were escorted, none too gently, to our living accommodation. This consisted of a large wooden hut, about 80 feet long by 30 feet wide; into this space were packed almost two hundred bodies, all airmen. Our new home was numbered 57. Most of the available space was taken up by double rows of bunks, about 6 feet long and 2 feet wide, in three tiers, so that a floor area of 72 square feet could accommodate eighteen bunks. Narrow gangways between the double rows provided access. Straw palliasses adorned the bunks, and that was all. Apparently our captors considered that their 'guests' would not need luxuries like blankets, as sufficient body heat would be generated to keep them all warm. The remaining floor area, about 10 feet wide and running the length of the hut, was adorned by a few trestle tables and wooden benches, enough to seat perhaps forty. Simple arithmetic showed that when the inmates were confined to the hut, only one in five could sit at the tables, while the remainder had to lie on their bunks. Sitting on the bunk was almost impossible, except for a dwarf or a contortionist, as the headroom was very limited. There was nothing else in this palatial apartment; no chairs, no lockers. Indeed, the latter were hardly necessary, as no one had possessions, apart from a small Red Cross cardboard box each. There was a tortoise stove near the end of the building, but as there was hardly ever any fuel available, it was almost superfluous! Beyond this a doorway, with no door, led to a narrow tiled area, along the walls of which were rows of metal troughs with taps at either end, providing running water for ablutions, drinking and the washing of small items of clothing; needless to say, the water was cold: only sissies would need hot water! There were also four elementary urinals. Into this, then, our new abode, stepped the nine of us.

All this lack of luxury was not apparent at first, for we were greeted warmly and each given the inevitable cup of acorn coffee and a slice of stale black rye bread. We did not realise at the time what a sacrifice this was, for the daily issue to each POW at the camp was an eighth of a loaf per day, while a ration of 100 grams, nearly 4 ounces, of margarine was issued weekly. It would have been difficult to weigh and distribute a daily ration! The coffee was certainly not plentiful. A bowl of watery soup formed much of the rest of the daily allowance. A few ounces of potatoes, fish-paste, vegetables (mostly dried), millet or barley and about an ounce of cheese, our 'entitlements' for the week, were issued to the cook-house, which was staffed by POWs, and incorporated into the sparse diet. An infrequent allocation of meat was welcome, even though it was not prime beef or pork. In fact it was probably horse or dog. Inmates tried to forget that cartloads of dead dogs were delivered to the camp each week. Fruit was never available. The occasional arrival and issue of Red Cross parcels, however, did alleviate hunger and saved many from near starvation. Unfortunately the receipt of such luxuries was far from regular, and one issue a month was the most that could be hoped for. We new arrivals had yet to experience the longing for the arrival of the next delivery and the excitement of the receipt of the food the parcels contained.

Jock, Steve and I were allocated three of the few vacant bunks, on which we flopped down and slept and slept. When we awoke, the first to greet us was Ivan, a navigator from our own squadron, whose aircraft had failed to return from an operation in October. Ivan had been the only survivor. News was exchanged and the three of us learned more about the camp, Stalag 4B. Apparently it had been built as a transit camp only, but no one ever seemed to be transferred to a more permanent one. As a transit camp it was not inspected by Red Cross representatives, so the rules of the Geneva Convention could be conveniently 'bent'. There were five compounds: one for RAF personnel, one for British Army prisoners from the North African campaign, transported via Italy; one for other western Europeans; one for Russians; and one for Polish Jews. It was rumoured that many of the latter had been gassed or executed and that over three thousand of them were buried beneath the soil of one of the compounds. It was said that a total of about twenty thousand prisoners were held in the five compounds. The Russians' and Jews' compounds were inaccessible from the others, but inmates of the other three were able to communicate during daylight hours on the occasions they were allowed to leave their huts. The area within the confines of the main fence was surrounded on all sides by a low wire, beyond which one would pass only at the risk of instant lead-poisoning from the machine-guns of the guards situated in sentry boxes perched high over the outer fences at intervals of about 40 yards. These twin outer fences consisted of intertwining rolls of barbed wire, to a height of about 10 feet. It was evident that our captors didn't want their guests to leave!

The RAF compound contained eight huts, all of the same size and each accommodating nearly two hundred airmen, ranging in rank from sergeant to warrant officer. Many of these airmen wore wooden clogs, issued to replace their old-type flying boots that had been lost in the clouds. The compound itself was a rectangular enclosure about half the size of a football pitch. The inmates were generally permitted to leave their huts during daylight hours and take exercise by walking around the perimeter, and to make use of one of the four communal lavatories in each compound, sited close by the fence. These were hardly the epitome of luxury, containing two facing rows of ten wooden seats, with the necessary apertures. Almost needless to say, the sanitation was elementary; the results of users' labours, so to speak, dropped directly into a long trench below. The trenches were emptied regularly, via openings in the exterior walls, by a group of Russian prisoners, escorted by guards, and then removed from the camp by cart. Fortunately, the lack of food ensured that a visit to one of these edifices was necessary only infrequently; once or twice a week was usually sufficient, unless the intake of food well past its 'best by' date prompted urgent visits. However unsavoury it may seem, this description of the facility is necessary, as it was to become a focus of attention later.

Life in the camp became a boring routine. During inclement weather and in the evenings there was absolutely nothing to do, except wait and long for the daily issue of stale black bread and vegetable soup, brought to the entrance of the huts for the inmates to distribute. As bunks occupied most of the available space, a system was evolved to ensure that all had the occasional opportunity to sit on a bench. Fortunately for those who remained reasonably alert and optimistic, there were some who stayed on their bunks all day and every day, except to collect their rations. On the increasingly rare occasions that Red Cross parcels arrived, even these depressed airmen shared in the excitement. The parcels, containing such luxuries as tinned meat, usually 'Spam', dried milk (labelled 'Klim'), condensed milk, tinned jam, tea and biscuits, were distributed and gloated over; the contents were examined and re-examined and decisions made as to what to eat first. Often three or four particular friends would share parcels, so that an opened tin of meat lasted the group two or three days. Although it was a great temptation to eat all of a parcel's contents in a few days, most airmen made them last at least a week. Some empty tins became drinking mugs, while others were carefully and laboriously fashioned into plates. Nothing was wasted. On one occasion a Red Cross issue contained packs of cards and books, enough for four packs and six books for each hut in the RAF compound. Those occupants of Hut 57 who were fortunate enough to be able to read at least one of the books enjoyed the temporary escapism, while bridge players made good use of the cards during most waking hours. I played a lot of bridge and read *Alice in Wonderland*!

The other great excitement was the arrival of mail from home, which was collected by the senior officer in each hut. Jock, Steve and I had to wait almost three months for our first letters. Only then did we learn that our parents had been informed of our safety at the beginning of January, nearly two months after we were reported missing. We realised how traumatic the wait must have been for our parents, wives and fiancées, and felt very sorry for the families of the rest of the crew who had not survived. As the letters were censored, the news received was confined to family matters, but the receipt of the letter mattered more than the content. Writing letters to our nearest and dearest was more of a problem. Usually a postcard was issued, irregularly, but not more than once a month. With pencils provided by courtesy of the Red Cross, we prisoners wrote our messages on the postcards. We could not describe the conditions in which we lived: not only would the German censor obliterate any such references, but also we felt there was no point in burdening those at home with further concerns as to our welfare. Therefore most cards, and the occasional letter-sheet, contained cheerful comments, without actually saying or implying that our treatment was of a satisfactory standard. One particular incident did give us the opportunity to assure loved ones that all was well. One of the inmates, a Belgian who had joined the RAF, had been a hypnotist in civilian life. One evening he consented to give a performance, which was truly amazing. Subjects leaned over to impossible angles, sat without chairs and became inebriated on water. Letters home were then able to include, without actually lying, the comment that 'We thoroughly enjoyed a concert'. No doubt some recipients thought the prisoners were having a comfortable time, and had no wish to escape. They could not – and should not – know of our deprived conditions or that escape was constantly in the thoughts of most of the incarcerated airmen, second only to the need for food!

Christmas 1943 came and went. It was a non-event in terms of any kind of celebration, other than the event itself. Extra food and drink were conspicuous by their absence, although our thoughts naturally turned even more to home. Shortly after this Ivan received his first letter from his parents, mentioning that Alan, his twin brother, had recovered from the necessary twenty-five visits to the lavatory. Although the German censors must have been puzzled, the comment was not obliterated. As Alan was also a navigator on another Lancaster squadron in Lincolnshire, Ivan concluded that he had returned successfully from that number of operations over Germany, with five more to do before a welcome and deserved respite. However, Ivan was not thrilled with the news that his twin had almost completed his tour,

Hardly a wish-you-were-here postcard! Communications had to be innocuous to pass the censor. This card tells of 21st birthday celebrations lost owing to their enforced separation. (*Harold D. Church*)

Kriegsgefangenenlager

Datum: 27/3/1944.

My Darling, I wonder if you were able to spend your 21st birthday at home yesterday. I was thinking of you more than ever, which is saying a lot, and hoping you were having a good time. We did plan to celebrate it together too, didn't we? Never mind! All my love Darling. Harold.

for only on the previous evening he had made a point of coming to me to voice his concern. He said that he knew without doubt that Alan had, just at that very moment, been killed! I did my best to reassure him, but to no avail. Ivan knew, and that was that. Astonishingly, Ivan was right: later he learned that Alan had indeed lost his life, on his thirtieth and last operation, on the very evening that Ivan had had the premonition, or perhaps telepathic message. I had heard, or read, somewhere that identical twins usually shared experiences, even when apart. This occurrence was surely proof that such telepathy existed. I was saddened by the news. I had completed most of my training with the twins, from Initial Training right through to our postings to squadrons some 18 months later. It was only at that stage that authority had decreed that the twins must serve on different squadrons. It was probably a wise decision. Neither twin had made any comment to me, but I could speculate as to their feelings had they been on the same squadron and one had stayed at base when the other was flying on ops. It must have been traumatic for their parents, too, having both their sons in Bomber Command. They were two fine young men, full of fun. During our stay at Scarborough they had shared the same girlfriend for two weeks. Alan would go out with her one evening, report to his brother where they had been, and then Ivan would take his place on another evening. The aim of this exercise was, of course, to attempt to fool the young lady for as long as possible. They managed two dates each before they were dismissed with dishonour! Almost inevitably they were nicknamed Castor and Pollux (the heavenly twin stars).

As has been observed, the lavatories in the compound were close to the inner fence and the contents were emptied regularly by Russian prisoners who scraped the effluence through apertures along the outside of the buildings. Moreover the guards never bothered to enter those palatial premises or to check comings and goings. These facts prompted considerable thought. Given the necessary tools, and ignoring the unpleasant surroundings, a tunnel could be dug from beneath one of the lavatory seats, under the fences to the field beyond. It had to be assumed that the field would contain growing crops by mid-summer and that these would be tall enough to hide escaping prisoners from the traversing searchlights after the barbed wire fences had been negotiated.

Although in our particular camp there were no means of providing false documents or civilian clothes, the optimists among us were convinced that once out, other difficulties could be resolved. Plans were made. The occupants of the hut would need to be told and involved. Every airman would be asked to contribute bed-boards to help prop up the sides and roof of the tunnel. The bed-boards were about 2 feet long and 4 inches in width, so about five hundred would be required for a tunnel up to 60 feet long. The soil was soft, particularly at the beginning of the tunnel, so there was no great need for digging tools any more sophisticated than empty tins from Red Cross parcels. Dispersal of soil presented no insuperable problem; it could be dumped in the other apertures or 'filtered' through trouser legs on to the compound.

Jock and I were involved from the planning stage, as were ten or a dozen others. Who else should be included? If possible, it would be wise to confine the knowledge to those who had to know; the more people that knew of the proposal, the greater the chance of a leak. As it was, there was no way of telling whether an infiltrator had been planted in order to learn of such plans. Prospective escapers could make their way, individually, to the building in the evening, before nightfall. After all the others had left, they would have ample time to negotiate the tunnel, break through the soil above and begin their journey to freedom before their disappearance was discovered. Once out of the camp, they would travel in pairs, but it was left to each pair to decide on their preferred route. Jock and I agreed we would travel north-west along the east bank of the River Elbe, and attempt to reach Lübeck on the north coast. We had no maps, but estimated the distance to be some 200 miles. At least following the Elbe would ensure we were going in the right direction. I remembered from my Mercator charts that Dessau and Magdeburg were on the proposed route, with Berlin to the east. There should be few other large centres of population. Perhaps we would be able to board a boat travelling to Sweden? The Lübeck–Sweden escape route had been one of those suggested by the intelligence officer in lectures on escape procedures back at base. A major problem was the lack of any disguise, but we could do nothing about that at this stage. Stealing clothes was a possibility, while purloined bicycles could provide transport. However, there were still difficulties to be overcome before the break-out. We would need to ensure that the chosen lavatory seat was not used during the excavation. We would have to contrive a means of keeping our clothes reasonably clean to avoid suspicion both while the tunnel was being dug and for the period after the escape. We could dig in the nude, but how would we clean ourselves afterwards? The issue of seat use was soon resolved: the chosen latrine block was the nearest to the fence and we were confident we could contrive a method to prevent people using the chosen seat, whether or not they were aware of the digging going on below. The last seat in the line would simply be 'damaged' in such a way as to persuade men to avoid sitting on it. No one would wish to risk splinters in the rear! The problem of clothing for the digging was difficult, but eventually a possible solution was found, albeit a risky one. At least two pairs of overalls would be required, one for the digger at the tunnel face and one for the person transporting the soil back to the beginning of the tunnel. With only two airmen working in the tunnel at any one time, the operation would take a long, long time – but time we had in abundance. It so happened that Wireless Operator Jim Hobbs, one of the instigators, was quite fluent in the German language, having spent several holidays in the Black Forest area before the war. Jim had discovered that one of the guards, who had been wounded on the Eastern front, lived in that district and he had cultivated his acquaintance, with the obvious ulterior motive of bribery. The occasional gifts from home of cigarettes, using the Red Cross facilities, were used for this purpose, as they were greatly prized by the captors, some of whom were not averse to exchange when it involved little risk. In contrast to the coarse, half-filled, noxious weeds they smoked, even in 1944, British cigarettes were indeed nectar. It was decided that Jim would attempt to procure the overalls from this source, pointing out to the not over-intelligent guard that they were required for use in cleaning the floor of the hut with the two brooms provided for that purpose. After all, the airmen's uniforms were all we had and they were scruffy and dirty enough already. Once obtained, the overalls could be smuggled to and from the latrine block under our uniforms. Jim would begin negotiations when the opportunity presented itself, so that the overalls would be accepted as commonplace. Most potential difficulties now appeared to have been overcome, although there were many minor points still to be considered. These could be left to a later date, however, when the participants had been chosen and all the details finalised. It was decided that the digging would commence in May 1944, when there would be longer hours of daylight.

Life at the camp continued its boring routine. Inmates had to will themselves to walk round the compound as the shortage of food made them weaker, knowing that some exercise was vital in order to remain reasonably fit. Two circuits were usually enough for most. Part of the routine was a daily parade of bodies, usually around breakfast time. (Breakfast time it may have been, but there was certainly no breakfast at that time. The first and only meal would not be available until mid-day.) At this daily assembly the occupants of each hut were required to line up in five rows in the compound, prodded by dangerous-looking bayonets, in order to be counted. It was surprising how a group of well-drilled servicemen could be so awkward in such a simple exercise! It was also surprising how difficult it was for the German unteroffiziers (non-commissioned officers) to count up to two hundred! Any slight disturbance in the ranks or another distraction would result in a recount. Unfortunately the 'goons' possessed no sense of humour, at least not one comparable to ours, so they often gained their revenge. Thus on particularly cold and frosty mornings the inmates of a specific hut would be kept standing for hours, while two or three German soldiers searched their hut for anything that ought not to have been there. Nothing was found, as there was nothing to find, but some of the captors did have the annoying habit of scattering the airmen's few possessions – mugs, tin plates and carefully preserved contents of parcels – causing much annoyance and resorting after the interminable parade. Strangely enough, the soldiers did not attempt to steal the contents of the parcels. It became a point of honour not to collapse from cold or hunger during such occasions, and surprisingly few did. Apparently the unteroffiziers did not like their smart uniforms to get excessively wet, so, happily for the airmen, such lengthy parades were confined to dry weather. Even then the 'goon-baiting' continued; the prisoners would not allow their captors to relax.

Another relief from routine was provided by occasional visits to the showers. These excursions were most welcome, for after about a month the odour of almost two hundred young men in a confined space did become rather offensive, although, given time, one can get used to anything. On these infrequent occasions the occupants of each hut were escorted from the compound to the brick buildings that contained the showers (the same buildings that the nine of us had been taken to back in November). Unfortunately the prospect of the cleansing process was somewhat spoiled by a rumour that the brick building also contained the gas chamber used for the Jews reputed to be buried at the camp. However, we were reassured by the knowledge that, so far at least, all RAF personnel had returned safely to their huts after showering! New occupants of the huts soon learned the routine: as the showers were blissfully warm, it was the practice to undress and drop one's clothing at one's feet, to be washed also.

Then, when the typically efficient warm air was produced to dry the bodies, the clothing was also dried, albeit only partially. Our captors did have the decency to leave both the showers and the hot air running for some time. In retrospect, the infrequency of the showers was understandable. Even if the facility were extended only to those who were neither Russians nor Jews, there were still some 10,000 or 12,000 people using the showers. Presumably there was some sort of roster.

Inevitably, in a camp of that size, there were illnesses and deaths. Only the less serious cases could be dealt with in the small basic hospital, which was mainly staffed by British and other European prisoners who had had medical experience during or before the war. Of course, nothing could be done for those suffering from malnutrition, a problem that affected all the inmates of the camp, but minor operations could be performed. A captured British medical officer was available for dental work, but unfortunately for the patients any urgent treatment was a painful experience, as no anaesthetics were available. Needless to say, only those in constant pain asked to be escorted to the dental surgeon to have a tooth extracted; there were no facilities for fillings. No medical facilities at all existed for the Russians and Jews: if they were ill they were ill, and if they died they died. Cartloads of deceased and naked prisoners were often seen leaving the camp, piled one on top of another.

During the early spring months plans for the proposed tunnel were complete. After much deliberation it was decided that twenty should be the maximum number to make the initial attempt. If all went well, others could follow, until the absences were discovered. The plotters and diggers would go first. Occupants of the hut who wished to be involved drew lots for the remaining initial places. Jim had negotiated for and procured not two but three sets of overalls from the guard. The overalls and brooms were on constant display; the hut had never before had such clean floors. The vital bed-boards had been promised readily, in spite of the fact that the bunks would be even more uncomfortable without them. The lavatory seat had been deeply scored and inspections showed that it was no longer in use. The Russian detail had evidently not noticed, or didn't care that they had nothing to extract from under the last aperture in the line. Work on the tunnel began in early May, and a routine was soon established. The first two diggers of the day would saunter to the latrine, with overalls under their uniforms and empty cans in their pockets. Another airman would follow, to act as look-out. After about an hour the first workers would be relieved by two more would-be escapees, who would change into the overalls while the two finishing their shift changed back into uniform, taking with them in their tucked-in trouser legs the soil they had excavated, to be shaken out in the compound. The look-outs were also changed frequently. The last pair to dig before the evening confinement took back the overalls. Transporting the bed-boards to the scene of operations was left until twilight, so that stiff-legged prisoners would not be so readily spotted by guards in the towers or patrolling the compound.

The first few days of digging were extremely unpleasant, as the first foot or so of soil removed was liberally mixed with excreta. However, it had to be done. The work was shared and the going was fairly easy. The diggers soon became accustomed to the use of the tin cans as tools and quickly evolved an efficient system. The 'topsoil' was scattered beneath the other lavatory seats, until the hole became deep enough and wide enough to insert bed-boards vertically to support the shaft. Then the construction of the horizontal tunnel began, sloping downwards slightly for the first few yards, until it was estimated to be about 4 feet below the surface of the compound, leading towards the fences. After each few feet of construction vertical bed-boards were inserted, with a horizontal board pushed, banged and persuaded into place above each pair. Mistakes were made and minor collapses occurred, but novice diggers gradually became more proficient as we progressed, slowly but surely, towards our objective. Slowly was the operative word, as the method of execution, the need for secrecy and the tools available were not conducive to speed and efficiency. No doubt one man with a modern machine and an efficient support system could have constructed a much safer and neater tunnel in a few hours. Our masterpiece, it was estimated, would take weeks, if not months, at the initial rate of about 2 feet a day, on those days when it was safe to work. As the tunnel became longer, the excavation, transportation and removal of soil would take more time. Still, we had nothing else of importance to do; although the conditions were claustrophobic, the tunnel diggers did have the satisfaction of knowing they were 'digging for victory', so to speak.

Those who have never had occasion to dig an elementary tunnel, 2 feet wide and 2 feet high, with nothing more sophisticated than tin cans, wriggling forwards and backwards in a claustrophobic space, in a fetid atmosphere, cannot possibly understand what the experience is like. Those few of us who have had occasion to do so were probably slightly mad! Of the twenty original volunteers, some withdrew, either from illness or claustrophobia, to be replaced by others. The work continued, albeit slowly.

By the middle of May it was estimated that a total length of about 50 feet would be sufficient to ensure that the exit would clear the barbed wire fencing and take us safely into the field beyond, but only just. The crop growing in that field was watched anxiously and soon identified as wheat. By mid-June it would be tall enough to hide crawling bodies. Searchlights constantly swept along the outer fences after twilight, so it would be a tricky operation for the escapees to run, one by one, across the frequently lit area, before reaching the haven of darkness. Each such dash would need to be timed to coincide with the brief dark intervals between the sweeping beams.

One reason why we felt it necessary to shorten the tunnel was one that had not been thought of! After only a few days of excavation, the interior of the tunnel began to darken, so that the job in hand became more and more difficult. Some form of lighting was necessary if the diggers were to see what they were doing, and indeed to maintain a straight line. One wag suggested we should beg, borrow or steal a searchlight, but this was ill received, while a shortage of glow-worms precluded that form of illumination. It was soon decided that Jim Hobbs's bribable guard should be approached with a view to obtaining a few candles and a box or two of matches. The need could be explained easily. The lights in the huts were turned off after dark and it was sometimes necessary for an inmate to visit the urinals during the night. How much more considerate to others it would be to do so without making a noise in stumbling towards the objective. So, in exchange for a packet of cigarettes, candles and matches were obtained.

Progress continued, but even more slowly as the tunnel lengthened. Fortunately for the purpose in hand, we diggers were all very slim, even skinny, because of the meagre diet, but even so the laboured crawling to the work-face, empty tin in hand, and the even more laboured crawling backwards on knees and elbows, with a full tin in each hand, was a time-consuming procedure. Our target was to clear 2 feet per day. That does not sound very much, nor is it, until you realise that the soil dug out and transported amounts to 8 cubic feet. A medium-sized can holds about 45 cubic inches, so it was necessary to dig out and transport about 300 cans-full to reach that daily target. It was also necessary to dispose of the soil. This then, was a further reason to shorten the tunnel, as the labourers became even wearier and output decreased. Another fact that had not been considered was the shortage of fresh air as the tunnel became longer. In spite of the increasing difficulty, the tunnel lengthened by about a foot per day and spirits became higher. Optimists estimated that an upward shaft could be excavated by mid-June, while the more cautious reckoned that the end of June was a more realistic target.

During the first week of June, when it was calculated that the tunnel had reached a point somewhere below the first rolls of the outer barbed wire, the Germans demonstrated their childish sense of humour and their capacity for deceit. One fine morning, when the first shift had begun their labours, the look-out was surprised by the rapid arrival of an armoured truck, from which descended, equally rapidly, several guards armed with rifles, bayonets fixed. Four invaded the privacy of the privy, while two remained on guard outside. The two labourers in the tunnel were invited to come out, somewhat impolitely, prodded to the waiting vehicle, and taken away. Other prisoners did not see them again, but it was hoped they had been transferred to another camp no worse than this one. It was known, although no one seemed to know *how* it was known, that a camp only a few miles north was a concentration camp, mainly for Jews. Surely the two would not have been transferred to that place?

The occupants of Hut 57 were then paraded and informed, rather smugly, that the Commandant and his officers had known of the existence of the tunnel since the first soil had been removed, but as he had no wish to spoil the prisoners' enjoyment, they had been allowed to continue. Now he intended to give them the pleasure of filling in the tunnel again, using the available contents below the seats of the remaining lavatories. Of course, they could decline – but if they did so it was regrettable that no food would be made available until they agreed to his suggestion. The inmates of the hut, who nevertheless decided that a short period of unpleasantness was vastly preferable to further deprivation, did not appreciate this infantile sense of humour. Thus the tunnel was filled in, very sportingly, by several airmen who had not been involved in the excavation, but who took the view that enough was enough for those who had participated. Surprisingly neither the commandant nor his officers took any further disciplinary action against the occupants of Hut 57. There was little point in speculating how it had all gone wrong. Had the guard reported the bribery in obtaining overalls and candles? Had the comings and goings from the latrines had been noted? Had a German in RAF uniform been planted in our hut? Those seemed to be the main possibilities. It had to be admitted that the captors had at least ensured that several of their troublesome charges had been kept out of further mischief for a while. Our disappointment was great, to say the least. All that work – and hope – for nothing. However, we realised that we must not allow ourselves to become too despondent; despondency could lead to despair, and that must be avoided at all costs. After all, we had caused considerable trouble to our captors. We also reflected that a successful escape from the confines of the camp would have been only the first of three difficult stages; the long journey through Germany would have been extremely hazardous, as would egress through any of the closely guarded borders.

Other attempts to escape were made by those in other huts. One hopeful warrant officer concealed himself in the refuse being taken from the confines of the camp by escorted Russians, perhaps inspired by the efforts of Hut 57. Although he did manage to escape from the confines of the camp and then from the cart, he was soon recaptured, possibly because of the less than delicate perfume he emitted. His courage in taking this extreme method was much admired, although close proximity to his person was avoided until he had washed his clothes and himself in the cold-water troughs provided in the hut. Two other airmen exchanged clothes and sleeping quarters with privates from an Army hut. These privates were occasionally sent out of the camp on escorted working parties, labouring on the adjoining fields, so there was always the possibility that an escape could be effected. Alas, no opportunity arose, and after a week or so the pair returned to their original hut and their friends. They consoled themselves with the memories of fresh air, fresh surroundings and some food purloined from the crops in the fields in which they had worked.

It was around this time that the Camp Commandant informed us, via the senior British officer, that the German High Command had issued orders to the effect that future escapees, from *any* camp, would be shot when captured. This was the reaction to a recent mass escape from Stalag Luft 3, about which we had heard from new arrivals. This edict was rather discouraging, but we rejoiced at this sign of panic among our hosts; escapes and attempted escapes were evidently causing them much trouble.

News of the progress of the war filtered through as new prisoners were brought to the camp. These irregular arrivals were our only source of any information, as of course there were no radios or newspapers. In the middle of June a fresh batch of captured Allied airmen brought the glad tidings of the successful landings in France after the D-Day operations. Spirits soared and 'goon-baiting' intensified. Although no one was optimistic enough to think that the war would be over in a few weeks, at least the end seemed to be in sight. Then, gradually, more and more American Flying Fortresses were seen in the skies during the day. On one occasion Allied fighters strafed the camp; the toilets at the end of Hut 57 were hit, but fortunately no one was hurt. Evidently the camp was mistaken for an army barracks.

Now, at least, there was something to talk about. When a group of young men are confined to a small space for months and months, with no news of the outside world, no experiences of any kind to relate, no line-shooting to do, and no conquests to describe, stimulating conversation does become difficult, if not impossible.

One fine morning the first few to leave the hut for their daily exercise walking around the compound came dashing back quickly, exhorting all to come and look outside. Soon most of the occupants of Hut 57 and other huts too were lined up along the inner boundary wire, gazing longingly across the adjoining field. It was truly a sight for sore eyes. A solitary German woman, young and buxom, was hoeing some 200 yards away. Perhaps such intense interest was understandable, as many of the inmates of the camp had not seen a woman for two or three years! Some of the airmen stayed a long time, just looking, until the young woman was approached by a man, probably the farmer, and led away from the ogling stares.

One effect of the advance of the Allies across France was the increasing rarity of Red Cross parcels to augment the diet of bread, soup and acorn coffee. Even the issue of bread was reduced to one loaf for ten inmates. Those who shared each loaf would gather round the day's sharer, who would divide the bread into ten portions, as equally as possible. A roster ensured that turns to choose were in strict rotation, the sharer taking the last piece. He then had the privilege of first choice the following day. It was sad, even demeaning, that such measures had to be taken, but every crumb was important to hungry young men. Hunger became an obsession, so that we thought of little else, yet our sense of comradeship was so deep-seated and highly valued that there were few quarrels over the division of rations, or indeed about anything else.

During the summer months of 1944 the attitude of the German officers and guards had remained arrogant, but gradually we noticed a change. Fewer rifle butts were viciously used by the younger guards who had previously been only too willing to vent their spite on those who had dared to oppose their idol and leader, Herr Hitler. The more mature guards had always been more amenable, and they became even more so as they realised that eventual defeat was much more than a remote possibility.

One day in early autumn I received, through Red Cross channels, a present from Olive, my girlfriend back home. I had had cigarettes, also through the Red Cross, from her before, as well as from parents, other relatives and friends; while they had been much appreciated, this present, a blanket, was prized indeed. I could now take off my uniform blouse and trousers at night, and keep reasonably warm. Wearing the same uniform day after day, night after night, for almost a year was not only uncomfortable but extremely unhygienic. Rolled in my new blanket, even the straw mattress was more comfortable. I was the envy of many!

By this time most inmates had become inured to the discomfort and the lack of belongings. Those who have never gone without the basic requirements do not and cannot imagine life without them. Taken for granted are such needs as a change of underwear and socks, a spare handkerchief, comb, toothbrush, soap, flannel, razor, scissors (for nails and haircuts), towel, toilet rolls, sleeping apparel, sheets, a bed, a chair, hot water, cutlery, newspapers, books, radio, and of course a cup of tea with milk and sugar. The prisoners could not, however, become used to hunger. As hunger increased, so energy decreased. A plain white slice of bread, preferably with butter and cheese to accompany it, became a day-dream to savour; luxuries such as meat, fish, fruit and vegetables were not nearly so important as that plain white slice of bread!

As energy decreased, health deteriorated. Many confined themselves to their bunks for most of the day as well as during the night. Fewer and fewer took any exercise. Some died and were taken out of the camp for burial. New arrivals brought further news of the Allied advances on all fronts. Even these glad tidings failed to inspire many for whom food, food, food, was the only concern.

Christmas 1944 was just another date in the calendar. Although no calendars were available to the prisoners, the days were counted so that the date was always known. Early 1945 was extremely cold. The meagre ration of fuel for the tortoise stove in each hut was completely discontinued; our one consolation was that the Germans were also suffering the same shortages as their resources became more and more depleted.

Soon the first American airmen arrived at the camp, and they were in a sorry state. Many had dysentery, which spread among the existing inmates. More prisoners died and their bodies were taken away. It was better not to think of the poor Russians and Jews, who were even less well treated. It was reported that an Alsation dog had been put into one of the Russian huts to quieten the noisy inmates; the next morning its skin and bones had been found outside. It was also reported that retribution was swift and severe. There was no way of telling whether the story was true or invented.

The coldness intensified, as did hunger; the days seemed interminable. However, the now rapid advances of troops from the west and now from the east did begin to cheer us, and we began to be more optimistic that release from our tribulations was imminent. Then, one day in mid-April, as the weather improved, all British and American prisoners, some 5,000 or 6,000 in total, were paraded in a single compound. The Commandant, who spoke English, addressed us through a loudspeaker. He announced that he had received instructions from the German High Command that all prisoners of war were to be executed. This was very distressing news to the assembled airmen and soldiers, but before we had time to realise that such an announcement was quite unnecessary, as a mass execution could be carried out without any such warning, he paused, then went on to declare that he had no intention of obeying this order. He trusted that his clemency and humanity would be remembered, if and when the American or British troops liberated the camp. Those gathered there that day cheered, not because the Commandant had been so lenient, but because liberation must now be close and the war in Europe almost over. For the next week or so the guards continued to guard and the searchlights to search, but it became obvious that almost all the German captors were now completely demoralised. In most, arrogance was replaced by attempts at comradeship, which we rejected of course. A few still refused to believe defeat was near.

St George's Day, 23 April 1945, was a date to be remembered for the rest of our lives. In the very early morning the sound of exploding shells and machine-gun fire was heard throughout the camp. Prisoners awoke and warily opened hut doors. No guards, no accompanying dogs, were to be seen. The whole camp appeared to be deserted; there were no searchlights operating and the sentry boxes were unoccupied. Still we wondered what could have happened. Then the outer gates were flung open and a troop of Cossacks rode through, armed to the teeth with revolvers, rifles and swords festooned around them and with hand-grenades on their belts. Among them were a few young but tough-looking young women! They were singing loudly to the recognisable tune 'Song of the Plains'. The locked gates to the Russian compound were contemptuously broken and those imprisoned therein flooded out in greeting. In spite of their dreadful physical condition, they were herded out, presumably to join the advancing Russian army, of which the Cossacks were in the vanguard. The gates to the Jewish compound were also broken. Nothing was said to the remaining prisoners and we were left to our own devices, while the mounted troops departed.

Our first priority was to find food. What little there was in the camp kitchens was soon devoured, but the outer gates were wide open, so a large adjacent field of rhubarb became the focus of our attention. It was truly amazing how quickly the huge crop of rhubarb, not yet quite fit for harvesting, was completely cleared. It was not quite so amazing how quickly the almost-starving population of the camp suffered the effects of raw rhubarb on empty stomachs. Probably there were many who would never again eat rhubarb, and those who did would certainly remember this feast. To this day I am not at all fond of rhubarb.

Some of the occupants of Hut 57 decided to walk to the nearby small town of Muhlberg, some 2 miles distant, in search of something to eat. As we left the camp we noticed a row of poplar trees on the right-hand side of the road, which appeared to be adorned with hanging objects, one on each tree. As we approached closer, we could see that the hanging objects were uniformed Germans. They included the Commandant and the other officers and guards from the camp. Evidently the Cossacks had meted out summary justice, and the Commandant's plea for clemency had served for naught. The remainder of the journey to the town was not uneventful, either. Dead Germans were evident in several places, all men. Some were uniformed, others civilians. Some showed no sign of visible damage, while others had neat, black, round holes in their foreheads. These sights were most unpleasant, even though Germany had been, and still was, the enemy.

The town, a very pretty one, stood near the eastern bank of the Elbe. It appeared to be deserted. Despite our condition and the circumstances, we hesitated to break into houses to find food. It did not seem right or fair to do so. We tried knocking on one or two doors, but with no success. However, we did find, eventually, a baker's shop that had been looted, probably by the advancing Russians. In it was some black rye bread! Actually, it was reasonably tasty, as it was about a month fresher than that which had formed the bulk of our rations. So having eaten, we returned to the camp, to see what was happening. On the way back we noticed a group of Russian ex-prisoners lying beside a pig they had evidently slaughtered and on which they had been feasting. Their stomachs were grossly distended and they all looked very unwell; closer inspection revealed they were all dead. On reaching the camp, we discovered that precisely nothing had happened in our absence.

The senior British officer called the Army and RAF personnel together during the late afternoon. He told us all that he had been informed of the following facts. The British and American armies had crossed the Rhine and were making good progress eastwards; the Russian armies had reached the River Elbe (this, of course, we knew already) and were now heading northwards towards Berlin. There was no doubt that the war with Germany would soon be over. In the meantime the inmates of the camp were advised to stay where they were for the time being. The Russian liberators would make every effort to ensure that sufficient food was available for the immediate future, until arrangements could be made for repatriation. Alternatively those who wished to take the chance could attempt to make their own way westwards. A few of us, mainly RAF personnel with serviceable shoes, decided we had had quite enough of the camp and would prefer to take the risk of passing through the Russian and German lines in order to reach the British or American armies. We informed the senior British officer of our intention, collected our possessions (which amounted to practically nothing!) and set out. We took whatever food we could find, stowed in our cardboard boxes. I also took my blanket!

Ten of us travelled in a group along the east bank of the Elbe for several miles, through what appeared to be deserted countryside. We had no watches, but by the position of the sun in the sky we knew we had perhaps 2 hours of daylight left; during that time we would need to find food and drink and somewhere to spend the night in comparative safety.

Our physical condition was such that the short distance we had already walked had exhausted every one of us, so it was advisable to find somewhere to rest fairly soon. Fortunately what appeared to be a farmhouse lay ahead, so by mutual agreement we decided to investigate, with the prospect of satisfying our requirements. In the best tradition of the films we had watched in the dim and distant past, two of our number crawled ahead to 'case the joint', while the others waited in a ditch beside the roadside hedge. Our luck was in. After a short time the two scouts returned and reported that indeed it was a small farmhouse, with outbuildings, and that the premises appeared to be deserted. The whole group then approached the house and cautiously entered via an open door, which creaked eerily on its rusty hinges in the slight evening breeze. Quietly we filed along a corridor, passing open doors on either side. By unspoken arrangement we explored each of the four rooms in pairs; the living-cum-dining room contained a plain wooden table with six chairs, a clock, still ticking, a picture on the wall and nothing else; the front room, likewise undisturbed, contained a sofa and four easy chairs, some ornaments on the mantelpiece over the fireplace, and a few pictures on the walls. It seemed likely that this room was used only on Sundays. What was evidently a scullery contained a sink and the usual utensils one would expect to see; the fourth room, a kitchen, had a well-polished kitchen range for cooking, a scrubbed wooden table and a pantry. The pantry was empty. All the downstairs rooms were neat and tidy, and very clean.

The airmen who explored upstairs soon wished they had not. The bathroom was empty, but the three bedrooms were not. The farmer and his wife, aged perhaps about 50, were lying on their double bed, the sheets thrown off. The farmer was in his nightshirt, the wife was naked; both were dead, their throats cut from ear to ear. Both had horrified expressions, indicating they had not died in their sleep. The second bedroom provided an even more unpleasant sight. The occupants, two small children, one in a bed and one in a cot, had been ruthlessly murdered with knives or bayonets. The third bedroom was probably that of a daughter of the older couple, and mother of the two small children. Until recently, she had been a very attractive young woman, blonde and shapely. The two airmen who entered that room felt sick. They would never, ever, forget the sight; even if they lived to a ripe old age, her terrified face and mutilated body would still haunt their nightmares. This German family had not been the enemy, not of the British and western allies, nor of the Russians. Could members of the advancing Russian armies have possibly performed these atrocities? There was no other feasible explanation.

Upset and sorry as we were, life had to go on. We congregated in the living room to decide on our plans. As there was nothing we could do for the murdered family, we must leave them where they were. No doubt survivors in the area would find them and arrange for a proper burial. It seemed callous, but we had to think of ourselves; our actions in the immediate future would determine whether we had a longer future. Our priority was clearly the obtaining of food and water and shelter for the night, but none of us wanted to stay in the farmhouse! As it happened, all three of our requirements were soon satisfied. In an adjoining barn we found hens and hens' eggs, while in the corner of the same structure were piles of hay. A pump in the yard produced cool, clear water. The small stock of food we had set out with that afternoon had long since been eaten, but although we were very hungry, we knew that we must not over-eat if we were to avoid the fate of the Russians who had eaten so well but so unwisely earlier that day. So we made do with raw eggs and cold water. None of us fancied killing a chicken, plucking it and eating it raw! Hungry as we were, we were aware of the probable consequences of over-indulging. By this time it was dusk, so we stayed in the barn and made plans for the following day. Commonsense dictated we should split up. Obviously ten scruffy but generally uniformed young men would attract more undesirable attention than two such individuals, so we decided to proceed on the morrow in twos. Each pair would endeavour to cross the Elbe and then make progress westwards. With luck and a bit of skill we would be able to pass through the Russian lines and then the lines of the retreating German army to reach advancing British or American troops. We had a fair idea of our position, calculating that we were about 40 miles east of the town of Halle. The distance to probable safety was no great problem, but the obstacles in those miles seemed a bit daunting. Deciding to depart from the farm in the morning at different times, we said our farewells and lay down to sleep.

I was fortunate in having as my partner Jim Hobbs, whose fluency in the German language could help on our journey. In the morning Jim found two small canvas bags in an outhouse, so we transferred into them our few possessions, including four or five hens' eggs, from our cardboard boxes. We set off last, just as dawn was breaking; I never did like getting up early! Travelling northward, parallel to the Elbe, we looked for a bridge and after only a mile or two saw one in the distance. Cautiously moving closer, we noticed two Russian tanks on the near bank, guns pointing threateningly across the bridge. Coming to the conclusion that all bridges over the river would be similarly guarded, we decided there was nothing else for it but to approach, hoping that our uniforms would be recognised and that trigger-happy troops would refrain from firing. Apparently the two of us, obviously unarmed, appeared to pose no threat, so we were allowed to approach. We pointed to our uniforms and said 'English, English airmen'. Jim tried the same formula in German too, which could have been a serious mistake! It was almost an anticlimax when a Russian officer, lolling by the bridge, simply waved us over and said nothing, nothing at all, not even 'Good morning, and what a beautiful morning it is for a walk before breakfast.' So we simply walked over the bridge, although it must be admitted I had an itchy feeling in my back, or wherever this type of apprehensive feeling originates, that we might not reach the other side. Having crossed the Elbe, we walked along the road until we were out of sight of the bridge and then promptly sat on a bank to recover from what might have been a dangerous escapade. We almost felt cheated!

As the bridge had been guarded, it seemed likely that the Russian army was not ahead of us; it was equally likely that they intended to consolidate on the eastern bank of the Elbe. It therefore seemed quite probable that we would now have to negotiate our way through German troops retreating from the Russians, towards German troops retreating from the British or American armies! In the event it was much less difficult than that; in fact, it was so easy as to be unbelievable – a 'piece of cake' in RAF parlance. There we were, sitting on the bank minding our own business, when two American jeeps crammed with well-armed GIs approached along the road towards the bridge we had just crossed. As we rose rapidly to our feet, the jeeps stopped. From one an American soldier called across to the other, 'Just look at those two poor buggers!' Jim and I looked round to see who he was referring to, but could see no one else in the vicinity. Perhaps the Yanks were suffering from battle fatigue! Despite the rude remark, we were overjoyed to see them. We quickly identified ourselves and were lifted bodily into one of the jeeps, which was turned in the road and driven back in the direction whence it had come. The other jeep continued on its journey towards the river, after ascertaining from us that there was nothing of note between them and the Russians encamped on the other side of the Elbe. The GIs orders were to patrol as far as the river, and no further.

The journey to Halle that followed brought us tremendous relief, but our arrival and reception at a requisitioned hotel in the captured town was pure bliss, and the fresh white rolls, with real butter and real cheese, that we were each given was manna from Heaven. I had dreamed of such food for the last year and a half; now it was real. We were also each given a steaming hot cup of real coffee, with real milk and sugar. That, too, was appreciated far more than our liberators could have imagined. Having been treated so kindly, we could hardly ask for a cup of tea instead; we did not know, then, that Americans hardly ever drank tea! We were not allowed to eat anything else for the present, which was probably a wise decision, even though it was not fully appreciated at the time. Then followed hot showers and a debugging process, also greatly welcomed. Our clothes, such as they were, were taken away and undoubtedly consigned to an incinerator, but not before I had asked if my blanket could be debugged and saved for me. We were each then issued with a complete American army uniform, in a fetching shade of tan; even the underwear was of that colour. We were given pyjamas and escorted to a room with real beds, real sheets and blankets. We felt we were in Heaven in such luxury and then we slept, slept and slept.

The next day, after rising and washing, Jim and I were taken to a mess and given breakfast Again, we didn't have much, but the fruit juice, slice of buttered toast and coffee were really delicious. It wasn't that our hosts were short of food; rather they considered it important to introduce proper victuals gradually to our contracted stomachs (which were strangely distended on the exterior).

Then followed an exchange of information. We described our recent experiences to an intelligence officer, while he in turn gave us news of wider events. He told us that it had been agreed that the Russian armies would advance to the Elbe and no further, while the Americans would do likewise. Berlin had not yet fallen, but would do so soon. The war in Europe was in its last stages and until it was over all rescued prisoners would stay where they were. In the meantime we would be nursed back to health, as we weighed only about 7 stone each. We would be given paper to write letters home, and we would be issued with other luxuries such as a comb, a razor, a toothbrush and toothpaste. We should rest as much as possible and our intake of food would be increased progressively.

Jim and I wrote to our parents. These letters would not be censored, so we could now report our whereabouts, our new-found freedom and our expectations for the future without fear of erasure. Understandably only one letter each was permitted. We had thorough medical examinations, we rested and read, and we ate. We were joined by several other liberated prisoners, who did not look at all well on their arrival; in fact, they appeared to be emaciated 'poor buggers'. It was difficult to believe that the two of us must have looked like that only a week or so ago. Many of the newcomers had journeyed from the same camp, including four who had begun their travels with Jim and me.

On 8 May 1945, V-E day, Germany capitulated. Adolf Hitler had already been reported dead. In a week or so arrangements would be made to repatriate the former prisoners, first to Brussels and then home. It seemed almost unbelievable that the past was an unpleasant experience that could now be just an unpleasant memory. It would remain a memory of course, one that would never be forgotten.

During the following weeks we freed airmen gradually regained health and strength, thanks to the kind and compassionate treatment we received at the hands of the medical staff and all the other American personnel with whom we came in contact. We began to eat such luxuries as bacon and egg, pancakes, fruit, pies and cake. We began to put on weight. We also had plenty of time to think.

I, no doubt among many others, began to realise we had all learned a very significant lesson, a lesson in values, which are so often taken for granted. Possessions were not that important; what really mattered were the basic necessities of life. Freedom is a vital need, as are friends. One must have enough food and water in order to exist, while good health is very important. Shelter and warmth are other essential needs. Nothing else is absolutely necessary. Something less tangible is also necessary: a sense of humour! I vowed that never, ever again, would I complain at any lack of material possessions, and I hoped fervently that I would be able to keep that promise to myself.

In about the middle of May several Dakotas flew in to the nearby airfield to ferry the ex-prisoners to Brussels, from which town we were transported, also by air, to an aerodrome near Oxford. Even the unsentimental among us were affected when the white cliffs of Dover were seen ahead! All the repatriated airmen were then transported to Cardington for re-kitting. The first person I met on my arrival was a warrant officer from my own village in Norfolk, who had been based there for much of the war in charge of stores. The second was Ivan! 'What kept you?' was his greeting. He had been there for two days, having been sensible enough to wait at the Stalag until he was taken over the Elbe by Russian troops and handed over to the Allies. Those of us who had left the camp to make their own way need not have bothered!

By the end of May most of the British repatriates were home with their families, on extended leave and double rations for six weeks! Real freedom was wonderful, good fresh food was really appreciated, a proper bed with sheets as well as blankets was bliss and the weak wartime beer was nectar. Many of the repatriates would recover completely from their wartime experiences, while some would continue to suffer physically or mentally. Some quickly returned to civilian life, while others decided they would like to remain in the armed services, at least for the time being. Many would meet erstwhile comrades again, others would not. Many would marry, while others would remain bachelors. The end of an era was the beginning of another. None would ever forget the time they spent as guests of the Third Reich.

I was one of those who did marry and did contact some of my wartime comrades again. I joined the teaching profession, married Olive and we continued to live in Norfolk. We had a son and a daughter, of whom we were and still are, very proud, and grandchildren, of whom we are also proud. In enjoying a full and busy life, we had little time to reminisce about the past, although naturally old times were referred to occasionally. While we would never forget our wartime experiences, we chose not to remember the harrowing periods. Fortunately it seems part of human nature to have a selective and optimistic memory.

We three survivors of the crew of E-Easy kept in touch for several years, exchanging occasional letters and Christmas cards, but almost inevitably the letters became fewer and gradually ceased. Jock did phone me, quite unexpectedly, in the early 1990s to tell me he was dying of cancer. I then heard of his death.

The sixty or so years that followed the war have no part in this narrative, so these few lines are sufficient as far as I am concerned. Similarly the lives and fortunes of the others who were thrown together during the war are irrelevant to this story, which reached its conclusion when a 49 Squadron Association reunion took place more than fifty years later at Fiskerton. There had been other reunions over the years, but I had no idea that there was such an association until I heard it mentioned on a radio programme inviting those who had served on the now disbanded squadron to contact the secretary, Tom Gatfield. I did so, and was warmly welcomed.

I arrived at the car-park of the Carpenters' Arms in good time for the service at the parish church and the formal dedication of the bound book of remembrance containing the names of the 906 airmen of the squadron who had given their lives during the war. As I parked my modest saloon I noticed that several cars were already there, ranging from a Bentley and two Jaguars to a battered and elderly Mini. About forty men and a few women were gathered in groups, chatting; I joined them, introduced myself and in turn others came up and introduced themselves. I recognised no one's face or name, nor was I recognised. Sadly, I reflected, they all looked elderly, but of course, we were all elderly now.

We all walked to the church, to join many people from the village. The church was full and the service a moving one. Before the service began, I sat quietly in the pew, reflecting on old times and comparing, or rather contrasting, the old times with the present day. Nowadays many young men who play football for a living, earn hundreds of thousands of pounds a year, and are called heroes by the media and their fans for scoring goals. The young men whose names were inscribed in the book of remembrance earned a small fraction of that in a year, if they were lucky enough to live that long. Society in general had certainly changed, as had values. Money and possessions were gods now to so many.

Nowadays, so many young people took drugs – drugs were almost unheard of 50 years ago. The only drugs we had were the tablets that helped to keep the airmen alert on a long trip over enemy territory. In those days grass was green and was mown, ecstasy was a state of extreme pleasure, coke was put on the fire and a joint was a piece of meat. Yes, times have certainly changed, I thought, but change is inevitable. Anyway, I was harbouring unkind thoughts in the comparison; only a small minority of today's youngsters were addicted to drugs, while the great majority behaved much in the same way as we used to behave. After all, we did not always behave that well, I mused. When we were not on duty, the local residents must surely have found some of our conduct weird, if not reprehensible, particularly when we had 'had a few'. Whatever must they have thought of Wilf and his companions, when he chatted to a non-existent dog! Whatever did they think of our RAF slang: 'wizard', for first-rate, 'a black', for an error of judgement, 'black-outs', for WAAF underwear, 'blood-wagon', for an ambulance, 'close the hangar door', for stop talking shop, 'he's bought it' or 'he got the chop', when someone was killed, 'it's a piece of cake', for it's easy. Any reference to the 'camp bicycle' would have caused great puzzlement to anyone not in the know!

When the service was over, the association members returned to the inn for a chat and a pre-lunch drink. Tom, the efficient and dedicated secretary, had arranged that the Battle of Britain Lancaster 'City of Lincoln' would fly over the old base at noon, so just before that time we all trooped outside. Almost to the second the once-familiar roar of the four Merlin engines presaged the appearance of the last serviceable Lancaster still flying in the UK. Once there had been so many in the skies of Lincolnshire. The Lanc flew sedately over our heads, the pilot dipping the wings in salute. We all watched, we all thought our private thoughts, we all waved. The Lancaster, now elderly too, circled Lincoln and returned, once more dipping its wings, then disappeared in the direction of its base at Coningsby nearby. We returned to the inn for sandwiches and our modest glasses of beer or sherry. How times changed; but after all it was 50-plus years ago that those same men, and perhaps some of the women, had gathered there evening after evening, drinking, chatting and singing songs. I read and re-read the names of my friends: a separate list, compiled painstakingly by 'Uncle' Will Hay, the chairman of the association, showed me that the remains of the four members of my crew who had been killed on that fateful night so many years ago were interred at the

Reichswald Forest War Cemetery near Kleve in Germany, having been initially buried in the Nordfriedhof, Dusseldorf.

After a while, before embarking on the journey home, I drove down the quiet country lane to find the old airfield, passing two fairly new housing estates on the way. Arriving at the entrance, I switched off the engine and sat there thinking and remembering. Surprisingly a few of the old buildings were still there, albeit in a dilapidated condition. I recognised the officers' and sergeants' messes, facing the road, and saw that other buildings remained beyond them. As the place did not look particularly private, on impulse I drove in and parked the car. Several lorries were scattered on the forecourt but there were no signs of occupancy. I walked a few yards to inspect the area more closely, when a man and a dog appeared from around a corner. The dog wagged his tail in greeting.

'Hello: can I help you?' said the man, who appeared to be about 60 years of age. 'I'm sorry to have intruded, but I was stationed here during the war and could not resist a look,' I replied. 'You're more than welcome. My name is John Brown and I run my transport business from here. Do come in and have a closer inspection.' We walked in to the old sergeants' mess; pictures of Lancasters covered the walls and items of memorabilia were scattered on the benches. Incongruously a large engine reposed near the centre of the floor. Mr Brown explained. As a young lad he had lived close by during the war, and had watched the bombers take off, night after night, and listened out for their return. In those days the village had revolved around the airfield. After the war he had watched as the runways, control tower and hangars were removed and the fields restored to arable farming. As his business prospered, he decided to buy the remaining land and buildings, using them as a base for his business as a contractor. He had vowed to keep the now dilapidated buildings in their present state, as his own little tribute to the squadron.

I signed the visitors' book that he held out; looking through the names, with addresses far and wide, I recognised no one that I had known. 'Before I take you on a tour of the rest of the buildings,' said Mr Brown, 'I must tell you about my ghost. Even if you do not believe in the supernatural, please hear me out. The mess really is haunted. You see that engine; perhaps you recognise it as an old Merlin engine from a Lancaster. I found it near the site of one of the squadron's hangars. I had it brought in, years ago, intending to strip it down and smarten it up a bit, but I never did get around to doing anything with it. Well, one morning, two or three years ago, when I came in, it had disappeared! Just like that – gone! I just could not believe it, as it was not possible to lift it manually. Besides, who would want an old aircraft engine? I dashed through to the office to tell my wife and she came in to look. I wasn't away for more than a minute, but when we came back, there it was in its usual place. Obviously, she thought I had been dreaming. Then tools began disappearing during the night, and appeared again the following morning in a different place from where I had put them. Joan, my wife, was convinced of this after I suggested that she put the tools somewhere of her own choosing when we left the premises after work, and to check for herself the following morning. She did so and sure enough, the tools were in a different place. The ghost seemed attracted to my pipe, too. I would put it down and find it somewhere else later. There was nothing malicious and we both quite enjoyed the game; it was like playing hide-and-seek with a child.'

Mr Brown continued: 'Then, for a time, my ghost became unfriendly. Tools were taken and not replaced for days. My pipe disappeared and I never did find that. The telephone in the office, next door, was unplugged and the computer, on stand-by, was turned off. I wondered why, because my ghost had always been such a friendly joker. Then, suddenly, there were no more unkind pranks after I had returned the safety helmet I wear for demolition jobs to its usual place, over there.' He pointed to a corner bench. 'Surely there could be no connection between a missing helmet and a ghost's irritation? Anyway, I left the helmet there and used another one. I cannot think why a ghost would value a pipe and a helmet, or for that matter, play hide-and-seek with an old engine.' He insisted that it was all true: 'I'm not kidding, you know, it's all true.'

Of course, I showed interest in what Mr Brown was telling me, making suitable comments, but I did not air my views as to a possible explanation that had occurred to me during the tale; it just seemed too far-fetched! How on earth (although perhaps that is the wrong phrase) could anyone believe that a youngster of 18, killed in 1943, had come back to haunt his old squadron's premises? If his ghost did exist, why did he (or it) wait 50 years before coming back to his old mess? It just did not make sense.

Just then the dog came through the doorway, wagging his tail. Mr Brown told me that he spent a lot of time in the old mess, just lying there quietly. Sometimes, if he was outside, he would prick up his ears as if listening, then run into the mess and wait expectantly. 'So you are still at it, Wilf, old friend,' I murmured. Only this time the dog was visible and Wilf wasn't.

While driving home from Lincolnshire, I realised that my experiences at the old airfield during the last hour or two had caused me to reconsider my views on the supernatural. It wasn't that I had been a complete sceptic, as I had read and heard of several incidents that seemingly defied logical explanation. Nevertheless I did have my doubts, because I had never had such an experience myself. So much has been said and written about ghosts and spirits, but the only spirits I had contacted were poured from a bottle! So many hoaxes had been perpetrated, too, which hardly encouraged belief. However, I do accept that we still know little of the mysteries of life and the universe, let alone an after-life or the possibility of reincarnation. Examining the evidence, I became convinced, at least partly, that Wilf's ghost was genuine, so to speak. The pipe, the helmet and the dog, all reminders of Wilf's constant companions, both on ops and on squadron premises, seemed to provide too many coincidences, and Wilf was certainly a joker! Mr Brown and I had never met before, so his story could not have been an elaborate leg-pull. There was no possibility that he could know anything about Wilf. Why did his dog visit the old sergeants' mess so frequently? Surely there must be a rational explanation? But I could not think of one!

A year or so later Olive and I travelled to Lincolnshire for a short holiday and Olive expressed a desire to visit the old squadron premises. On our arrival we met Mrs Brown. Her husband was away on business, but she was quite happy to show us round the buildings. In passing she mentioned that they used to have a mischievous ghost, but he had suddenly disappeared about a year ago! I wondered if Wilf had been waiting for a fellow crew member. I began to wonder even more about the supernatural.

For more than fifty years I had no intention of writing about my wartime experiences, partly because they were similar to those of so many others and partly because I had no talent for writing, except for personal and business letters. As I found these particular occurrences half a century after the war so fascinating and extraordinary I decided to relate them. However, without recounting some of the wartime events that preceded my later visits to the squadron premises, it would have meant little to any readers and would certainly have been too short to be of any interest to anyone. Therefore I decided I must begin at the beginning, or rather from the time that we set out on that fateful night, 56 years ago at the time of writing. The facts are basically true, except that some names and some places may not have been properly identified. For example, I do know that I was posted to various other RAF bases, including Saxby and Swinderby during my training. I remember most of the places, but cannot remember the purpose of the postings. Memories do fade after all that time, and the detail of some of the described happenings may have been forgotten or even suppressed for more than half a century. Had I claimed complete veracity, no doubt I would have been challenged on some aspects, or even committed some kind of infringement of the rules, in writing a section of my autobiography. Readers must now decide for themselves whether the story itself is completely true, whether it is almost true, or whether the writer is suffering from senile dementia. By the way, although I am not sentimental by nature, the blanket did service in my car boot for many years, and I still have a small piece of a parachute and a tattered receipt for an Omega watch! I wonder what happened to that watch?

CHAPTER SIX

First Men Down

The Rattlesden-based 447th Bombardment Group entered the maelstrom of European air combat in December 1943, and flew its initial mission on Christmas Eve without marring the following day's festivities with the loss of any aircraft. Such luck could not last and the Group's second mission on 30 December 1943 would see the first men shot down on board a brand-new B-17 named 'Maid to Please' by its pilot, First Lieutenant Ed Beaty.

Pictured on 30 October 1943, this is Crew 54, the first 447BG crew to fall in combat. (Left to right): Lieutenant Julian Y. Schrero; Lieutenant Merle L. Kent; Lieutenant Joseph J. Lamansky; Lieutenant Lowell A. Doan; Staff Sergeant Howard D. May; Staff Sergeant Homer L. Miller; Staff Sergeant Dee L. Troxell; Staff Sergeant John C. Bitzer; Staff Sergeant Herman F. Holland; Staff Sergeant Walter E. Dickerman. (*John Bitzer*)

Such were the vagaries of crew assignment – 'the decision of some desk jockey' – that Ed was not given his 'own' aircraft to fly that day. He recorded in his diary: '12-30-43. Briefed at 4:30 AM. Attempted to take off for mission to Ludwigshaven, Germany. Assigned an inoperational 873 ship and did not get off.' Ed lived to fight another thirty missions, and his was one of only two original 447BG crews to complete their tours. Ed then flew another forty-seven sorties in P-51s with the Scouting Force, but fate may have taken a different turn had he been given his 'Maid to Please'. Instead she was allocated to First Lieutenant Julian Y. Schrero and his crew. Flying with Schrero was Staff Sergeant John C. Bitzer, who had stretched the odds to be there. He was born, ironically, in Tuebingen, Germany, and when he first attempted to enlist as a Naval Air Cadet, intent on flying the F4U Corsair, he passed the mental tests and most of the physical examination, but was washed out for being too short – by half-an-inch! He was 'fit to be tied', such was his frustration when he returned to his work as a design specialist in General Electric's Cleveland Equipment Plant. Colleagues tried to console him, and one more knowledgeable than the rest offered some advice on how to attain the height required. His friend knew the human frame stretched during sleep and did not readjust to daytime height immediately upon wakening. Johnny should also try the Army Air Corps instead of the Navy, as the Army had no height restrictions that he was aware of. That night Johnny slept virtually on the recruitment centre's doorstep and was first in the following morning. Amazingly, he passed and his diminutive stature was soon found ideal for one of the most difficult air-crew assignments – the ball turret gunner. John Bitzer takes up the story of his first, and only, mission.

You are sound asleep, suddenly the C.Q. [Charge of Quarters] awakens you at 4:30 hours and tells you to drop your teddy bear and grab your socks, you are flying this morning. Breakfast is at 5:00 hours; briefing is at 6:00 hours. This is when you find out what and where your target will be for today. Today we are going to Ludwigshaven, Germany, to bomb the IG Farben chemical factory. You will get intelligence reports on where flak concentration and fighter activities are located, also if there will be any fighter escort. Length of the mission is about eight to nine hours. Type of munitions today are incendiary bombs. You board a truck as a crew and are taken out to the aircraft you are assigned to. Take off is at 8:35 hours.

You visually check guns (I was a ball turret gunner). The ball turret has twin fifty-calibre guns; each has five hundred rounds of ammunition. We get the order to board the plane; the engines start up and check out OK. We taxi to where the planes are assembling and get ready to go. The flare fires and the first plane takes off. As we taxi down the runway the engines are working hard to get the plane off the ground with a full bomb-load. Just as you are running out of runway up you go and keep climbing to a given altitude, which today is 25,000 feet, and form up. At this time I am able to enter my turret. In order to do so you position your guns pointing to the rear and then point straight down. This allows me to open the hatch and enter the turret. After entering you close the hatch and then you can position the turret in any direction. You head over the

Barely 20 years old and marginally too short, John C. Bitzer stretched the odds to enlist. (*John Bitzer*)

English Channel and hope ordnance did a good job and have put your guns in good working order. As you approach France there is no more idle chatter on the intercom except to keep your eyes open and report any fighter sightings. There was an Me110 (a German twin-engined fighter) sitting out of gun range and probably reporting our position, speed and direction to flak batteries and fighter bases. As we fly over France and Belgium little black puffs of flak start to appear and as we come closer the puffs become larger. Every so often a burst of flak comes close and really shakes the plane up. As we approach the target flak ceases and we see fighters coming in from different directions. The whole attack lasts but a few minutes but to us it seems like hours. We approach the IP (Initial Point) where the bombardier takes over and the bomb run begins. This is where we are most vulnerable; no evasive action can be taken while on the bomb run. After 'bombs away' we turn to come home.

It was kind of a repeat coming back until we got to the outskirts of Paris. We were hit by flak, lost an engine and tried to get under the cover of clouds. An Me110 fighter hit us hard. In the ball turret the power went out and panic set in: WHAT DO I DO NOW? You start to think. Oh yes, there is a mechanical means to rotate the turret. Just above my head in the turret are two cranks that can bring the turret guns facing to the rear and down which allows you to open the hatch and exit the turret. I grabbed my chute and snapped it on, saw the radioman was hit bad and fire was raging in the bomb-bay. At this point those up front were not aware of what had happened to us in the rear of the plane and vice-versa. Both waist gunners were ready to exit the waist position and I was the last one out of the rear of the plane just as it exploded. I remember pulling the ripcord and then I blacked out.

Several thousand feet below, farm worker Robert Degrez was beginning another afternoon's work. The weather was typical for a winter's day with high dense clouds helping to keep the climate above freezing and ensuring a slightly more comfortable afternoon on the tractor. The constant drone of aircraft engines was so normal in the skies above Henonville that those on the farm at Le Coudray paid no heed. Then a distinctive change in tone caught Robert's attention, and a note pitched higher than the rest. The aircraft

Robert Degrez, in 1946. He remembered pieces of the aircraft that 'fell from everywhere' and how the crew 'left their youth and their life' on a farm in France that day. (*Robert Degrez*)

themselves were in that other world hidden by cloud, but the sound told Robert that an aeroplane was diving as the shriek of its engines carried far over the landscape. Then came the staccato clatter of cannon and machine-gun fire followed by 'a long and muffled humming sound from quite high', then seconds later an explosion reverberated earthwards. Robert knew immediately that the Boche had caught yet another unfortunate homeward-bound bomber. Then, confirming his fears, odd black shapes tumbled crazily from the clouds as small pieces of wreckage dropped into the surrounding fields. Suddenly the sky seemed full of falling debris as Robert raced to the farm gate. Pieces of wing, sections of aluminium, all tumbled to earth, with the lighter, fluttering fragments seeming to hover before impact as if resisting being robbed of flight. The tail section with its gunner's station smashed into a recently ploughed field some metres from the roadside and close to the farm entrance. The force of its landing broke the tall tail fin which fell to one side of the crumpled fuselage. Robert recognised this but other shattered parts still showering down were unrecognisable, some smearing the sky with ragged, smoky trails, others plummeting like meteorites. Lighter parts drifted as far as Arronville, over 3 miles distant, while the heavy engines slammed into the soil near the Backeland distillery of Henonville, nearly a mile away. This wide distribution of debris confirmed that the bomber had broken apart or blown up at altitude. Had there been any survivors? As if in answer to his question, Robert saw two parachutes. These were not drifting like dandelion-seed over the landscape but falling swiftly, perhaps not fully unfurled, maybe damaged. Even as he stared, one parachute, still 60 feet above the ground, was struck by a piece of falling wreckage and came perilously close to nearby power lines. The unfortunate flier whose parachute had been struck by falling debris made no movement to break his fall or protect himself – perhaps he was dead or unconscious. He thumped heavily to earth near the barn and his body bounced several times before he lay still with the folds of his parachute now settling gently over him, like a shroud.

The other survivor, co-pilot Second Lieutenant Merle L. Kent, had already detached his harness and was scooping up his parachute. Despite his heavy landing and a bullet wound to his foot, Kent was still mobile and helped Robert pull the still unconscious Johnny Bitzer into the barn where they were hidden from view as the victorious Me110 arrived to circle overhead, undoubtedly marking their position. The co-pilot, obviously in pain, used one of the morphine syrettes from his emergency kit while Robert went to check for other survivors in the bomber's crushed rear fuselage. Crossing the field, Robert and other rescuers found one crewman wedged in the tail gunner's position; his head was covered in blood but he was still alive and just able to move. Other farm workers took an axe and began clearing an opening through which to extricate the injured airman, now believed to be the radio operator, Staff Sergeant Dee L. Troxell. German soldiers, soon arriving on the scene, took a very callous stance; pronouncing the airman dead, they ordered the Frenchmen away.

Scattered pieces of the bomber were still burning and Robert made his way some 250 yards into the field to a crater that was emitting oily black smoke. It was surrounded by wreckage and amid the debris he found two airmen who had fallen or perhaps jumped too low. Both

A picture taken without his knowledge shows a German officer studying the still-smouldering remains of 'Maid To Please'. A 447BG report by Captain Charles G. Davis stated that the B-17 had been attacked by an Me109 and left the formation with her no.1 engine smoking. Subsequently she was again attacked from astern by the Me109. (*Via John Bitzer*)

were embedded upright in the soft, dark soil – and both were clearly beyond help on this earth. One of the bodies had split open but Robert noticed no blood on the young airman's clothing and surmised that he must have been dead before the aircraft fell. A label on his flying suit identified this fallen hero as Second Lieutenant Joseph J. Lamansky, the B-17's navigator. Robert could not identify the second airman but remembered Merle Kent speaking of casualties before they went down. Neither body was burnt and later deduction indicates that this second casualty was Second Lieutenant Lowell A. Doan, the bombardier. This left several airmen still not accounted for and the Germans were anxiously searching the surrounding countryside. Bitzer and Kent were captured at the farm. About an hour after the crash, a small open truck arrived and the Germans bundled both the living and the dead on board, showing scant respect for either. The search for other airmen continued and the next day Robert discovered the burnt wreckage of the bomber's cockpit. Inside were the remains of another flier, later identified as Julian Y. Schrero. In the ashes now being gently washed in soft rain, Robert spotted a small foreign coin and picked it up. One cent, tiny in value but symbolically priceless to him because it represented the sacrifice being made to help his beloved France by men from a land far away.

Self-help was also under way beneath the noses of the enemy and one method was to aid Allied airmen who were trying to evade the enemy. One crew member from 'Maid to Please' was fortunate in avoiding both death and captivity thanks to the heroism of a French farming family. Michel Doutreleau was then aged 10 but would never forget the events of that dark December day. Four aircraft fell in the area that day; by the end of hostilities the number was nearer 200. Among them, 'Maid to Please' would always be prominent because it fell on his parents' farm and he remembers the fast and furtive activity involved in hiding one survivor from the Germans. Staff Sergeant Walter E. Dickerman, the tail gunner, was quickly hidden by the Doutreleau family and soon was passed on to the Resistance in the care of Miss Rossi, a young woman living in Beauvais who received and harboured more than sixty Allied airmen. Further aided by a Mr Demarque, Dickerman slid along the escape line to eventually reappear at Rattlesden, where his experiences undoubtedly boosted morale and provided vital intelligence. As Dickerman began his home run, Johnny Bitzer remained in a coma, unaware of anything since pulling his ripcord.

I regained consciousness the next day in a German hospital in Beauvais, France, and became POW #817. I was riddled with flak, mostly in my right leg. Treatment at this hospital, in spite of being German, was very good. I was in the hospital until mid-January and then was taken to Frankfurt, Germany, where the Luftwaffe interrogation centre was located. I was put in isolation for about five days and questioned. I was amazed at the knowledge the German intelligence had regarding my background, even down to the high school I attended. I was then transferred to a transit camp where they decide to which POW camp you will be sent. We went by boxcar to a camp near Memel, East Prussia, which took about four or five days. This was in the winter and there was no heat in the boxcars. We were the first Americans to open up a compound at this camp, which was Stalag Luft VI. There was another compound of British, Australians, New Zealanders and Canadians. They were instrumental in helping us to get organized, with the permission of the Germans of course. The treatment was not bad, food was lousy, but the Red Cross parcels saved the day.

In July 1944 Russian armour had broken through the German lines south-west of Leningrad and was hurrying through Estonia toward Lithuania. Stalag Luft VI lay directly in the path of the Russian advance. German authorities decided to evacuate the camp. On 14 July 1944 Stalag Luft VI was evacuated and we hoisted our packs and were marched off to a railroad siding and were loaded into boxcars. We were taken to the port of Memel. We boarded the SS *Insterburg*, a rusty old tramp-steamer. POWs disappeared down the hatch to the coal bunkers below. We were jammed into the hold with no room to lie down. Sanitary arrangements consisted of a bucket hauled up and down by a rope. Men became very sick, vomiting, etc. After three days and nights without food or water we docked at Swinemunde. 'Raus, raus' were the guards' orders for us to climb the ladder to fresh air. We boarded boxcars again, forty to fifty men in half a car, with one guard with an automatic weapon in the other half. They took our shoes and belts and handcuffed us in pairs. After 24 hours of travel we stopped. The 'Heydekrug Run' was about to begin! There was much shouting by guards and barking by guard dogs as we scrambled from the freight cars. Our boots, belts and so on were found in a big pile on the ground and then we hurried to the little station of Kiefheide. The guards were commanded by an officer who acted like a mad man and urged everyone else into a frenzy. (We later found out that the officer's wife and daughter had died in a Berlin air raid.) The guards resorted to bayonet stabs, rifle butts and dog bites to increase the pace. (I still carry scars on my backside from the bayoneting.) Packs were discarded and men began to fall by the wayside as the run quickened. Along the route men shouted encouragement to each other and warned against attempts to escape into the woods. Machine-gun nests were strategically placed in the woods to counter any attempt to escape. The guards were really trying to provoke us into making a run for it but we held fast. Word came down the line that if you could no longer run and were exhausted (this was in the middle of July), you should fall by the wayside and lie still. After 3 kilometres of running up the hill we reached the camp. We laid exhausted in the forelager with no food, water or medical attention. Later a truck went out to pick up those that had fallen and the discarded bags. The next day they finally brought us some water and soup. They searched us but we had no idea what they were looking for, it was mostly just to make you more miserable, if that was possible. We settled into Stalag Luft IV, Lager D, and it was the same story: lousy food and Red Cross parcels again saving the day.

Recently I was asked what Christmas was like as a POW. I really had not thought about it for many years. Looking back I realize it was a time when you understood the true meaning of Christmas. There were no commercials and no questions such as what gifts are you going to get me and what gifts do you want. At this point you felt closer to your fellow man and shared the same thoughts and prayers regardless of your religion. This was my first Christmas as a POW and my third Christmas away from home. Home is something that was always in the back of your mind but especially at that time of year.

When I first arrived at this camp there were 3,000 POWs and by late December the number had risen to almost 10,000. The Germans were working feverishly building Lagers E and F. The weather had turned bitterly cold and temperatures were below zero. There were twenty-four men in a little room with one pot-belly stove. I was in Lager D and we had eight three-tiered bunks per room. Each bunk had five slats and a straw mattress, which you learned to arrange for maximum comfort. The Germans had issued us two horsehair blankets that you could almost see through when they were held up to the light. We usually slept with our clothes on to help us keep warm. Each room was issued twelve peat bricks a day which we used sparingly. We had a radio (although very few of us ever saw it) and the reports were that the war was going well and that the air war in Europe was really in full swing. Maybe this would be our last Christmas away from home. I did not know it at the time, but later found out that we had to get permission from the German Commandant to sing Christmas carols as a group and to walk around the inside perimeter of the compound. Permission was granted and after all the carols were sung someone suggested singing, 'My Country 'tis of Thee'. The German Commandant and guards did not know this was not a Christmas carol, and we felt that we had put something over on them.

Some POWs made 'Kriegie cakes' using water, powdered milk, margarine and crushed graham crackers from the Red Cross parcels. This mixture was put in a Klim can and baked. (Klim is milk spelled backwards and is what you buy today as powdered milk.) There were no limits as to what the empty Klim cans were used for. Another cake was made from German bread mixed with Klim and sugar into sort of a baked bread pudding. Raisins were added and chocolate icing was made from Red Cross candy bars. We had been saving our raisins from the Red Cross parcels for a 'Christmas drink'. Some of the guys were pretty inventive and knew how to make Raisin Jack. This process started several weeks prior to Christmas, and after fermentation it became quite a potent potable.

This was passed around and believe it or not we all slept good that night. The next day was a different story. We heard via our radio the news of a German breakthrough and learned that the Battle of the Bulge was on, and the Allies were in retreat. MERRY CHRISTMAS!

On 6 February 1945 we got word again that we were moving out due to the Russians advancing and we started the infamous Death March. When you hear the words 'Death March' most people's first thought is Bataan. But there was another death march that lasted almost three months and covered some 600 miles. In early 1945 again the war was going badly for the Germans. They decided to move those in POW camps further west. The men from Stalag Luft IV have probably the most gripping tale of this death march. Stalag Luft IV, in eastern Prussia, held an estimated 9,000–10,000 POWs. The order to evacuate came down in early February. The departure of sick and wounded by train came first and then more went by rail a few days later. On 6 February 1945 the remainder of us set out on foot. We were given Red Cross parcels and many men started out carrying heavy loads. After a few miles the roadside became littered with items too heavy to carry, although we were told the march would only last for three days. The German guards divided us into groups of 250–300 men. Each group travelled a different route and at a different pace. During the day we marched four or five abreast and at night we were herded into barns. If no barn was available we bivouacked in fields or forests. Water was available but often polluted. We were given little food and had to search to find whatever we could to eat. We sometimes stole food that had been thrown to farm animals. We often marched all day with no food, water or rest. Snow was piled knee-deep sometimes and the temperature went well below zero. This was one of the coldest winters on record. We all became infected with lice, and pneumonia, diphtheria, pellagra, typhus, trench foot and tuberculosis were common among the troops. Almost everyone had dysentery caused by drinking contaminated water. Blisters, abscesses and frostbite were also common. Sometimes the Germans provided a wagon for the sick but there was never enough room. Other times they brought a wagon but no horse to pull it so weary GIs would step into the yokes. Sometimes the guards would take a straggling marcher into the woods, you would hear a shot, and the guards would come back alone. Even though a buddy system was in place, everyone tried to help everyone else. Day after tortuous day the march continued. Finally, in the late spring of 1945, it was over, on 26 April to be exact. From beginning to end it spanned 86 days and 600 miles. Many of the marchers suffered illnesses for the rest of their lives. Worst of all, several hundred POWs, possibly as many as 1,300, died on this senseless march to nowhere. The Baltic Cruise, the Heydekrug Run and the Death March were considered war crimes and are recorded as such.

John kept a diary during his first heady days of freedom. Euphoria, elation and optimism still spring from its pages, tinged with an understandable desire for retribution – but it was very minor on the scale of chaos elsewhere.

LIBERATION DAY. April 26th 45. I wish I could impress on those that read this what is in our hearts and minds. Today is Liberation day and I will never forget it. After being on the march for two-and-a-half months, since Feb 6th 1945, we marched into Bitterfeld as free men and as I write this I am sitting in a German office in Bitterfeld, minus the Jerries of course. We left Gross Tyschow Pomerania the 6th of Feb and marched to Stalag XIA at Attengrable by Magdeburg. We evacuated XIA because the Yanks were getting too close – incidentally the Russians were chasing us up till then. From there we came down towards Leipzig to Annaberg. There the Russians chased us again. We finally stayed at a farm and it was rumoured we would wait there till the Yanks took us – we couldn't hardly believe that and we didn't. We left there again because Jerry didn't want to be taken by the Russians. Being in their position I can't blame them. Finally the great day came and we left this place and marched to Bitterfeld where we disarmed the Jerries. We shook hands with the first GI at 2.45, marched further and saluted the first officer at 3.20. We bummed our first cigarette at 3.45. This has been a great day for all of us and a long awaited day. For myself it's been 17 months. To be a free man once again is hard to believe. The town here is ours and we can have what we want – we got our K ration supper tonight. K rations has been on our lips for the past week . . . tonight was a dream fulfilled after eating what we have since we have been on this march. Hancock, Miller, McClure and myself saw this day together. I've known these boys since they have been POWs. Miller came to Stalag Luft VI with me and 78 others. It's all been pretty rough but we saw it through although we had our doubts at times. It's good to see 2000 men running around with a good meal in our bellies and happy as a lark. Yes – I can't think of much more because my mind is not in shape to do any writing so I'll close once again . . . they say we will go out of here the quickest way – as far as I'm concerned the quickest way is not quick enough but soon we will all be home. This day will be big in our hearts. Many was the time when I thought I would not see home again but here I am as good as home once again. All I care to do now is go home and the hell with Germany – they have everything coming to them that has come in the past and what is to come in the future. We are sitting now on top of the world Yippee!!! Once again we live like men and eat like men. The 26th of April will live for a long time inside me. Thanks to God I will see home once again.

April 27 1945. I didn't sleep a wink last night but I just don't particularly care. I am still in Bitterfeld waiting to move out which should be this morning. We went into the town and raided a bakery. There were seven of us and the owner, who was a little on the scared side, wanted to give us old bread, we wanted fresh bread so we took the fresh bread and walked out. We didn't give him anything for the bread because we wanted to get back at the Jerries for the treatment and rations we got while on the march. The MPs told us anything we want to just go and take it. Cameras and field-glasses were supposed to have been turned in – any we found on the civilians we took away from them. At 11.00 the trucks came and we took off – it really was good to ride in a good old GI truck. We came from Bitterfeld to Halle in 45 min. Here we got set up for a few days to get deloused and get clean clothes and then homeward bound. It's still hard to believe that you're a free man again after a year and a half of running round in Germany. Today was a full up day and everything that happened pointed to going home once again.

April 28 1945. The second day of liberation and it's still a dream. Got my first good night's sleep in three days and I felt like a million. Hoping to get on our way soon. We got registered this morning – name, rank, ASN, POW no, where and when shot down, etc. We went up and ate chow and boy it's sure different from what we have been eating from the Jerries. It just does not seem possible – all of this – after living the life we have after so long a time. It will be hard for a person back home to realize what we have been through. After chow we went up to a house where there was a nice coal-burning stove and made us some coffee. Later on we went to the buildings where the Jerries used to be and raided their clothing store and I got a good pair of pants which I needed bad and some underwear and a sweater. There sure is a lot of stuff like clothing, army equipment, etc., left here. This used to be a good-sized air base until we came along. There are a lot of planes on the field burnt and full of holes. We sure knocked hell out of this place. The way things look Jerry sure left in a big hurry. This is an awful big place right by Halle. There is millions of dollars worth of equipment here. If only I could have a GI truck I'd haul a bunch of this

Robert Degrez (left) and John Bitzer during the memorial dedication ceremonies, June 2001. (*Ernest A. Osborne, 447BG Association UK*)

The memorial on the Le Coudray farm was established thanks to the efforts of Michel Doutreleau, who never forgot the men who perished on his family farm. (*Ernest A. Osborne, 447BG Association UK*)

stuff home and it would be worth a lot of money. Well, another day closer to home. Good night!

After several more days at Halle, John eventually found himself homeward bound and very glad to have left the land of his birth. He went first to Rheims in France, then on to Camp Lucky Strike and Camp Philip Morris at Le Havre, from where he boarded a Liberty ship to take him home. It would be many years before events triggered John's return to Europe.

Michel Doutreleau was greatly moved by his encounter with the B-17 'Maid to Please' and her heroic crew. Growing up, he was haunted by the spectacle of wreckage spilling from heaven and the smell from the burning bomber. He felt that the unfortunate souls who had died on land he had now inherited should be properly honoured at the scene so he started to research their story. His efforts soon put him in touch with the 447BG Association and Ernest Osborne, whose boyhood fascination with the raiders from Rattlesden turned into a lifetime's research honouring their achievements. Ernest helped open a door into the past and Michel was overjoyed to make contact with Johnny Bitzer. Aided by his family and friends, Michel planned and designed a memorial to be dedicated where 'Maid to Please' had fallen.

Michel's efforts culminated on 9 June 2001 with the formal unveiling of the memorial and a commemorative service attended by some 2,000 people. Those in attendance included representatives from the United States Air Forces in Europe, old comrades from the Resistance, civilian dignitaries and people from all over France who had turned out to pay tribute. Distinguished guests from overseas included Ernest Osborne and Byron Schlag, President of the 447BG Association, but the guest of honour was a man of small stature and great spirit as Johnny Bitzer returned to honour his crew. He had aged while they had not, but Johnny had always remembered them through the long years of a life fulfilled. He had married in 1948 and had five children before his wife passed away; he later married again. Speeches marked the event and reminded both nations of the enduring fight for freedom. Sharing the unveiling, Michel and John also shared the emotions evoked by 'Taps' and a flypast by a KC-135 Stratotanker of the 351st Air Refuelling Squadron saluting one of its lineage. Hardly had the noise of its four jet turbofans faded when the sound of engines from an earlier era announced the arrival of B-17 'Pink Lady'. Curving gracefully through airspace that once witnessed the horrific final moments of a sister ship struck down in battle, 'Pink Lady' saluted the crowd and especially the small figure of Johnny Bitzer – one of the first men down, but one of the lucky ones.

CHAPTER SEVEN

The Last Ride of the Valkyrie

Naming your aircraft after a goddess whose role was to choose fallen warriors and carry them off to Valhalla might seem like inviting trouble. After some debate Crew 22 of the 733rd Bombardment Squadron, 453rd Bombardment Group, had done just that and this story tells of the woes that befell them during the last ride of the 'Valkyrie'. To the US Army Air Force, the crew's anthropomorphic treatment of their machine was allowed but irrelevant. Consolidated B-24H Liberator serial number 42-52176 was a heavy bomber on the inventory records for Station 144 at Old Buckenham in Norfolk. Apart from the serial, the aircraft's only other distinction was an individual call letter N carried beneath the 453rd Group's dark blue J. This letter, encircled with an off-white background and boldly worn on each rudder and on the port upper wing, distinguished the 453BG more clearly when the machines were assembling into the massive formations that shook the air over East Anglia in 1944. For Crew 22 who rode the aircraft into battle, trembling inside, it was their Valkyrie.

In Norse mythology the Valkyrie – 'beautiful shieldmaidens on winged horses armed with helmet and spears' – chose the best heroes to assist the war-god Odin in his battles. The word meant 'choosers of the slain', and Lieutenant Jackson S. Tisch was well aware of the meaning when he proposed the name for their B-24: 'Part of the thought was romantic. We equated ourselves with Odin's battle-watching maidens who picked out the warriors who were to die and took the worthy to Valhalla. We could have lived up to that ideal much better than we did . . . [Valkyrie] won the token vote partly because there was no competition.'

Jack Tisch had flown fourteen missions by 8 May 1944, but that day was, ominously, number thirteen for the 'Valkyrie' and the rest of the crew. Jack always felt, 'I needn't have been a party to it – "let 'em enjoy their own luck", I thought. But on the one occasion when our crew went on a mission without me, I worried a lot.' Jack had actually joined pilot Robert P. ('Pete') Catlin's crew as navigator shortly before the 453BG left the USA. Jack later recalled how Catlin's original navigator 'became "unglued" at high altitude (I wish I'd thought of that) and was transferred to Staff Navigator at Hamilton Field . . . a cushy job that he could have sold for a brevet general's job. I was a casual at Hammer Field in Fresno and they shipped me down to take over. By this time the Group was in staging

The crew pictured before coming overseas. (Back row, left to right): Robert Catlin, pilot; George Wear, co-pilot; Jack Tisch, navigator; Joseph Aiello, bombardier. (Front row): Ken Drapeau, radio operator; Morris Irby, top turret gunner; Ray Bates, right waist gunner; Arthur Behne, nose turret gunner; William Moore, tail gunner; Franklin Suders, left waist gunner. (*Jack Tisch*)

for overseas shipment (flight, in our case) and I just got in on a final two or three weeks of training. So I never got to know everybody as well as they all knew each other. But I'm an old shoe and we all got to know each other pretty well enough. We got into some adventures in Midland, Texas, West Palm Beach, Florida, Aguidilla, Puerto Rico, and tried in Natal, Brazil. Once we got to Dakar, we knew to leave well enough alone and kept good until Marrakech.'

They arrived in England on 22/23 December 1943 and gradually accumulated missions, mostly as a crew but with other individuals occasionally filling in elsewhere as required. Strangely, their 'nose art' never adorned the actual aircraft. Jack recalled in 1978 that it was applied to the blackout boards in the enlisted men's mess and he commented in a letter to historian Chris Gotts, 'You will observe that the Valkyrie was painted on ordinary plywood – and there's even a handle, bottom right. The horse looks a little more like my idea of a German or Norse handmaiden and the girl looks a bit delicate but our tastes were thoroughly

A Valkyrie, as depicted in an image created for the crew. Modern interpretation depicts them as Odin's beautiful handmaidens, while earlier mythology describes the Valkyrie as 'gruesome and war-like', riding wolves and picking over the bodies on the battlefields like ravens. (*Jack Tisch via Chris Gotts*)

satisfied at the time.' They never even applied mission symbols: 'It wouldn't have meant much anyway, because other crews might use "our" plane if we were stood down . . . although we as a crew always used the same plane.'

For the mission of 8 May Catlin's crew was not made up of its usual complement, as Jack relates:

The crew members this day were Robert P. ('Pete') Catlin, pilot; George Wear, borrowed co-pilot (George Cahill was ill); Joseph ('Little Evil') Aiello, bombardier; ? Seay, nose gun turret; Ken Drapeau, radioman; Franklin Suders, engineer and left waist gun; Morris Irby, top turret; Ray Bates, right waist gun; William ('Bill') Moore, tail gun turret; and me sitting in the navigator's seat.

There was nothing remarkable about the mission or the flight until after we had dropped our bombs. We got up at 1:30 AM, washed, shaved, breakfasted and were briefed. Then on to the plane waiting on its hardstand until take-off time and form up. We took off as usual after dawn, to avoid unfortunate mid-air meetings. By 7:00 AM we were on our way to Brunswick – Braunschweig on my map.

We flew to Braunschweig without incident. We dropped our bomb-load and turned for the boring trip home, 'fat, dumb and happy'. I moped in the navigator/bombardier/nose gunner compartment alone, keeping a very casual log. Until this mission, we'd hardly even been approached by enemy fighters. We knew there <u>were</u> some but our actual experience with them was minimal. We were the lead plane in the upper right echelon, I believe. The lead navigator was doing fine. I watched Germany passing by beneath us, and looked for other plane formations in the sky through the front turret. There would have been a gunner in the turret ordinarily, but somebody had left it unlocked the night before and it had vibrated out of place when we took off. There was no way we'd have found out that the nose turret wasn't going to be operational anyway, because nobody manned it until we were forming up to head for our target. I doubt that we'd have turned back even if we had been lead ship. Incidentally the gunner who should have been there was a substitute for Behne who flew only a few missions with us. The new guy was named Seay, and spoke only southern talk. Every time he warmed up his guns over the Zuider Zee, he would come on the intercom and mouth some gibberish to Pete, who also spoke southern. I never knew what they were talking about until the damn guns started – and, of course, I started! I never caught on either . . . I had tried to edge in [to the turret] far enough to turn it on and adjust it, but couldn't so it made a good window on the world. The gunner stayed on the flight deck, to lend a hand where needed.

From my admirable vantage point, I was able to watch a formation come up, line abreast, ahead of us. Fighters or bombers I couldn't say, but there were too many of them to be anything but Americans. I watched them get bigger – rapidly. Good, I thought, that's our fighter cover arriving early. Sure enough, they were fighters. I could tell that when all their wings lit up with flashes and faint smoke. Well! THAT startled me. There were dozens of them! Actually, there must have been at least 30, but it looked like the whole damn German Air Force. It made a person nervous to watch it – all that shooting – they might hurt somebody!

At a closing speed of over 500mph, I had little time to worry before they were gone. Wow! That had been close. It was lucky they'd missed us – or so I thought. I was glad that was over. The intercom hummed with comment, none of which I understood. I already had a slight hearing problem, enhanced by the fact that half the crew had a southern accent and the rest were easterners. I never paid any attention to their gabble on the earphones.

I can't say when anything in particular happened because I couldn't feel anything. The number 2 engine might have been hit on that fly-by; I just didn't notice. What I did notice was another flight of fighters coming up alongside, way to our left. Great, now these damn Germans will leave us alone! This <u>must</u> be our escort. But then our 'escort' turned right, and right again, and came barrelling through on another pass! It seemed so fast that I had less time to worry, but now I was concerned on a wider front. On this attack, I noticed that something had happened to our number 2 engine – it was feathered – and we were flying on only three engines! It is very unsettling – not because you're in any immediate danger, but because you now have a narrow margin of safety. I had a word with myself: 'Not much additional can go wrong, you hear? Try to keep safe the rest of the trip, and be glad they didn't hit the gas tanks!'

By now the intercom was a shambles of garbled communication. Everybody was talking, nobody listening. There were orders and advice and alarms and curses. There was nothing I might have done with the information even had I been able to understand what was said. I busied myself with a mordant entry in the log: 'Fighters – enemy'. I'm glad nobody saw it – it strikes me as a bit smarmy now. The log survived the attacks, the crash and souvenir hunters. I picked it up at the crash scene later and got rid of it.

I thought the third attack had missed us until I spotted our number 3 engine feathered. This was the one that supplied power for numerous accessories plus the hydraulic power for other systems. Good grief – two engines out? I glanced very nervously at the number 2 engine again and, by gosh, they had it going again. Whew! I eyed the engine and cowling and spotted the trouble. Some 20mm shells had blown the top (master) cylinder virtually off; the cowling was bulged up a LOT on both the 2 and 3 engines. Yes, they'd started the no. 3 engine again, too. We had two 14-cylinder and two 13-cylinder engines, for a total of less than three power plants – and we were still flying. God bless Pratt and Whitney!

The third attack was the last that I saw and I thought the formation was all right. The fact was that we lost 10 planes out of 24. It's just as well I wasn't able to see the action. While I relaxed in the belief that we were out of danger, the Germans were making side and astern attacks, and Pete and George were struggling to subdue 30 tons of recalcitrant aircraft that was determined to carry us all to an early grave. I didn't feel any bumps or vibration or any flight behaviour that alarmed me. All the while Pete and George were wrestling with controls that flipped up and down as cannon shells shredded them, retrimming the ship as engines ran away and had to be feathered, and doing it again when they could restart the engines, mindful that anything could blow up or break off at any moment.

The rear attacks created havoc. Shells shattered the Plexiglas of the rear turret, ripped up the ammunition racks to the tail gun and wounded the right waist gunner, Ray Bates. They also jammed the elevator and rudder together, making the plane climb, and cut some of the control cables at the same time. Pete and George were attempting to muscle the big clunk level, but what with the loss of the cables and the damage, the boys weren't making it. We had to get out of the climb attitude darn shortly, otherwise we'd stall and never have a chance to regain control. Pete's tremendous training paid off here. He switched on the auto-pilot to help, since every little bit might make the difference. And it did – actually in a surprising way. Pete later reconstructed the situation like this: the auto-pilot, which had become useless for its intended purpose, was all that could supply the super-power needed to crush through the ripped aluminium at the tail and normalize the elevator. Had the auto-pilot been working as designed, it would have [been] a gentle servant, overcome by any resistance and of no avail against the broken controls. As it was, the pilots found that flying entirely on the auto-pilot was the only effective means of operating the airplane. They were happy to fly it any damn way it liked. We went the rest

Debris strewn over the Norfolk landscape at Morningthorpe. The engines have been torn away and are visible in the centre and to the right of centre. During the late 1960s and early 1970s researcher Chris Gotts joined a team from the Norfolk & Suffolk Aviation Museum and found numerous parts from the lost 'Valkyrie'. (*Jack Tisch via Chris Gotts*)

of the way using the little half-inch knobs on the control panel with great delicacy. Another point for Pete. He had a poet's hand with the B-24. It flew like an angel.

Once our inner panic had subsided, we took stock of ourselves. Ray Bates's knees had been injured by shell fragments, I don't know how badly, but he was bearing up. Bill Moore, in the tail, gave up on his job after being flipped out of the turret twice when the concussion of the exploding shells bounced him down the walkway into the waist. The first time this happened he went back and manned his good gun again. Next time he stayed in the waist. Que sera sera. As we looked over our situation, I noted: 1. We seemed to be flying south-west instead of west. I wouldn't want the lead navigator to think I would correct him but west was best. After three minutes' fretting it dawned on me that the sun was wrong. By gosh, we <u>were</u> going west. The compass never moved after that so I presume the master compass in the rear was damaged. 2. The crew seemed to be gathering on the flight deck behind the cockpit. 3. I saw the rest of the formation some hundred feet above and ahead of us, and realized we were sinking. 4. What are we going to do? It's up to you to show us the way to go home, Jackson!

The torn-off tail section with oxygen bottles littering the meadow. (*Jack Tisch via Chris Gotts*)

We still had some of Germany and all of Holland to fly over, not to mention the whole 105 miles of North Sea. We also had company in the shape of a little pest in an Me109 who must have shot off all his ammunition but was convinced that, if he hung around a couple more minutes, we'd fall out of the sky in the normal course of disintegration and he could take the credit. As he came by to see why we were still in the air, Morris Irby laid a couple of effective shots into him and got the credit for the only kill we ever chalked up. So, ha! The worst that now stood in our way was Ijmuiden, flak capital of Holland – and the 105 miles of North Sea, of course.

My prime contribution to our welfare came off when I flew us 10 miles north of our usual route and the sharpshooters of Ijmuiden ignored us. We were uplifted a bit more by a lone P-38, which hung about 'just in case' and tried to reassure us. 'Big brother' he called us. Some big brother – with a bloody nose, torn stockings and a hole in both knees of our trousers. Perhaps he couldn't see what was holding us together and just wanted to help our morale. He flew on at last, radioing for Air Sea Rescue. On the flight deck it was like a reunion. Seven of us, all talking together except the pilots, who had their hands full. They might also have been a bit nervy over having to operate without their chest packs on. The rest of us were ready to bail out instantly if anything untoward occurred – what else could happen?

Once we were safely away from the continent we began to cheer up. We had about 14,000 feet of altitude to trade off for low power and speed. We used it judiciously. I want to be sure to give proper credit to Pete and George (who was first pilot with his own crew) for getting $100,000-worth of performance out of what can't have been more than $126-worth of airplane. When Pete heard the hideous damage report from the waist, he had to go look to believe it. He then hurried back to help nurse the shuddering wreck along. Pete may have considered making a belly landing or gliding in without any power to make a dead-stick landing, but I can't think that idea lasted once we got the rest of the bad news. I wasn't there then – and he didn't try – so he proved to be of sound mind at the end.

By now we were approaching England! Our spirits soared. The sky was clear, the sun shone. We still had enough altitude to manoeuvre, if necessary. We lightened the ship by throwing out anything loose, including Pete's combat boots and the radio, so Pete wasn't in contact with the tower any more. We assembled in the waist to bail out, Irby following with final instructions. Ken Drapeau was brashest and closest to the camera hatch. Everybody was watching, so he straddled the hatch, smiled and pulled his feet together and dropped. We all saw his chute open and breathed a sigh. It had worked! I found myself next in line, and also being stared at. So I dropped my B4 bag with my jacket and my navigation instruments through the hatch (What for? So I could pick it up on the way down? What was I thinking of?) and followed it out of the plane. But I didn't open my chute! I forgot the guys in the ship were still watching. They were quite upset.

Well, why didn't I open my chute? Well, because the plane was cruising along at 150 knots and I was waiting for the wind to die down. It occurred to me at last that I wasn't likely to notice any difference between that and 140 knots, the average navigator's terminal velocity. So I then followed the hearsay, 'Pull the bloody ripcord or walk the whole way down'.

And here's the account of the longest, nicest ten-minute period of my life. I remember it well. I pulled the ripcord with great élan. You'd think I'd have the sense to visualize an elegant walnut plaque, carrying the red-handled ripcord with an engraved silver plate carrying date, time, mission and other data on the wall in my den, mute testimony to my great adventure. No, not me. I was above all that – I threw it away! (Did anyone report finding a ripcord at about that time? After all, they found my B4 bag!) The canvas opened quickly and the chute pack streamed up into the sky. That is, it looked up to me, although a ground observer might have corrected that notion. In the emptiness there, you are your own and only reference, which is not too reliable. I've never heard another bale-out victim mention it but, when you swing, it doesn't seem to be you swinging. It's the chute swaying above you. And there isn't any familiar 'little map' down below. It's just a wild disoriented countryside without a single identifying object. You don't know what to look for, and it wouldn't be there anyway. And I'm the navigator, mind you. I had been over this territory frequently, and was very good at pilotage, or spotting a place and identifying it.

The devastation of the Liberator was total. A wing section lies in the centre, the engine ripped away. There are undoubtedly fragments still to be found from the fallen bomber, each piece representing a flight into history. (*Jack Tisch via Chris Gotts*)

But I had a lot going for me in the plane because I always knew which way north was, and I always had a map to refresh my memory as to places on the ground. Without the map I was a stranger, but I knew I was within 10 miles or so of the base. I looked around for other chutes. None.

At the time, though, I was enjoying myself, except for one persistent discomfort. All I had to sit on was a thin, inverted-V-shaped web strap right under my crotch. There was no way to sit back and relieve the stress, no shelf to rest elbows on and lighten the load below. But for that, all would have been sheer bliss. But I suppose they don't intend you to enjoy yourself so much that the rescue becomes secondary. I recall that I was amazed at the silence – what a wonderful place to concentrate. I wished I had a copy of the *Chicago Daily News*, Thursday evening edition, with the patternless crossword puzzle, which was always a great challenge to me. But I had to do without it, and went back to my enjoyment of the drop. It was quite a long while before it became apparent that I wasn't just standing still in the sky. Until you are close enough to the ground to detect changes, you seem to float. But in the ground–sky relationship, around about 400 feet, your surroundings begin to close in and you start to wonder where you'll settle.

Illusions of controlling my descent and direction welled up – I would land with aplomb, remain standing and accept the homage of the throng. I wised up in time. There was a large wood in front of me but I couldn't get any idea of what was directly below. So be it. Be the big shot next jump! Take what comes even if it is a tree. I floated gently down on to a patch of thick grass and slowly lay back on the ground. I almost kept my balance but that didn't seem to matter as much as being safely aground.

I found it gratifying just lying on the earth. Warm, gentle breeze, soft grass, peace. I soaked in the delight for a minute before trying to get organized. I was wearing a sheeplined leather flying suit and boots over my electrically heated suit and I had a chute and harness – hardly good hiking equipment. I also had cigarettes. It seemed sensible to smoke one now. I lit up, and then gathered up my chute, harness and jacket. I was getting too warm. But I was lost. I hadn't a notion where anything was. I hadn't looked around to see whether there were any roads or habitations nearby. Dumb. And then I saw two cheerful Tommies coming towards me. They were an unofficial deputation from some nearby cantonment, and a welcome sight. They cadged an American cigarette apiece, gathered up my paraphernalia and set off for the nearest road, which turned out to be about 200 yards to our right. And surprisingly enough, in a few minutes, along came an ambulance to pick up whoever might be at the crash-site . . . Our ambulance crew was a couple of medics and a driver. I was about to tell them about our coming home . . . and suddenly we were driving over a big grass field, already full of people. I was told to stay in the ambulance while the corpsmen assessed the situation – lest I be shaken by what might be out there. Probably a good idea. I didn't have a notion what had happened after I left the plane.

The medics were quite efficient. They returned with Ray in their litter inside 30 seconds. He was still concerned about the pilot and co-pilot up front. He was connected to the plasma bottle and shot full of morphine before he had finished the sentence. The next news item was furnished by a kindly bystander. He told us, 'If this lad is all right, that accounts for everybody. We counted nine chutes.' I could see Ray's mind taking that in. 'Hey, I was all alone up there?' I was glad he was tranquillized. If they had told him that while he was urging everybody to help the pilots, it would have shattered him.

So, let's rejoin the crew in the waist. Six more Caterpillar Club members dropped from the camera hatch after me and landed all over the countryside. But when the time had come for Ray to jump (he now had Morris Irby's chute because his own had been torn up by German firing), he decided his knees were too injured to land on. Deliberately or accidentally, he popped open the chute Irby had just given him. This put Irby in a fix. He decided to go up front and see what Pete would do now. With a guy in the waist and another with no chute, some changes had to be made! Meanwhile, Pete and George were not even considering a landing.

Here's what they had to work with: we'd been losing gas all the way; two engines were dying; the control cables were half gone; there was only one functioning elevator, rudder

Morris Irby (left) and Pete Catlin study bullet holes in the nose-wheel tyre. (*Jack Tisch via Chris Gotts*)

and aileron; one wheel was down (which alone makes for an extremely hairy landing); all they had to fly with were the tiny knobs of the automatic pilot; AND it turned out that the down tyre was flat! So that was the rest of the bad news I mentioned earlier.

As soon as possible after the crew went aft, Pete sent George out to exit through the bomb-bay doors. These are flexible, and supported by dozens of little wheels, fore and aft, that are designed to break off under undue stress such as 220lb of co-pilot. But, like the temperamental auto-pilot, it didn't work that way. Pete watched as George jumped heavily on the stubborn door. Suddenly, he shot through, seeming to scrape his face on a narrow slot beside the central catwalk and the door. Once George was out, Pete put on his chute, wormed out of the cockpit and through the flight deck and down into the bomb-bay. He carefully kicked out a lot more wheels to avoid scraping his face off, and unceremoniously abandoned ship.

Now, when Irby came forward a few seconds later, I can't imagine what went through his mind. After all, he'd been good all day – conscientious and efficient, even valorous in shooting down our German tormentor, and exceedingly generous in letting Ray have his own parachute – and what does he get? Shafted! But fate wasn't all finished with miracles that day. Never before and never again afterwards, did we carry an extra chest pack. On this mission only, there was a spare chute lying in plain sight on the flight deck.

The survivors of the 'Valkyrie' pose by the remains. Left to right: Jack Tisch, George Wear, William Moore, Robert Catlin, Morris Irby, Joe Aiello. (*Jack Tisch via Chris Gotts*)

I don't know whether Irby remembered Bates out the back, and there wasn't anything he could have done for him anyway. Irby had the chute on and was out of the bomb-bay doors in the nick of time. The ship was now so low that, as his chute opened, he found himself on the ground. I've heard that after the first snap open, a chute closes up again in a sort of reaction, and for the next 40 or 50 feet the chutist speeds up again. Morris jumped at the precise second that ensured he wouldn't be injured. And, boy, he deserved it if anybody did . . .

Meanwhile, back at the wreck, Ray was medically cared for and the morphine made him comfortable, if not sleepy. So, when the pub hove into view, there was a unanimous vote to take advantage of it. If there hadn't been, I'd have made it an order. We stopped there for a nerve restorative, and that's how we found our glib radioman, Ken Drapeau, haranguing four or five regulars and the barman. He'd landed in what we'd call their back yard and so shocked the owner that he stood him a free drink. Ken repaid his generosity with an exciting account of his day up to then. By the time our contingent arrived, the barman had recovered, and I <u>paid</u> for our brew. I'm sure they considered he'd earned his free drink, but they really got an earful now because we were both big talkers. We were the first two crew members to get together and compare notes on the flight. By now everything was overlaid with humour, the scarier parts with wry irony. There was so much to talk about, I wonder how we managed to be out of the bar by nightfall . . .

Once we got the ambulance under way again, we went right to the base where Ray went into surgery. I joined the other Valkyrians in a small empty ward wherein we found two bottles of rye and several glasses. I forget whether we ate or drank lunch, but it was a great reunion whichever! Someone sent for our night gear and we found that we were to be 'under observation'. Our flight surgeon, an amateur 'shrink', probably thought we'd do something weird after such a traumatic experience. Ha! We all checked out normal and loused up all his theories. He's the man once quoted in the *Chicago Times* as saying 'That gunner [Ray Bates] had guts'. Guts! What the hell else could he do – fly away? He didn't ride the plane down from a glorious sense of adventure – he didn't know everybody else was gone!

While Jack's last ride of the Valkyrie contains a deliberately humorous vein, it camouflages the bitter reality for the 453BG that day. German fighters hacked eight aircraft from the heavens while others, like the 'Valkyrie', staggered home with battle damage and carrying wounded air-crew. Of the 27 ships leaving Old Buckenham that morning, only 17 returned. There were 81 casualties, of whom 36 were POW and 45 were dead. The reality of the telegrams that tore apart loving homes across the USA was far removed from the glorified mythology of Valhalla and Odin's handmaidens. The shattered remains of the 'Valkyrie' lay strewn through hedges and across meadowland near the Norfolk village of Morningthorpe. That Ray Bates survived is incredible, but it appears that he was thrown clear as the aircraft disintegrated.

A new Liberator soon appeared and the crew, excluding the injured Bates, continued flying further combat missions until they achieved their allotted tally that August. Soon after, the four officers shared the same vessel home and took up their lives again without Liberators. During the mid-1970s some of the survivors got in touch and began to share occasional reunions where they reminisced about their 'Valkyrie''s last ride. Time has since taken its toll and most who flew in the 'Valkyrie' have gone on to rejoin their comrades in Valhalla – where one hopes the handmaidens are as beautiful as legend says.

CHAPTER EIGHT

Stinger Stung

By 21 June 1944 the Axis powers were reeling from the Allied offensives worldwide. The Russians were about to launch an enormous summer campaign; the Americans had inflicted heavy casualties on the Japanese in the Battle of the Philippine Sea, and less than two weeks had elapsed since the Normandy landings. Great gales pounding the special Mulberry harbours had hampered the build-up of men and materials but the beachhead was now established and the initial objectives secured. The skies over western Europe reverberated continuously as both the RAF and the USAAF flew thousands of operations against a variety of targets. Prominent among the missions were those related to the German synthetic oil industry, because oil was the lifeblood of modern mechanised warfare. Cutting the German jugular would bleed the Third Reich to death on land, sea and in the air – but the Germans knew this full well and ferociously defended such targets. In the battle for oil both sides suffered tremendous casualties and one of the steps taken within RAF Bomber Command to alleviate losses was the increasing provision of night-fighter protection for its bomber streams. For months the night skies had seen British bombers being stalked by German fighters, which were themselves now stalked by more British fighters. All three fought in skies riddled with flak that was largely indiscriminate despite the German endeavours to avoid hitting their own.

The scale of aerial activity was massive, with hundreds of machines involved, but each battle boiled down to a war waged between small clusters of men either manning flak emplacements, crewing bombers or flying night-fighters. One such night-fighter, a Mosquito, took off from West Raynham in Norfolk that night intending to sting the enemy. Instead, it was the Mosquito that got stung.

Pilot Officer Peter A.E. Coles and his navigator, Pilot Officer James A. Carter, had merged into a fine combat crew after some very specialised training, and were now reckoned among an RAF elite, the men of 141 Squadron within 100 Group. Peter had volunteered in 1940 and commenced his career in 7 Air-crew Receiving Centre in Torquay as a 'prospective pilot'. His induction and medicals satisfactorily completed, he moved to Cambridge aerodrome to join 22 Elementary Flying Training School at Marshall's famous flying school. Here he met the delightful de Havilland Tiger Moth. This superb little basic training biplane propelled him over Cambridge and the fertile fenlands thereabouts at a steady 80–100mph, depending

No. 141 Squadron air-crew at West Raynham. Jim Carter is second from the left, facing the camera, and Peter Coles is second from the right. The others are unknown, although the airman on the right was called Henri. He was subsequently killed in action. (*Mrs Joyce Carter*)

on wind strength and direction, and he started to learn the essentials of flight. The Tiger Moth and its tutors were fundamental to the *ab initio* instruction of countless 'prospective pilots' such as Peter. More than sixty years later this remarkable little machine still operates from the same airfield and modern pilots can learn the idiosyncrasies of a 'tail-dragger'. Having passed this part of his training, Peter's next move was north-east to RAF Cranwell, where he received advanced aeronautical education with the Service Flying Training School. This later included training at RAF Middleton St George on the Lorenz Beam, the grandfather of modern instrument landing systems. Its use required the pilot to fly along a radio beam, guided by the noises from his headphones. A steady tone told him his approach or course was correct, while a series of dots or dashes indicated he was veering to one side of the beam or the other. This system facilitated landings in poor visibility. Peter completed the Lorenz course and later continued his tryst with technology in a somewhat bizarre manner when he crewed up with Jim Carter, a fellow Brummie.

In September 1941 Jim had reported to 3 Air-crew Replacement Centre at Lords Cricket Ground and, having been sieved through the system's health and intelligence tests, he moved on to 3 Initial Training Wing. This unit occupied a cluster of seaside hotels at Paignton in Devon and Jim found himself in the Palace Hotel, although conditions were hardly palatial with several recruits crammed into the larger rooms. Here the rigours of training included cadets clad in full flying apparel climbing to the top of a diving board before leaping into the water and then striving to clamber into an upturned dinghy. This was exhausting but all knew it might one day be for real in far less hospitable surroundings. Completing this aspect of his training, Jim espied the opportunity for an early posting when he volunteered for 'special duties' and soon found himself at Staverton in Gloucestershire with 6 Air Observers School, where his education intensified. Hours plodding around the West Country on board the unit's well-worn Avro Ansons were interspersed with additional hours doing the same thing in the sleeker, if slower, twin-engined de Havilland Dominie biplanes. Gradually Jim absorbed more advanced methods of navigation and learned to understand the increasing use of technology demanded for the task. An additional hint of his 'special duties' emerged in March 1942 when he found himself at Prestwick in Scotland on a radar training course. Here he became airborne in some ancient Blenheims and the even more mature Hawker Audax biplane, a derivative of the famous Hawker Hart bomber. This further education encompassed use of the still relatively new AI equipment and groomed him for a move in May to 51 Operational Training Unit at Cranfield, where he crewed up with Peter Coles. The crewing process practised within the RAF tended to be informal, based on little more than availability and a brief assessment of the 'chemistry' between personalities. Happily the system worked, and the bonds between airmen whose lives were interdependent would often be like a marriage, 'until death us do part', and many shared even this final frontier.

Peter and Jim worked in concert and together wrung what they could from 51 OTU's battered Blenheims and its newer but still worn Beaufighters. In addition to the Bristol products, there was a new aircraft on the airfield in the shape of the Douglas Havoc. This American-manufactured twin-engined aircraft, with its tricycle undercarriage, was originally intended as a light bomber and was first ordered by the French government, which hoped to bolster its own antediluvian bombers pending the arrival of more modern indigenous designs. Their plans were overtaken by events and widespread use of the Havoc in French service never transpired. Following the defeat of France, production orders were diverted to the RAF. One unusual use for the aircraft saw its armament removed and replaced with a nose-mounted 2.7 million candlepower searchlight, powered by a hefty generator set back in the fuselage. Conceived by Wing Commander William Helmore, an RAF pilot, distinguished engineer, song writer and radio broadcaster, the Helmore Light was manufactured by the General Electric Company. The concept was for the Turbinlite Havoc to operate in conjunction with a pair of Hurricanes. Using its on-board AI radar, the Havoc would close in on the enemy before illuminating it for destruction by the attendant Hurricanes. Hopefully the German aircraft would behave like a rabbit caught in headlights and simply freeze until it was shot down.

After completing their training on the Havoc with 51 OTU, Peter and Jim were posted to 1451 'Turbinlite' Flight at RAF Hunsdon in Hertfordshire, a satellite station for

North Weald. On 2 September 1942 the flight became 530 Squadron but sadly the premise of the aerial searchlight was deeply flawed. The targets were understandably uncooperative and threw themselves in aerial contortions around the heavens. Even a German bomber could out-manoeuvre the Havoc, which in its attempts to follow the target frequently got in the way of the enthusiastic Hurricanes. The Havoc was also clearly visible to the German gunners. After floundering through the skies on several sorties with no reward, 530 Squadron disbanded in February 1943 and Peter and Jim were posted to 141 Squadron. The Turbinlite Havoc disappeared from front-line duties with little to show for the effort and expenditure. With 141 Squadron Peter and Jim returned to a more formidable night-fighter, the pugnacious Bristol Beaufighter. Enthused by the change, both were eager to patrol the night skies from their new base at Ford in Sussex. However, their new commanding officer, Wing Commander J.R.D. 'Bob' Braham, was reviewing the situation and felt that his squadron lacked the necessary depth of experience for combat, so he had them withdrawn to Predannack in Cornwall. There they endured an intense period of practice AI interceptions blended with night 'Ranger' operations attacking German transport on the Brest peninsula. The squadron also foraged far out over the Bay of Biscay seeking combat with Ju88s and Focke-Wulf Condors, which were busy harassing Allied shipping and aircraft of Coastal Command. During this period 141 Squadron also added U-boats and E-boats to its list of targets. The experienced Coles–Carter combination accumulated additional experience and the whole squadron became more efficient and deadly. It was this expertise that facilitated the squadron's selection for 'Serrate'.

Serrate was the code-name used for a new electronic device being developed to counteract the German night-fighters now taking an increasing toll of British bombers. The idea of sending British night-fighters abroad to protect the bombers had previously been broached but the technical capabilities for detecting the enemy were lacking. Even with Serrate, there were many dangers. Bomber crews could not afford to hesitate and would shoot at anything resembling a night-fighter because *any* delay in determining friend from foe put their own lives at risk. Bob Braham and his men understood and accepted this fact. They also knew they would be operating over regions containing some of the strongest anti-aircraft gun concentrations in the world. Then, of course, there were their German counterparts – skilled, well equipped and 'playing at home' – but something had to be done to alleviate the bomber losses. The boffins at the British Telecommunications Research Establishment had been studying the technological issues, particularly the problems and opportunities relating to homing on emissions from the German night-fighters' 'Lichtenstein' radar sets. To help solve some of the problems, they needed to confirm the Lichtenstein's operating frequency, which intelligence had deduced as 490 megacycles – but how were they to prove it? Endangering their own lives, one crew from 1473 (Wireless Investigation) Flight heroically set themselves up as a decoy with radar detection equipment on board their Wellington to monitor the suspected frequency. Like a sacrificial tethered goat, they eventually attracted the attentions of a marauding Ju88 and the Wellington was savagely shot up – but they secured the vital information. Fate favoured the brave and miraculously the crew survived, despite ditching off

Built at Leavesden, this Mosquito NF Mk II HJ911 is similar to the one flown by the Coles/Carter crew. (*BAe via Martin Bowman*)

the English coast on their return. Serendipity then played a mischievously belated hand in May 1943 when the defection of a German air-crew presented the British with a prime working example of the deadly Ju88 night-fighter and its apparatus. This secured all the information required for Serrate and 141 Squadron was selected for its introduction.

After installation of the new equipment, 141 Squadron trained rigorously with Defiants and other squadron members acting as the enemy. Serrate was not a 'stand alone' system and required coordination with the Beaufighter's own AI radar once Serrate had secured a likely target. Deploying their new toy during the summer of 1943, the squadron enjoyed a remarkable rate of success, claiming twenty-three enemy night-fighters downed. That year events in electronic warfare had moved so swiftly that the RAF decided to concentrate its increasing expertise in this area under one command and thus created 100 Group, which was formed in November 1943. Comprising thirteen squadrons flying a selection of aircraft types, 100 Group's role was to use electronics effectively and offensively and provide counter-measures against the strengthening enemy talent in the same field. No. 141 Squadron was ideally suited to join the new Group but the faithful Beaufighter was proving increasingly inadequate, lacking both range and a sufficient speed advantage over its enemies. The decision was taken to re-equip with the de Havilland Mosquito and the first examples arrived during the autumn of 1943. This superlative aircraft, built of balsa and plywood and powered by twin Rolls-Royce Merlins, enjoyed a fearsome reputation and fully deserved the many accolades given to it for speed, manoeuvrability and effectiveness in many roles. Increasing use of this wooden wonder eventually caused German night-fighter pilots to feel themselves becoming much less the hunters and much more the hunted. The fast moving and heavily armed Mosquitoes ranged far and wide, duelling in the darkness and creating a crisis of confidence among its adversaries.

For Peter and Jim, by then both commissioned as pilot officers, the Mosquito's arrival was exciting even if the early examples were second-hand from other units. For the operation of 21/22 June 1944 their allotted aircraft was NF Mk II serial DD732, which was typical of those then bearing the squadron's TW codes. It had first entered service in 1942 and had flown with both 85 and 151 Squadrons. Earlier in its career it had apparently shot down a Do217, and Peter and Jim were hoping to notch up another kill that night so they gave the machine a thorough workout during its routine night flying test (NFT). The NFT was a discipline for evaluating the aircraft and its systems before an operation so the skilled technicians among the ground personnel could complete any minor adjustments required before battle commenced. The machine performed sweetly and gave Peter the impression it was newer than the airframe hours denoted in its records. Satisfied, he signed the aircraft acceptance documentation and followed Jim to the billet they shared to have a rest before setting off in the evening to the briefing. Tonight was planned as a 'Maximum Effort', so the briefing room was a 'full Bomber Command effort with all the trimmings'. Amid the gently swirling haze of cigarette smoke, various specialists outlined the targets for Bomber Command and the forces engaged that night. Some 133 Lancasters and 6 Mosquitoes would strike the synthetic oil plant at Wesseling, with a further 123 Lancasters and 9 Mosquitoes hoping to pulverise another synthetic oil complex at Scholven/Buer. Routes, timings altitudes, known flak concentrations and Luftwaffe resources were all highlighted. The meteorological officer had read all available reports and studied the weather fronts and confidently predicted clear conditions. This was a boon for the target-marking force, whose bright flares would, it was hoped, fall with precision from low altitude to guide in the bombers. In order to create confusion among the enemy air controllers, 32 nimble Mosquitoes would speed towards Berlin and stretch German defences even further. Moving more ponderously but in comparatively safer climes, a force of elderly Stirlings would be bumbling around Guernsey, St Malo and St Nazaire doing some 'gardening'. This activity escalated German shipping losses and made a valuable if unsung contribution to Bomber Command's efforts to defeat the enemy. Penetrating inland, 10 Halifaxes would aid the Resistance forces by dropping containers of supplies and munitions to that unseen army now openly challenging and harrying the German troops moving up towards the recently established second front. There were many flights into history that night. It was the summer solstice so the air-crews had less darkness to hide in. In practical terms, Bomber Command reduced the choice of targets to those that could be reached in darkness but it would still be a busy night. This fact was also apparent to German controllers and strong retaliation was anticipated in a concentrated area of activity. The crews of 141 Squadron sorted out the duties assigned to them and each crew studied the task that lay ahead. Peter and Jim were to 'free-lance' in the Ruhr area with the purpose of 'diverting and/or intercepting enemy night-fighter forces'.

To accomplish their orders, they had a repertoire of techniques. One employed on previous occasions was to act as a decoy close to the bomber stream. Simulating a bomber's radar signature, they would reduce the Mosquito's speed to that of a lumbering Lancaster and paddle along imitating its flight movements. Pretending to be a bomber on the fringes of the main stream, they would appear to have strayed from the protection of the herd. It was well known that such singletons were more vulnerable and provided rich pickings for prowling night-fighters who hunted like hungry tigers and mercilessly culled the unwary. As the bait in this trap, Peter and Jim had to coordinate their activities with split-second timing or risk being shredded by a storm of cannon fire. Peering into the twin cathode ray tubes of their Serrate set, Jim looked for the two fishbone-shaped images that were displayed when the apparatus picked up signals from the German Lichtenstein AI unit. On one screen the 'ribs' of the fishbone would be longer on the side nearest the enemy but became of equal proportion when the target was dead ahead. The other screen conveyed the same image but worked in elevation, so Jim knew whether the target was above or below them. This would be when – and if – they assumed the offensive. Meanwhile they had another electronic aid in this deadly game of cat and mouse. 'Monica' was the code-name for a rearwards-looking radar designed to warn of an aircraft approaching from astern; this emitted a series of bleeps that intensified in frequency as the German closed in for the kill. Dawdling along beside the bomber stream, their role was to appear innocent, unguarded and vulnerable as Monica's shrill warning squawked in their headphones. With perfect timing, just before the German opened fire they would accelerate and whip round behind the enemy, suddenly becoming the hunter not the prey. Such manoeuvres required excellent teamwork. It also tested to the limit the capabilities of their advanced electronics, but they had no monopoly on this. The German 'Flensburg' radar was now homing-in on Monica, in another example of technological leapfrog. British bombers also carried Monica. By carrying out tests with an example of a Flensburg device captured in July 1944, Bomber Command realised to its horror that its operator could obtain a precise signal clearly indicating the target's direction. This was not so much of an issue for a nimble Mosquito pretending to be a bomber, but probably fatal for a bomber unwittingly telling the enemy where it was. Sadly, Flensburg was unknown to the crew of DD732 as they prepared to go hunting the hunters.

Following the briefing, Jim spent half an hour drafting his route for the night's operation. Then, folding his charts, he went back to the billet and both men rested as the evening's shadows heralded the shadowy world of night-fighter combat. Inner tensions tweaked their outer calm when, at around 10pm, they set off for B Flight dispersal. It was in both their natures to allow plenty of time so the pre-flight activities could be precise and unhurried. The colourfully declining daylight clutched the western heavens as Peter conducted his pre-flight inspection of the Mosquito. Jim climbed the small, retractable, aluminium ladder, stowed his parachute and dinghy pack, and then dropped back down for a last draught of fresh evening air. The next few hours would be spent breathing tired, stale oxygen through a mask. As Peter conducted his external check of the aircraft, Jim ran through his own mental checklist. An escape kit had been drawn but he fervently hoped not to need it. He also rechecked the night's 'sisters'. Obtained through intelligence sources and printed on easily eaten rice paper, these were the enemy's 'colours of the day' – signal flare codes for the next 24 hours. An aircraft engaged by flak might use these flares to dupe enemy gunners into ceasing fire. Lastly Jim made a final check of his pockets to ensure he had no personal belongings that might provide 'unofficial means of identification', and then he was ready. Fortunately the Mosquito was a relatively warm and cosy aircraft; heat was drawn into the cockpit from the port radiator through a vent behind Peter's seat. This meant both men flew more lightly attired than other less fortunate aviators of the period. There was no need for heavy flying jackets and Jim simply wore his battledress with a light roll-necked pullover, although he was wearing a pair of 'escape' flying boots. These were full length and fleece-lined, but they had a detachable top so they could be quickly converted to resemble civilian shoes should the need arise. Peter opted for a Sidcot suit. Ironically this would cause him a few problems before the night was out. Drawing up the ladder, Jim closed the hatch and Mosquito DD732 prepared for take-off.

A few minutes later both Merlins were making Rolls-Royce music. To us, living in the next century, this sound offers an unforgettable evocation of the era but it was deafening to the air-crews who lived in close proximity to it for hours on end. Peter was running through systems functionality as each engine was independently evaluated. Opening each to 2,000rpm, he lowered and raised the flaps, watching for any suggestion of sluggishness that might indicate hydraulic pump failure. The electrical system was charging happily at 29 volts indicated, and all other checks gave DD732 a clean bill of health. It was about 11pm when call sign Gomar 25 got clearance to take off and power surged through both engines as the Mosquito swiftly accelerated, eagerly seeking its element. Deftly Peter checked the aircraft's characteristic tendency to swing left by advancing the port throttle slightly ahead of the starboard. As the aircraft lifted smoothly away, the undercarriage tucked tightly into the nacelles and the now uncluttered aerodynamics saw the aircraft moving swiftly beyond 200mph. As they climbed away from West Raynham, Jim gave Peter their course for Germany.

Navigational techniques had developed rapidly since the early nights of 1939/40 and Jim now had the benefit of more sophisticated electronics through the use of 'Gee'. Following the damning revelations in the Butt Report, British scientists had developed this new electronic system based on an imaginary grid that overlaid much of Europe. Signals transmitted from suitably spaced stations in the UK were received on board the distant aircraft, whose navigator, using special charts corresponding to the electronic grid, could plot his position to within 6 miles or less, depending on his distance from the transmitters, by checking the time differences between the radar pulses received. Gee gave the RAF an advantage until German countermeasures inevitably caught up and started jamming the signals, rendering the system ineffective for bombing. However, the jamming was weak on the approaches to the continent so Gee still proved a useful navigational aid and Jim plotted their course using Gee until the jamming curtailed its value and he switched to more traditional techniques. Unfortunately the weather once again proved capricious and the predicted clear conditions failed to materialise. Faced with ten-tenths cloud, the bombing force used another electronic device from its armoury known as H2S, a ground-mapping radar capable of reading through cloud and displaying an image of the terrain below.

By now Jim had calculated that they were some 40 to 50 miles west of Cologne. Aware of the likelihood of German night-fighter activity, he was now focusing his attention on the Serrate set. Until now, the cathode ray tubes had been dormant but the flickering of excited pixel activity indicated the presence of a nearby German night-fighter. Studying the fishbone illuminations, Jim estimated their target to be at 2 o' clock and advised Peter to alter course for an interception. The hunt was on and the Mosquito banked towards its prey. Watching the flickering screens, Jim guided Peter in as they carefully pursued their target, which was, they hoped, completely unaware of their presence. They had been trained to kill and set about the task with precision – there was nothing chivalrous about aerial combat in the night skies over Germany. Closely monitoring the variations in signal strength, Jim tracked the target and waited for their AI to register a contact. No one wishing to live flew straight and level for long so their pursuit involved a series of course and altitude corrections, but the continuing Serrate signals indicated they were slowly gaining. The minutes ticked anxiously by as the Mosquito manoeuvred stealthily astern of the enemy night-fighter, creeping up like a dark assassin. The minutes passed as they weaved around the sky, metaphorical dagger in hand. All the time they remained alert for any alarm from Monica. Tension flew as their third crew member. The Serrate signals were strong, but could not indicate the distance to the enemy – but where the hell was the AI contact? They needed AI, then a visual, before the kill. The night skies were crowded and the risk of 'friendly fire' was high.

Jim was sure the distance was diminishing and calmly waited for the AI to register. Then suddenly it all went wrong, giving them no time to react. One moment they were slipping smoothly along on air undisturbed but for their tracking undulations and the occasional bumps from fading propeller wash. Suddenly, and without warning, flak tore the heavens asunder in the most savage and sudden barrage they had ever seen. Normally there were searchlights and feelers of flak that they simply avoided. This time it surrounded their aircraft in a maelstrom of flashes and explosions. Buffeted by blasts, it felt like they had been deliberately drawn into a trap. Peter had no time to take evasive action before the Mosquito was hit. Both men heard the sickening crump and a storm of shrapnel was felt striking the aircraft. Amazingly not one shard struck flesh but the stench of cordite was followed immediately by the reek of high-octane fuel. At any instant they expected their 'wooden wonder' to flare like a giant match, incinerating its crew in a matter of seconds. But miraculously there were no flames and the tumult of exploding shells ceased as suddenly as it had started. Jim and Peter were shocked, frightened but still alive, and the reassuring rhythm from both Merlins made them wonder if the flak attack had really happened. However, Peter knew they had not escaped entirely unscathed. Following the last burst, the aircraft had been so buffeted that it took him a few moments to realise it was not settling back into its normal flying attitude. Instead, it sagged wearily back on its tail and he could only maintain control with strong forward pressure on the control column. This was evidence of damage, but they had no way of visually ascertaining the extent beyond what they could see from the cockpit. An indication of further trouble quickly became evident when Jim checked their fuel gauges. He was aghast to see the indicator for the 150-gallon fuselage tanks draining rapidly towards empty. Their aircraft was haemorrhaging its lifeblood into the heavens. Just as the tank registered zero, Peter switched to draw from the inner wing tanks and prayed for a smooth transition. It was not to be. While their power was uninterrupted, the fuel status for these tanks was also diminishing faster than allowable for normal consumption. Their wing tanks were also leaking. More slowly, maybe, but still at a noticeable rate so the damage had to be extensive. Any hope of continuing their patrol was now transformed into a struggle for survival as Jim set a course for home.

They were at 20,000 feet and had been flying straight and level for longer than was healthy but weaving would reduce their range and Peter was also unsure about the aircraft's structural integrity. Reducing power and trimming as best he could for better economy, Peter commenced a shallow glide on the westerly heading given by Jim. Far from home, both realised their vulnerability in an aircraft that might disintegrate under the duress of any evasive action or even through the simple process of lowering their undercarriage. Furthermore they could no longer rely on the normal mathematics of fuel consumption converted into range and they might not even have enough to reach home. Chasing their Serrate contact had taken them towards Duisberg and Jim now desperately needed confirmation of their position to plot the shortest course home. As expected, Luftwaffe countermeasures were swamping the Gee signals making the equipment virtually useless at this range. Their heading, although westerly, now lacked the precision needed to optimise the situation for the ever-dwindling amount of fuel left in the leaking tanks. Jim knew that the German jamming of Gee weakened near the enemy coast and, sure enough, as they approached the North Sea the Gee signal strength intensified so he was able to obtain a better fix on their position. He told Peter to adjust course. His navigation had been sound and he was inwardly relieved when only a minor correction proved necessary for an increasingly anxious run towards West Raynham. Jim calculated that there was a narrow margin for error and believed that they stood a chance providing the rate of fuel lost did not increase. Leaving the enemy coastline behind, they now contemplated the additional anxiety of a long North Sea crossing.

Far below, the brooding darkness of the North Sea had swallowed countless aircraft but Peter was determined not to join the many unfortunate aviators who would forever have no known grave. He tuned to the emergency frequency and broadcast the words uttered by so many airmen in distress, 'Mayday, Mayday, Mayday', followed by their call sign. In an instant the reassuring voice of the Air Sea Rescue controller came through. He confirmed their position and took control of guiding home the wounded hunter. Jim now had good Gee signals so kept up a running commentary of their coordinates on the emergency frequency. Calmly the ASR controller vectored the Mosquito towards its base and, as they crossed the English coast, bade them farewell and wished them good luck, before passing them neatly into the hands of the air traffic controller at West Raynham.

By now their commanding officer, Wing Commander Charles Vivian Winn, knew of their predicament. As an experienced pilot himself, he understood their situation and their emotions. As they lost altitude towards the airfield, Winn and Peter talked about the known aspects of the Mosquito's condition. Nearing the aerodrome, they faced the problem of lowering their undercarriage. This might cause the aircraft to become dramatically unstable or even to disintegrate when the wheels emerged. Even under normal conditions the Mosquito had a tail-down attitude when the undercarriage and flaps were lowered and it lost height rapidly. Jim and Peter were not enthusiastic about the idea of baling out, and after a further discussion they decided to risk a standard approach and landing, hoping there would be no catastrophic failure when the landing gear was lowered on a machine that was perhaps already structurally weakened. Peter recalled the Pilot's Notes for the Mk II, which cheerfully advocated, 'Before Landing. If the flight has been of any duration, operate the undercarriage up and down a few times before finally lowering for landing.' Not this time – it would be like stressing a piece of bent metal until it broke.

Peter had good brake pressure and everything else seemed fine as he eased back below 180mph and selected undercarriage down. The indicators sat slap in the middle of Peter's control console and both airmen stared at it, nervously awaiting green lights. Moments later Peter felt the aircraft slew awkwardly. He corrected the yaw but there was no comforting green light from both indicators. It was grimly evident that the port wheel had lowered normally but the starboard leg had stuck, probably halfway down. It was difficult to be sure. Jim craned against the cockpit Perspex and tried using a torch to see but the angle was difficult. What he could discern offered little comfort and Peter leant over to check for himself. Judging from the torchlight's beam, it seemed as if the entire starboard wheel and undercarriage compression legs had been blasted away, leaving only the battered stumps of the undercarriage legs. Where the main wheel tyre ought to have been there was simply air. With only part of the strut visible, the wheel might have been left behind in its nacelle but it was impossible to tell, and either way they were in serious trouble. Wing Commander Winn had already sent for the engineering officer and a three-way conversation ensued, with Jim apprehensively eyeing their dwindling fuel supplies while Peter discussed how to land. Some months ago he had landed an Airspeed Oxford on one wheel without serious mishap, but that docile trainer had a far lower landing speed than the Mosquito. In addition, there had been no ragged, partially descended stumps to stab in to the soil. In this condition the Mosquito risked digging in on its starboard side and then cartwheeling, with both airmen and aircraft being torn apart in a splintering, burning trail of death and destruction. These unspoken thoughts soon scotched the idea of landing on one wheel. It was then suggested that Peter should slam the aircraft down so hard that the port undercarriage would break under the impact, allowing them to belly in and slither to a standstill on the grass before emerging like Hollywood heroes. Peter felt this idea was crazy and far too dangerous, so he decided to gain altitude and allow Jim to bale out.

Baling out of a Mosquito was no easy matter. The emergency exit was in close proximity to the whirling blades of the starboard de Havilland hydromatic airscrew, so this engine had to be shut down before anyone baled out. Otherwise it would be like leaping into a bacon slicer. To avoid diced airman, it was standard procedure to feather the starboard propeller and then bale out. Simple!

Peter climbed away from West Raynham. Jim had calculated that Peter would have enough fuel to get back there to attempt a crash-landing once he had jumped out. Checking that Jim was ready to jump, Peter reached over to the prominent feathering buttons on the starboard side of his instrument panel. Firmly depressing the right-hand button, Peter held it until it engaged, then released it, closed the starboard throttle and firmly counteracted the power loss with his controls. The aircraft was becoming increasingly difficult to handle as the propeller came to a standstill. Moving quickly, Jim released his seat harness, wished Peter luck and then discarded his helmet and r/t connections. Unstowing his chest pack parachute, he clipped it to his harness before kneeling down in the door well and tugging the emergency release on the door handle. This was supposed to snap free the hinge pins and send the hatch tumbling clear but nothing happened! Angry, Jim put his shoulder to it and pressed hard. It still stubbornly refused to release. Sweating with exertion and fear, Jim clambered halfway back into his seat and gripped the edge for more effective leverage. Withdrawing both legs, he then kicked out hard at the offending panel. It vanished. With no time for further farewells, Jim dropped to his knees and rolled headfirst out into the night sky. Even though it was dark, his adrenalin-stimulated senses took in some of the damage invisible from the cockpit. Where the starboard nacelle should have had undercarriage doors and a main wheel, there was simply a void with strips of rubber and splintered wood thrashing in the slipstream.

Tumbling away, Jim tugged his ripcord. To his relief the parachute burst from its pack, cracked open and seemed to haul him upright with a painful stab in the groin where the harness ran between his legs. From the thunder of twin Merlins and the cockpit drama of a few seconds ago, he was suddenly suspended in the night sky with the sound of the Mosquito dwindling into the distance. He felt very lonely, yet there was no sensation of descending; it also felt very tranquil, almost comforting. The darkness took on a misty hue as he floated into a cloud layer that robbed him of any horizon as a reference for his height. From his altitude on baling out, he estimated himself to be at about 4,500 feet. Drifting gently through the calmly caressing clouds seemed somehow soothing, but at about 1,000 feet he drifted clear. Below the cloud base it was drizzling uncomfortably and, peering earthwards, Jim could just make out something of what lay below, making his nerves jangle and his pulse race. He cursed himself for not attaching the dinghy to his parachute harness. A straightish line below, shining silver-grey in the gloom, looked like a river, perhaps the Great Ouse near King's Lynn. Unsure how to alter his direction of drift, he descending with mounting alarm towards the threat of drowning. As he got closer he saw a light that appeared to be proceeding along the river. Instinctively he called out but his shouted 'Hello, Hello' received no answer, nor did the light alter course. He became aware that the light was hardly following the motion of a boat, the movement was not right. Relief now blossomed as he realised that what he could see was a road, with moonlight reflecting off the wet tarmac; the light was the lamp from someone's bicycle. However, his shouts still drew no answer, and he was now drifting away from the road with the darkness below growing to engulf him.

Having seen films about parachute jumping and undergone some training, Jim expected to land hard and was mentally preparing to roll in an effort to absorb the impact and avoid broken bones. But then, without any noticeable jolt, his heels touched terra firma and he found himself standing upright in a field. He felt almost obliged to roll for effect but it was more of a gentle sag at the knees from sheer relief – his landing had been like thistledown as the parachute folds fluttered lazily to earth and the rigging lines collapsed. Standing up again, Jim twisted the lines and smacked the quick release box for the parachute and shrugged himself clear of the harness. Stepping away from the lines, he took a few paces to survey his surroundings. It was dark and still in the countryside with no hint of any nearby human habitation. The hours spent practising and protecting his night vision helped as he identified a hedge and field gate nearby. Gathering his parachute, he bundled it beneath the hedge then clambered over the gate into a narrow country lane. Guessing which way to go, he chose left and set off walking through the drizzle, damp but down in one piece. His main concern was whether Peter had survived the crash-landing at West Raynham.

After walking for about 10 minutes Jim came to a house set back about 30 yards from the road on his right. It was an attractive, Georgian detached property served by a semi-circular gravel drive along which he now crunched. Reaching the front door, he knocked firmly and heard the sound echoing away inside. Stepping back, he waited. The door remained closed but there was movement overhead then a window opened and a woman's voice carried nervously from an upstairs window asking who he was and what he wanted. Understanding her anxiety, Jim gave his name and a brief explanation, and then asked if she had a telephone he could use to call West Raynham. The woman hesitated uncertainly before asking him to leave, explaining that she was alone in the house with a baby. Politely persistent, Jim explained that he understood her concerns but requested that she at least call the police and advise them of his whereabouts. There was no time for a response before Jim heard footsteps on the gravel behind him and turned to see several figures emerging from the darkness. One man asked if Jim were the airman who had baled out, and, just as he was replying, a light came on and the front door opened. The woman emerged to greet her husband, who was one of the search party, and they all hurried inside.

Jim found himself in a large, spacious hall. Before he knew it, a tumbler of whisky appeared in his hand. The woman's husband then explained that he had departed earlier to report for voluntary duty with the local Royal Observer Corps. He had been cycling along the lane when he heard someone calling, but never for a moment thought to look skywards. Still perplexed, he continued to the ROC post where he learned that a Mosquito had crashed in the vicinity and at least one of the crew had baled out. This explained the 'heavenly' voice so he hurried to retrace his route with a search party from the ROC. They had not found Peter but the search was continuing and military personnel were scouring the surrounding countryside. As the man spoke, his young son was brought down to meet the airman and it was obviously a great event for the excited toddler. Meanwhile a call to West Raynham resulted in Wing Commander Winn and Jim's flight leader, Flight Lieutenant Anderson, shortly arriving by car. They told Jim his Mosquito had crashed at 0240 hours at Litcham in Norfolk but there was some concern because Peter had still not been located. They decided to go and view the wreckage. Pausing en route to collect his parachute, Jim saw in the gathering daylight just how lucky he had been. He had drifted down into a small paddock adjacent to a railway line and enclosed on three sides by tall poplar trees. He had floated in on the open side, narrowly avoiding becoming entangled in the trees which would have meant at least an uncomfortable arrival and would have greatly increased his chances of being injured if he had fallen when trying to extricate himself from the branches.

Reaching the crash site, they found Auxiliary Fire Service tenders were still trying to douse the flames. Wreckage was strewn across the countryside, unrecognisable as a Mosquito. Stepping from the car, they were approached by a worried-looking AFS officer who told them that his men had just found the body of the pilot amid the debris. Jim was shocked – what could have gone wrong?

We shall never know for sure. When his navigator vanished into the darkness, Peter Coles again called the control tower to report Jim's departure. He was having serious misgivings about trying to slam his aircraft down so hard that it broke the one descended wheel, and then sliding the machine along on its belly. Realistically the outcome was more likely to be his charred remains spread among a smear of smouldering debris. His commanding officer had similar misgivings and now ordered Peter to try to bale out, rather than restarting the feathered engine for an approach.

Following a brief acknowledgement of this instruction, nothing further had been heard from the pilot. After learning of Jim Carter's safe arrival, Winn hoped that good news about Coles would soon follow. However, hearing nothing after the call confirming Jim's safety, Winn decided to go and collect the navigator, still hoping that the pilot would soon be found safe and well.

What had once been a sleek twin-engined night-fighter was now no more than splintered fragments of burning balsa and plywood surrounding the smouldering carcasses of its twin Merlin engines. The AFS officer informed them that the charred torso of the pilot had just been discovered, burned beyond recognition. Telling Jim to remain in the car, Winn and Anderson went to confirm the unfortunate pilot's fate, leaving the distressed navigator wondering how it had happened and feeling the terrible guilt of the survivor. He now knew the idea of crash-landing the Mosquito had been abandoned, so what could have happened after Peter had acknowledged the order to bale out? Why had he remained on board? These thoughts chased anxiously around his mind as the two officers returned. Winn was looking very annoyed. Nearing the car, he told Jim not to worry – they had not found Peter's remains. Winn was angry because the worry had been unnecessary. The 'pilot's body' pointed out to them had transpired on closer examination to be the molten remains of the red rubber dinghy, not Peter's roasted flesh. In the firemen's defence, it had looked grotesquely similar to a headless, limbless and very burnt human torso. The main question now was where *was* Peter? Had his parachute failed? Was he lying injured or dead somewhere?

Peter held the aircraft steady, undid his seat harness, disconnected his headphones and double-checked there was nothing to snag his seat-type parachute to prevent a swift egress. Trimming the aircraft as best he could, he held it steady until the last moment and then pulled himself swiftly from his seat. Given that there was power only on one side, he would have only moments before the aircraft rolled over and plummeted earthwards. Just as the aircraft started to twist over, he dropped into a crouch over the exit hatch then rolled headlong forward for a textbook tumble into the night. Gripping the ripcord, he hesitated for a moment to ensure he was clear of the machine and then tugged hard. The canvas pack burst open to release a stream of pale yellow nylon that whipped out behind him then ballooned overhead. His descent was arrested in a jaw-jarring jerk and he found himself floating between two layers of cloud. The fate of Mosquito DD732 was evidenced by a flash of flame that suffused into a brief bright flower spreading across the cloudscape before wilting into the night. Peter drifted into the lower layer of cloud and, after a brief interlude, floated serenely clear and descended gently into a healthily ripening cornfield. The tall rain-soaked stalks dampened his Sidcot suit but he was otherwise unscathed and grateful for a safe descent. Releasing his parachute, he reviewed his surroundings as best he could, but the tall crops gave no clue as to which way he should go. Tossing a mental coin, he set off in what ultimately transpired to be completely the wrong direction because he circumnavigated almost the entire field before finding the gateway only a few yards from where he had touched down. This gateway opened on to a country lane. After less than a mile he came across an army post, a searchlight or AA detachment, with a sentry on duty.

Startled by the sudden appearance of this damp, dishevelled and disreputable-looking character claiming to be an airman, the sentry did not conceal his suspicions and Peter promptly found himself on the prodding end of a bayonet. There was little by way of insignia on or beneath the Sidcot suit to confirm his story and news of the lost Mosquito had not yet reached this outpost. The guard simply did not believe Peter's story and, despite the latter's protestations, the prodding continued until he found himself in the sergeant's quarters where the soldier awoke his superior. Both soldiers were wary but, as dawn brightened the sky, they could see his apparel more clearly and Peter had to concede their behaviour was militarily correct under the circumstances. His flying suit gave no real clue as to which side he belonged to, and soon after the Normandy invasion there had been rumours that the Germans would try to infiltrate saboteurs to attack Allied airfields or other targets in East Anglia. These troops were quite properly taking no chances. Keeping Peter under guard, the sergeant attempted to radio his headquarters but it seemed that the radio had either failed or there was no one on duty at the other end. This caused even more concern; perhaps the enemy had sabotaged communications? With no radio, the sergeant now sent a despatch rider but Peter's fortunes were about to improve when the motorcyclist met an American patrol searching for the missing Mosquito pilot.

Peter was pleased when the briefest of negotiations saw him handed over to the USAAF patrol who took him to collect his parachute. Only in daylight did he see that one of the panels had split and the canvas pack was torn. On examination, it seemed shrapnel from an exploding shell had cut through the pack and torn into the canopy. Quite apart from the fact the shrapnel had to have penetrated the cockpit with some velocity, its proximity to an essential part of his anatomy evoked eye-watering contemplation. He considered himself very lucky and was delighted to accept some American hospitality at a nearby airbase where he eagerly consumed a substantial US-style breakfast while his hosts contacted West Raynham. Peter was soon picked up by Flight Lieutenant Anderson and was reunited with Jim Carter. The sum total of their injuries was a slight cut to Jim's face, probably gained when he exited the Mosquito.

Mosquito DD732 was no more but the hatch that had stubbornly refused to jettison was discovered intact and subsequently saw service as the squadron scoreboard. Compensation was available for the farmer on whose land the aircraft had fallen but airmen sent to salvage the wreckage said the elderly rustic was somewhat philosophical about the event and commented that aeroplanes were crashing on his land all the time! This was true for the region overall but few crashes had such happy endings. Peter and Jim were given two days survivors' leave which they spent in the Norfolk coastal resort of Hunstanton. They resumed operations on 27 June and completed their tour without further mishap before being posted to 51 OTU at Cranfield to instruct others on the Mosquito. Among other tips, Jim passed on the method of shifting a stubborn escape hatch using both feet as a faster and more effective method than the procedure written in the manual.

Following their time at Cranfield, Peter and Jim faced several options regarding their future in the RAF. Having now completed two tours together, they were offered a return to operations or the choice of non-operational flying. It was now February 1945 and the war was clearly in its closing months. Following some discussion, Peter and Jim decided to go their separate ways. Jim had opted for combat, and a further five sorties with 85 Squadron. Peter went to RAF Montrose for miscellaneous flying duties and by the end of the war he had amassed a total of more than 1,000 flying hours.

Peter Coles and James Carter had been an excellent combat team in an elite service, each trusting the other and both putting faith in their Mosquito. While they had been fortunate, the night of 21/22 June 1944 had been a grim one for the RAF with 46 aircraft lost – 12.7 per cent of the attacking force. The Lancasters of 5 Group were particularly hard hit by night-fighters, with 44, 49 and 619 Squadrons each losing six machines apiece despite the endeavours of 141 Squadron and other countermeasures. Their Mosquitoes had set out to sting the enemy but, for Peter and Jim, it had been very much a case of the stinger stung. Matters might have been a lot worse, though, and their flight into history could all too easily have resulted in two more names on the war memorials instead of a note in Norfolk's Civil Defence Records.

Both men returned to busy civilian lives, although Jim Carter continued flying part-time from Castle Bromwich with the RAF Volunteer Reserve until 1955. The two men lost contact until thirty years later Jim tried to locate his former pilot. Aviation historian Chris Gotts helped but it was not to be and the crew of Mosquito DD732 were destined never to meet again as Jim died in March 2003. This story is a tribute to their courage.

CHAPTER NINE

Clobber College

During the summer of 1988 the East Anglian harvest yielded more than just food for the nation. Through August and September the East Anglian Aircraft Research Group recovered a Republic P-47 Thunderbolt, parts from a B-17 and three P-51 Mustangs. Two of the latter were lost in a mid-air collision, the type of mishap that occurred with tragic regularity in the congested wartime skies over Eastern England.

Tuesday 27 February 1945 saw the Leiston-based 357th Fighter Group leaving Suffolk to support the bombers over the ever-diminishing remains of Hitler's vaunted Thousand Year Reich. Dubbed the Yoxford Boys by German propaganda because of their airfield's proximity to that town, the 357FG was one of the USAAF's premier fighter groups. It had numerous aces in its midst, including their top-scoring Captain Leonard K. 'Kit' Carson, now the operations officer. Kit had served with the Group from its inception and eventually completed two tours. His prowess saw him achieve 18.5 victories and he amassed considerable combat experience, which he and other combat veterans imparted to newly arrived neophytes through the 554th Fighter Training Unit attached to the 362nd Fighter Squadron, 357FG, and known to the pilots as 'Clobber College'. Through the auspices of this unit, veterans like Kit took the tyros aloft to test their abilities and help indoctrinate them into the European Theatre of Operations. More simply, they provided area familiarisation flights intermingled with combat training so the more experienced tutor could determine whether new arrivals were ready for combat operations. This was the task undertaken by Kit that clear winter's morning.

Kit telephoned for flight clearance and briefed his four fledglings regarding the plans for their brief local training sortie. Kit wanted to complete the flight and return before mid-day when the skies would become crowded with aircraft returning from operations. The weather was favourable, with good visibility that would help his brood learn the local landmarks around Station 373, while there was also room for some combat practice beneath the clouds at 5,000 feet.

The pilots were freshmen but the aircraft allocated to Clobber College were war-weary machines retired from front-line combat. The USAAF recognised this status by adding the letters WW to the aircraft's official serial number. Second Lieutenant Ralph E. Eisert was

John C. Howell stands by the starboard tailplane of Shoo Shoo Baby contemplating a very close call. His participation in Operation Chatanooga was almost the last for him and his favourite Mustang. The purpose of Chatanooga on 21 May 1944 was to destroy enemy locomotives, railway stock and as much rail infrastructure as possible before D-Day. (*Merle Olmsted*)

given P-51B-15NA, serial 43-24766WW, a tired type of over 606 hours that had only just returned to service following the replacement of the main wheel assembly, perhaps abused by some rather hard landings. Checks prior to the aircraft's re-entering service saw the manifold regulator replaced and crew chief Corporal Ercil O. Parletts was now satisfied that the aircraft in his custody was once again ready for its training role. Second Lieutenant Robert R. Hoffman was given a Mustang that had achieved a little more distinction in the Group's battle annals. P-51B-10NA, 42-106447WW, with nearly 579 flying hours, had been the mount for First Lieutenant John C. Howell and was personalised as 'Shoo Shoo Baby'. On 21 May 1944 Howell had taken serious flak damage while strafing trains but Shoo Shoo Baby had struggled home safely and further earned its spurs during shuttle missions to Russia. Now, still proudly wearing its nose art, the Mustang had retired into the ranks of Clobber College and had flown at least fourteen times with various trainees. Throughout this period Shoo Shoo Baby had suffered only a minor problem when the wheel well doors failed to retract, but this was soon addressed by crew chief Corporal Leonard Traber.

A fine study of Shoo Shoo Baby taken from the 385BG B-17 'Spirit of Chicago'. (*Merle Olmsted*)

Jostling behind Kit, the Merlin engines of the four Mustangs rasped and crackled as they taxied out, waddling like quarrelsome ducklings. Airborne a few minutes later, they formed behind their leader and cruised easily over the countryside with Kit pointing out features like a tour guide. Then they conducted some basic manoeuvres and Kit decided to assess their capabilities in a 'Lufbery'. This defensive aerial manoeuvre was accredited to the American First World War ace Raoul Lufbery but the tactic's true provenance is uncertain. Essentially, disadvantaged fighters would fly in a tight circle, each protecting the other's tail from enemy interceptors. Knowing the Lufbery might save young pilots in a tight spot, Kit prepared his flight to practise the control and coordination required but things went horribly wrong. He later described what happened in his statement.

On February 27 1945 I took off with a flight of five ships for the purpose of a transition formation flight.

We had flown in our local area for about forty minutes when I got the flight into a right echelon formation and peeled off into a Luf Berry [sic] circle at about five thousand feet. In the course of the Luf Berry I looked back to check the interval between ships and seeing that it was satisfactory, I tightened the radius of the turn. We had lost altitude down to three thousand feet and I was going to level out and have them rejoin formation in preparation to land when I looked back once more and saw two ships spinning out of the circle. One had lost a wing tip and aileron and in the course of descent the whole left wing folded. The other ship was intact but was spinning violently; he made a partial recovery a few hundred feet off the ground but re-entered the spin and they both crashed within two hundred feet of each other, neither pilot getting out.

I did not see the immediate cause of the accident but the pilot who was at the tail end of the circle stated that one pilot was attempting to turn directly inside of the other, thus putting the other ship on the outside of the turn in his blind spot, that is beneath his wings.

In view of the fact that the possibility of material failure is very small, I believe that the pilot making the shorter turn snapped out of the turn and collided with the other, or each having the other in a blind spot made a fatal move which caused the collision.

Each of these pilots had approximately 200 hours in P-40 type aircraft, one having 1,000 hours in training command and the other having 430 hours. Each had 9 hours in P-51 type aircraft before their last flight.

I had every confidence in their pilot ability and judgement.

Eyewitnesses on the ground ran to assist. Police Constable Wallace Charles Allum also made a statement to the Accident Investigation Board:

At about 1150 hours I was in my garden when my attention was drawn by the noise of planes in the air. I saw in the direction of Darsham about six planes; they appeared to be flying in a circle, when I saw two planes collide . . . from my position, it appeared to me as though they had collided wing tip to wing tip. As soon as the collision occurred, I saw pieces fall from both planes, and the planes made a dive to earth. There was then a slight explosion, and a huge volume of black smoke went up in the air. I arrived at the scene of the crash about ten minutes after. Nothing could be done, as the ammunition was exploding, and the heat was intense from the burning planes . . .

Allum's official East Suffolk Police Report added that both aircraft had fallen beside the Darsham road near Westleton village.

Another eyewitness, young Cyril Fuller, was even closer and was among the first on the scene. The sight of the five Mustangs had given him a welcome excuse to pause in the laborious task of cutting saplings from Wilderness Wood for army latrine poles. Being near the edge of the trees, his view was uninterrupted and it appeared that two of the fighters had turned into each other, smashing together cockpit against cockpit. Frightened by the noise, Cyril and his companions dived into the nearest ditch as the two machines screeched earthwards and exploded in neighbouring fields.

Cyril was quickly on his feet and raced towards the nearest machine but he soon realised there was no hope for the pilot. The nose had embedded deeply into a meadow and it was

Some of the 357FG veterans visit the crash-site of Shoo Shoo Baby, where their erstwhile comrade Ralph Eisert was lost.

burning furiously. Standing back from the intense heat, Cyril never forgot seeing the pilot slumped forward as flames consumed the cockpit. Would-be rescuers were forced to retreat as ammunition exploded and two columns of acrid black smoke merged to hang, shroud-like, in the sky overhead.

After the USAAF had removed the bodies, a local gamekeeper, Walter Lee, received 10s for filling each of the craters. Rumour had it that little effort was made to clear the wreckage below plough depth, and that rumour was substantiated when EAARG searchers obtained powerful responses on their metal detectors and planned the first recovery. Coincidentally, former members and families of the 357FG were visiting England for their 1988 reunion tour and on Sunday 21 August the recovery team had the exciting privilege of a visit by equally enthusiastic veterans and their wives. On arrival, the veterans found a crater some 8 feet deep, in which the digging team had exposed the rear of the Packhard-Merlin, which stood almost vertically. To reach the engine, much of the work had been by hand, painstakingly slow but essential to ensure smaller artefacts were not overlooked. This process had taken them through what remained of the burnt cockpit where they found some

These few personal items are poignant reminders of the young airman. A gold ring and a Zippo lighter were found in the remains of the Mustang's cockpit.

The angle of impact and the depth of penetration are clearly illustrated in this picture as members of the recovery team dig around the engine by hand.

The dry summer resulted in tough digging conditions but at last the Merlin was hoisted free from its long entombment.

Warbird harvest. David Wade guides the propeller boss with its single blade clear of the crater as Pat Ramm dextrously manipulates the digger's controls.

When the armour-plating from behind the pilot's seat was lifted away, it revealed a concertinaed cockpit.

Dog-tags belonging to both pilots were found. Their service numbers are shown. The inscriptions T42-43 and T43-44 refer to their anti-tetanus inoculations, while the single letters 'O' and 'B' give blood group information for medical personnel. The letter 'P' at bottom right denotes Protestant faith. The key is thought to be a locker key, its contents forever unclaimed.

Silver wings glint in the morning sunlight after being excavated from the Suffolk soil that had hidden them for so many years. These were once proudly worn by young Robert Hoffman.

Jeff Carless, one of East Anglia's leading researchers, supervises the recovery of the oil-soaked engine.

This flare pistol would have been used to fire recognition colours, perhaps to identify the aircraft as friendly to over-enthusiastic anti-aircraft gunners.

A machine-gun (centre) embedded almost vertically in the ground. Any weapons found were handed in to the local constabulary.

poignant reminders of the young pilot. One of Eisert's dog-tags confirmed whose machine it was, and careful sifting of the soil revealed a ring and a Zippo lighter. Although the veterans were keen to stay, their tour itinerary had already been disrupted and they could not wait to see the engine of Shoo Shoo Baby hoisted clear later that afternoon.

On 4 September the continuing harvest enabled EAARG members to return to excavate Ralph Hoffman's aircraft. Some of the best items to appear were found near the surface during early hand digging. Less than 4 feet down the solid thunk of spade on metal revealed the armour-plating from behind the pilot's seat. When this was removed both of Hoffman's dog-tags were revealed, still on their chain with what was presumably his locker key. In the earth nearby was an even more symbolic discovery – the young aviator's silver wings, still glittering in the sunlight.

Strong detector readings to one side of the crater produced a burnt tyre and undercarriage leg, part of the new assembly fitted all those decades earlier. Returning to the centre of impact, they uncovered a very mangled Packhard Merlin V-1650-3 engine, serial 43-49314, which records later revealed to have flown for 236 hours. It was beyond any hope of restoration. The supercharger been ripped away and the front banks of cylinders splayed into an incongruous Vee pattern, indicating the force of the impact, as did further chunks of shattered engine pulled from the crater. One blade was still located in the propeller boss and two more were found nearby.

The hands on this corroded watch face, frozen in time at the moment of impact, tell of a young airman who did not get the time he deserved for his life, for children and grandchildren. His was a flight into history, a flight into eternity and a sacrifice that must never be forgotten.

Fate and inexperience had cruelly robbed these two young pilots of their lives – of family fulfilment, future careers and the chance one day to return as veterans. The remains of Lieutenant Ralph E. Eisert Jr were repatriated by his family and reinterred back home, while Lieutenant Robert R. Hoffman rests today in the beautiful US Cemetery at Madingley near Cambridge. The headstones and the Wall of the Missing there are mirrored by RAF names at Runnymede and on the tablets for the fallen in the Deutschen Soldatenfriedhof at Cannock Chase. These losses left shattered families in a world at war. Their young men had flown into history, but the work of aviation historians, researchers and archaeologists seeks to ensure such flights are no longer anonymous and unrecognised. We owe them that – and so much more.

Bibliography

The Blitz Then and Now, Battle of Britain Prints International, 1990

Chorley, W.R., *Royal Air Force Bomber Command Losses*, Midland Counties, 1992

Edwards, Squadron Leader Ralph, *In the Thick of It*, Images, 1994

Falconer, Jonathan, *Bomber Command Handbook, 1939–1945*, Sutton, 1998

Freeman, Roger A., *Mighty Eighth War Diary*, Jane's, 1981

Goodrum, Alastair, *No Place for Chivalry*, Grub Street, 2005

Goss, Chris, *The Luftwaffe Bombers' Battle of Britain*, Crecy, 2000

Gunston, Bill, *Night-fighters*, Patrick Stephens, 1976

Olmsted, Merle, *The 357th Over Europe*, Phalanx Publishing, 1994

Price, Alfred, *Instruments of Darkness*, MacDonald and Jane's, 1977

Sharp, Martin C. and Bowyer, Michael J.F., *Mosquito*, Faber & Faber, 1967

Streetly, Martin, *Confound & Destroy*, Jane's, 1978

Turner, John Frayn, *The Bader Wing*, Midas Books, 1981

Wright, Stuart J., *An Emotional Gauntlet*, Pen & Sword, 2004

Index